ASP.NET 1.1 Solutions Toolkit

VICTOR GARCIA APREA, DANIEL CAZZULINO, RICK DELORME,
ROBIN DEWSON, FABIO CLAUDIO FERRACCHIATI,
DAVID GOTTLIEB, MATTHEW MACDONALD, SAURABH NANDU

Apress®

ASP.NET 1.1 Solutions Toolkit

Copyright (©) 2005 by Victor Garcia Aprea, Daniel Cazzulino, Rick Delorme, Robin Dewson, Fabio Claudio Ferracchiati, David Gottlieb, Matthew MacDonald, Saurabh Nandu

ISBN-13 (paperback): 978-1-59059-446-9
ISBN-13 (electronic): 978-1-4302-0001-7

Printed and bound in the United States of America (POD)

Trademarked names may appear in this book. Rather than use a trademark symbol with every occurrence of a trademarked name, we use the names only in an editorial fashion and to the benefit of the trademark owner, with no intention of infringement of the trademark.

Lead Author: Victor Garcia Aprea
Lead Editor: Ewan Buckingham
Technical Reviewer: Juan Carlos Elichirigoity
Editorial Board: Steve Anglin, Dan Appleman, Ewan Buckingham, Gary Cornell, Tony Davis, Jason Gilmore, Chris Mills, Dominic Shakeshaft, Jim Sumser
Project Manager: Kylie Johnston
Copy Edit Manager: Nicole LeClerc
Copy Editor: Linda Marousek
Production Manager: Kari Brooks-Copony
Production Editor: Mary Keith Trawick
Compositor: Kinetic Publishing Services, LLC
Proofreader: Patrick Vincent
Indexer: Michael Brinkman
Artist: Kinetic Publishing Services, LLC
Cover Designer: Kurt Krames
Manufacturing Manager: Tom Debolski

Distributed to the book trade in the United States by Springer-Verlag New York, Inc., 233 Spring Street, 6th Floor, New York, NY 10013, and outside the United States by Springer-Verlag GmbH & Co. KG, Tiergartenstr. 17, 69112 Heidelberg, Germany.

In the United States: phone 1-800-SPRINGER, fax 201-348-4505, e-mail orders@springer-ny.com, or visit http://www.springer-ny.com. Outside the United States: fax +49 6221 345229, e-mail orders@springer.de, or visit http://www.springer.de.

For information on translations, please contact Apress directly at 2855 Telegraph Avenue, Suite 600, Berkeley, CA 94705. Phone 510-549-5930, fax 510-549-5939, e-mail info@apress.com, or visit http://www.apress.com.

The source code for this book is available to readers at http://www.apress.com in the Source Code/ Downloads section.

To my father, Carlos, who has been the greatest model to follow in life. I'm working hard to someday become half the man he was and it's really a hard job! I miss you, ol' man.

To my mom, Marta, for always being there.

To my wife, Catalina, for her endless patience and support.

To my brother, Antonio, for sharing his incredible talent.

To Dr. Galo Pozzio, for all the times I've bothered him.

Contents at a Glance

Contents

About the Lead Author

VICTOR GARCIA APREA is cofounder of Clarius Consulting, providing training, consulting, and development in Microsoft .NET technologies. Victor has been involved with ASP.NET since early in its development and is recognized as a Microsoft MVP for ASP.NET since 2002. He has written books and articles, and also has done a lot of reviewing for Wrox Press, Apress, and Microsoft Press. Victor is also a regular speaker at Microsoft Argentina (MSDN DevDays, Ask the Experts panel, and other events) and in .NET local user groups.

You can read Victor's Web log at `http://clariusconsulting.net/vga`.

About the Technical Reviewer

JUAN CARLOS ELICHIRIGOITY was born in 1971 in a small town in the center of the Buenos Aires province in Argentina. At the age of 12 he got his first computer, a brand new Commodore 64, with which he started his first steps into computer programming (and computer games!). This interest, the great support given by his parents, and the technical formation he received at a technical high school set the foundation of his forthcoming career.

After becoming a mechanical-electrician technician in 1989, he entered the Universidad Nacional de La Plata where he earned an Analyst-Programmer degree in 1993 and a Systems Engineer degree in 2000. In those years, he demonstrated his capabilities by joining a university research group and obtaining several national and regional achievement awards.

In 1996 he chose to follow Microsoft technologies as his career specialization and he has been working as an independent software developer and consultant since then, providing his knowledge and experience to several medium-to-large companies in South America and working closely with Microsoft Argentina and Microsoft Corporation.

Introduction

Throughout this book we'll be developing a set of solutions (in the form of custom controls most of the time) designed to tackle the more common needs of Web Application development. These range from simple and self-contained controls, like the Spinner control developed in Chapter 2, to more advanced and complex solutions, such as the Search engine presented in Chapter 14.

While developing these solutions, we tried to demonstrate the most varied offering of different approaches as possible. For example, you'll find some controls that use a database for their storage needs while others will simply rely on an XML file to store any data. Moreover, you'll notice that some of them are designed to work only with a database as their data source while others are designed with a more flexible (and complex) approach in mind thus allowing almost any data to be used as its source.

You'll notice these different approaches not only regarding data access, but also with other aspects, like rendering. Some controls will just directly write literal HTML to the stream while others will rely on composition to do the same.

Our objective is to show you how the different topics in custom control development could be approached with the idea that, based on your specific requirements, you could choose whatever approach fits you best.

Who Is This Book For?

This book is targeted at Visual Basic .NET developers who have some experience with ASP.NET and are looking to start writing the real-world features found on most modern Web sites, like the *Voting* and *Reviewing* features of popular Web sites like Amazon.com.

Previous experience in writing custom controls for ASP.NET will help as most of the solutions developed throughout the book are based on them, but it's not a requirement as all solutions are "ready-to-run" and encapsulated into the form of controls or components that you'll be able to use right away in your Web sites even if you don't understand some of the inner workings.

For those just starting custom control development, we also offer a quick refresher (see Chapter 1) on key concepts regarding the subject.

Experienced developers may also find interesting the variety of different approaches taken throughout the book when coding the different solutions.

How Is This Book Structured?

The first chapter of this book offers a quick refresher about control development. Then most of the chapters go through the actual development of a given control, in the form of custom controls or User Controls. A few chapters are dedicated to other solutions that are not necessarily based on custom controls.

What follows is a summary of the contents of this book.

Chapter 1: Control Development

Before starting to code any controls, we do a quick refresher of some of the key concepts of custom control development to ease the comprehension of the following chapters. Differences between the main types of controls, an in-depth look at how viewstate serialization works, and recommended practices to build composite custom controls are some of the topics covered.

Chapter 2: Spinner Control

This is the first control we'll develop in the book and it will consist of a mimic of the NumericUpDown control available in Windows Forms. While developing this control we're going to show you how to embed the resources used by it (i.e., its JavaScript files) in order to simplify its deployment.

Chapter 3: Bindable Bullet List

This control is intended to simplify the listing of data in a bullet-oriented fashion, something that is currently supported by the HTML standard but didn't get built-in support in ASP.NET 1.x. During its development we'll take a look at how to code a DataSource property that allows binding to almost any kind of data.

Chapter 4: Data Navigator

We'll build the DataNavigator control as a companion of the built-in controls DataGrid, DataList, and Repeater. Our control will allow a set of records to display in a VCR-like fashion, thus making it a good candidate for a lot of database applications.

Chapter 5: File Uploader

As covered in Chapter 3 when coding the Bindable Bullet List, in this chapter we'll also cover some ground not supported in ASP.NET 1.x. By building a User Control (the first one built throughout the book), we allow a very simple reuse of this control in any page.

Chapter 6: Globalizable Page

This is the first chapter where we diverge from building controls and extend the built-in ASP.NET Page class to make it culture-aware. We'll also introduce how .NET handles resources and show you how to leverage this from your own controls.

Chapter 7: Validation Control

In this chapter, we develop a Validation control that takes a different approach from the built-in validators. While developing it we've separated the control code from the validation code thus offering a single control that you can use with multiple, different validation algorithms (that you can easily extend).

Chapter 8: Image Magnifier

The ImageMagnifier control extends the built-in ImageButton adding support for zoom. In its code we demonstrate how to use the GDI+ API in order to produce a zoomed version of a provided image, save it to disk, and access it from a browser.

Chapter 9: Chart

As we did in Chapter 6 when coding the Globalizable Page, we're also inheriting from the built-in Page class in this chapter. We demonstrate another use of the GDI+ API, this time to create different chart types on the fly. In contrast with Chapter 8 where we saved the generated image to disk, in this chapter we'll serve it directly from the page instead.

Chapter 10: Image Map Generator

The ImageMap control developed in this chapter offers support for client-side image maps. Within the chapter we'll code a custom design-time editor to graphically manage the "hot" regions of the image.

Chapter 11: Reviewing Controls

Two controls will be developed in this chapter that are aimed to offer the common review functionality found on most Web sites: LastReview and Average. The LastReview control will display the last or all available reviews for a given product and the Average control will show the average rating for a given product. SQL Server is used by these controls as the backend data storage.

Chapter 12: Straw Poll

This chapter aims to offer another very common functionality found in today's Web sites: that of a Straw Poll. Again, two different controls will be developed: XmlPoll and XmlPollResults. XmlPoll will offer the UI for taking votes and XmlPollResults will display the current results of a given poll. These controls will use a simple XML file as their backend data storage.

Chapter 13: RSS Reader

RSS is becoming more and more popular every day. The control developed in this chapter, RssReader, allows you to parse and display the content of RSS files.

Chapter 14: Search Engine

Within this chapter, we'll develop a simple and extensible search engine, which you could easily hook to your Web site. Two main components will be developed: SearchIndexer and SearchParser. SearchIndexer will crawl URLs and index the information found and SearchParser will perform queries against the indexed information.

Prerequisites

The following are the recommended system requirements for running the code in this book:

- Windows XP Professional Edition, Windows 2000 Server, or Windows 2003 Server (any edition)

- Microsoft SQL Server Desktop Engine (MSDE) or Microsoft SQL Engine

Note that although Visual Studio .NET is not a requirement, as you can use any other IDE (like ASP.NET Web Matrix), we highly recommend it.

Downloading the Code

In the code download for this book found at `http://www.apress.com`, you'll find one Solution containing two projects:

- A Class Library project with all the controls developed throughout the book (named `Apress.Toolkit`)

- A Web project including a Web application used to test the different controls (named `Apress.Toolkit.Demos`)

We have chosen to use two projects to allow the controls to live in their own assembly so they could be easily reused in any other Web application.

CHAPTER 1

■ ■ ■

Control Development

Before starting to code the several controls we'll be developing throughout this book, it's necessary to introduce you to some key concepts regarding control development. We'll use this chapter to clearly present the following to you:

- How to choose one type of control over another (User Controls vs. Custom Controls) when planning your next control.

- How to hack some basic design-time support for your controls without the need to actually write a custom `ControlDesigner`.

- How to optimize your viewstate usage by looking at the internal workings of the viewstate serializer in order to understand exactly what ends up being stored and to code your controls accordingly.

- How to avoid the most common pitfalls of composite custom control development.

User Controls vs. Custom Controls

One decision you'll need to face every time you start developing a new control is "Should I make it a User Control or a Custom Control?" The most important thing to consider when responding to this question is your control's UI requirements, as follows:

- If the UI is going to be static and could be created easily at design-time by dragging and dropping controls from the Toolbox window, then it will definitely be more appropriate to create the control as a User Control.

- If the UI is going to be dynamic and may vary, for example, depending on data retrieved from a database (or any other source for that matter), then a Custom Control will be a much better choice than a User Control.

Of course each type of control comes with its own pros and cons:

- User Controls are easy to write (as long as you know how to use drag-and-drop!) and they offer an easy caching story (by means of the `OutputCache` directive). However, they don't offer design-time support and were not designed for supporting a dynamic UI in mind.

- Custom Controls are much more complex to write, they require a better understanding of how things work (especially the control execution lifecycle), and there is no simple cache story for them (you'll need to write code to use the Cache API). However, they offer nice design-time support and are able to address (as they were designed to do) more complex scenarios than User Controls.

Within this book, we've chosen to code only two of our controls as User Controls: the `FileUploader` control (in Chapter 5) and the `ReviewerForm` (in Chapter 11). When reading about them, you'll notice they both perfectly fit the outlined reasons for when to choose a User Control.

Design-time Support

Design-time support is a big topic and one that merits a book on its own. For this reason, we haven't gone into much detail in this book and the controls will only offer a modest design-time experience.

When it comes to adding design-time support to your control, you have mainly two choices:

- Modify the control's code to make it aware that it may be running at design-time.

or

- Write a control designer to handle design-time support.

Here, the approach we've followed is to modify the control's code in order to offer some design-time experience. We've done this because it's the simplest way to offer some design-time support while not requiring you to have any experience with control designers.

This approach basically consists of modifying the `Render` method in order to check if it's running at design time and, if so, output a custom rendering. This usually translates into some code like the following:

```
Protected Overrides Sub Render(ByVal writer As System.Web.UI.HtmlTextWriter)
    If (Me.Context Is Nothing) Then writer.Write("Design-time rendering")
```

```
        Else
           writer.Write("Run-time rendering")
        End If
    End Sub
```

We're using one of the most common shortcuts for testing if the code is running at design time, which consists of checking the value for `Me.Context`. We can rely on this property being set to `Nothing` if the code is running at design time, so after checking that, we proceed with an appropriate rendering.

Note that, although simple, this approach has some major drawbacks:

- *Mixing design-time and run-time code*: This gets worse the more design-time checks and code you add. Plus, this has the effect of producing larger assemblies, as design-time code gets compiled along with your control's code.

- *Limited functionality regarding what you can do*: Basically, this is limited to just HTML output.

If you choose to write a `ControlDesigner` instead, you'll avoid the previous cons because

- You can move the design-time code to a separate assembly (i.e., `Apress.Toolkit.Design.dll`) that won't be required at run time.

- You can have more much control over the design-time experience, such as filtering properties, having several different renderings, controlling resizing and movement, etc.

If you want to learn more about writing control designers, please see the .NET Framework documentation.

The basic design-time support we'll be adding to our controls mainly consists of applying a few attributes to enhance their behaviors when being designed.

The following assembly-level attribute will specify which prefix to use to register the namespace for our controls:

```
<Assembly: TagPrefix("Apress.Toolkit", "cc")>
```

This is complemented by the `ToolboxData` attribute that will tell the IDE which markup to use when a control is dragged from the toolbox, as follows:

```
<ToolboxData("<{0}:DataBindBulletList runat='server' />")>
```

The parameter {0} will be replaced with the prefix previously specified in the
TagPrefix attribute. This will cause the following markup to be generated every time
a DataBindBulletList is dropped onto a Web Form:

```
<cc:DataBindBulletList runat='server' id='...'>
```

In addition, we'll use the Editor attribute to enhance the editing of some properties'
values, so when using the Properties browser the user may be presented with a custom
dialog to enter the data instead of having to edit its value in place and as a string.

For example, in Chapter 10 when developing the Image Map generator control, we use
the built-in ImageUrlEditor for the ImageSrc property by applying the Editor attribute
this way:

```
<Editor(GetType(ImageUrlEditor), GetType(UITypeEditor))> _
Public Property ImageSrc() As String
```

Now the user will be able to select an image by using a custom dialog instead of having
to remember the image location and directly typing it. Figure 1-1 shows what the dialog
looks like.

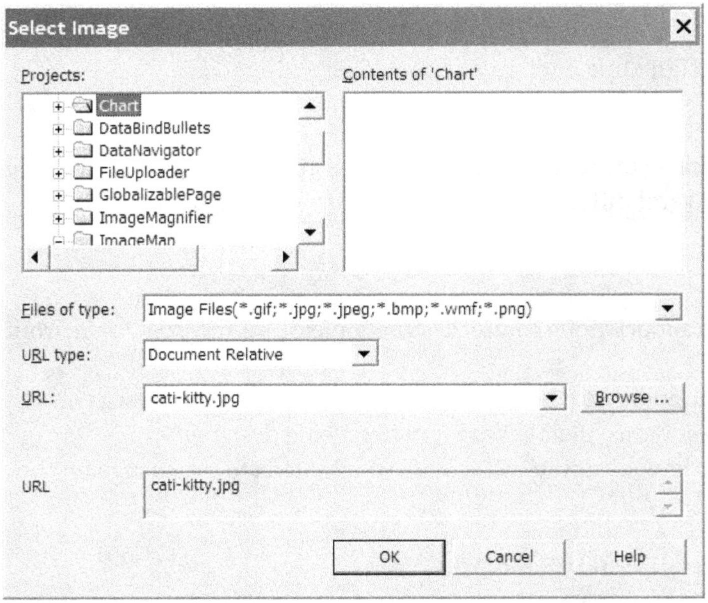

Figure 1-1. The ImageUrlEditor

Within Chapter 10 we went a little bit further and wrote our own custom editor to
edit the control's ImageMap property because that would make the control much more
usable.

Viewstate

If you want your control's properties to maintain state between postbacks, remember that you need to store them in viewstate, otherwise you can just use a private field to keep its state. For the controls in this book, you'll find that not every control's property is stored in viewstate, but only those that seemed necessary. Remember that based on your specific requirements, you can easily change this and alter each property's storage as you like with almost no work at all.

Setting and Getting Values

You'll notice that when implementing properties backed up by viewstate storage, all controls in this book follow the same pattern.

The Get method should try to get the data previously stored in viewstate and cast it to the appropriate well-known type (this is necessary as viewstate only handles Object types when storing and retrieving items), like so:

```
Get
    Dim obj As Object = ViewState.Item("SomeProperty")
    If Not (obj Is Nothing) Then
        Return CType(obj, String)
    End If
```

If no such data was found in viewstate, then a default value for the property is returned, like so:

```
    Return String.Empty
End Get
```

Usually, the Set method looks simpler as its only purpose is to feed the passed value into viewstate:

```
Set(ByVal Value As String)
    Me.ViewState.Item("SomeProperty") = Value
End Set
```

The Serializer

It's very important to keep in mind that although you can store almost any type of data in viewstate, doing so is not recommended at all because you may end up with a huge viewstate footprint and considerable serialization times.

As you already know, any value going into viewstate needs to be serialized first and that is the job of the public LosFormatter class. This class is optimized to work with the following types: `int`, `String`, `Boolean`, `Pair`, `Triple`, `Array`, `ArrayList`, `Hashtable`. Meaning that, if you restrict yourself to only store these types in viewstate, its footprint will be as small as possible and serialization time will be faster.

But you may need to store a different, non-optimized type. When this happens, the `LosFormatter` class will check if the given type has an associated type converter (by looking at its attributes for a `TypeConverter`). If one is found, it will be used to convert the data type into a string representation, which, ultimately, will travel into viewstate.

What would happen if the given data type had no associated type converter? In this case, the `LosFormatter` class will use the `BinaryFormatter` class to serialize the given value. This is—by far—the worst possible scenario, as the `BinaryFormatter` class will produce a binary and rather lengthy representation of the data, thus considerably impacting the size of the final viewstate.

As a result, it's very important that you always try to stick to the natively supported types and provide a type converter when handling nonsupported types.

You may find that not all controls in this book follow the previous recommendations; this was done so as not to overcomplicate the control implementation, and it's properly noted in each case so you know where to look if you decide to improve the control.

Composite Controls

These are the most complex kinds of controls to write, as they require a thorough understanding of the control execution lifecycle and particularities of child controls: how they are named, when they are created, and so on.

As various composite controls are developed within this book, we'll introduce, in advance, some of the key concepts that must be kept in mind while doing so.

Naming Your Children

Every composite control should implement the `INamingContainer` marker interface. Being a "marker" interface means that it doesn't include any method definitions and it's only used to "mark" your control as being a naming container. So with no methods to implement, all that's left is to implement the interface in the class definition, as follows:

```
Public Class MyWebControl
    Inherits WebControl
    Implements INamingContainer
```

What does being a naming container mean? If you mark your control as a naming container, ASP.NET will ensure that the `UniqueIDs` and `ClientIDs` of your control's children are prefixed with the ID of the parent, thus ensuring a proper unique identification for each one of them. For example, if you have a composite control whose ID is `LoginBox`, which contains a child of type TextBox whose ID is Username, the UniqueID for the TextBox will be LoginBox_Username. This hierarchical structure for IDs is what makes it possible for the FindControl method to actually get at the right control.

Being able to properly identify child controls is key to having them work properly, as core ASP.NET logic relies on this identification. For example, for postback event firing, a control won't be able to fire any event if ASP.NET can't find the control to tell it so.

Where Children Are Born

One of the most important things you should remember from the start is that the creation of your child controls needs to happen in the overridden CreateChildControls method and nowhere else.

Do not create your child controls at control definition time

```
Private WithEvents TextBox1 As System.Web.UI.WebControls.TextBox = New TextBox()
```

or in a constructor or any method other than CreateChildControls.

A good practice is to always clear any existing child control when entering CreateChildControls to ensure it runs with a blank control tree.

```
Controls.Clear()
```

Also, although possible, you should never call CreateChildControls directly in your code as ASP.NET will take care of this when necessary. If you want child controls to be re-created, then what you can do from your code is tell ASP.NET that something important enough to require re-creating your children has happened, so next time they're needed they'll be re-created; you do this by setting the ChildControlsCreated property to false.

There are two main points where ASP.NET will cause the creation of child controls:

- FindControl method: Inside this method, the controls' children are searched looking for one with a given ID; for this reason, it needs to ensure that the children are created before starting the search.

- PreRender event: At this point, if nothing caused the creation of child controls, then they need to be created now as the rendering stage is just around the corner!

Note that even if you don't call FindControl directly in your code, several parts of ASP.NET will call it (e.g., processing of postback data, raising of postback events, etc.), thus causing children to be properly created.

Getting at the Children

There is one well-known issue related to children access and it arises when trying to get at a child control by index:

```
Dim ctrl As Control = Controls(1)
```

If the child controls were already created by any of the previously outlined causes, then everything will work as expected; but if nothing has caused their creation yet, then the previous code will throw an exception because there won't be any control at index 1 (yet).

You can solve the previous issue by overriding the Get method for your control's Controls property and ensure the children creation before returning the collection, as follows:

```
Public Overrides ReadOnly Property Controls() As System.Web.UI.ControlCollection
    Get
        MyBase.EnsureChildControls()
        Return MyBase.Controls
    End Get
End Property
```

If you're going to create a bunch of composite controls, it's a good idea to provide a base class (i.e., CompositeControl) for them, which should include the previous code thus saving to implement it in every derived composite control. Also, as we have already learned, every composite control should implement INamingContainer, so this base class is a good candidate for implementing it.

The next version of ASP.NET (2.0) will already include a CompositeControl base class, which solves the previously mentioned issues.

What IDE to Use

Although not required for working with the code presented throughout this book, you may want to consider Visual Studio .NET as your IDE as it will save you a lot of time.

If you choose the ASP.NET Web Matrix IDE instead, keep in mind that it doesn't support the concepts of Solutions and Projects as VS .NET does, so it basically only knows about handling single files and it doesn't offer any compilation support. This means that you'll need to resort to using the vbc.exe command line compiler in order to compile the source files provided in the code download and build the necessary assemblies. To make it easier, we have provided a build.bat file to automate this. (You can find the code samples for this chapter in the Downloads section of the Apress Web site at http://www.apress.com.)

Embedding Resource Files

For a quick grasp of the differences between the ASP.NET Web Matrix IDE and the Visual Studio .NET IDE, and the extra work that may be required if you use the former, let's see what you need to do to embed files into an assembly, which is something we do in several chapters of this book. For example, in Chapter 2 we'll code a Spinner control that uses two embedded resource files: a bitmap file and a JavaScript file.

If you're using Visual Studio .NET, all you'll have to do is make sure the Build Action property for these files is set to Embedded Resource (using the Properties browser).

If you're using ASP.NET Web Matrix, you'll need to deal directly with the VB .NET compiler, and make sure you use the /res switch to embed both resource files, as follows:

```
vbc.exe /out:Apress.Toolkit.dll /t:library
        /res:Apress.Toolkit.Spinner.bmp /res:SpinnerLib.js
        /r:System.dll /r:System.Drawing.dll /r:System.Web.dll
        /optionstrict+ Spinner.vb AssemblyInfo.vb
```

TIP Remember that by typing vbc.exe /xxx, you can get the quick help for using the VB .NET compiler.

Adding Items to the Toolbox

In order to simplify the usage of the controls and components that we'll be developing in the next chapters, we'll add them to the Toolbox window that both VS .NET and ASP.NET Web Matrix support.

First, let's create a new tab so we can put the new controls in there, as we don't want to mix them with the built-in controls. If you're using Visual Studio .NET, right-click on the Toolbox window, select Add Tab (as shown in Figure 1-2), and enter **Apress.Toolkit** as the name for the new tab.

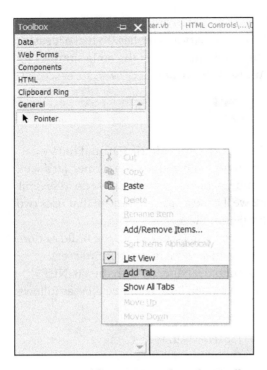

Figure 1-2. Adding a new tab to the Toolbox window

Now, right-click again on the Toolbox window and choose Add/Remove Items this time. The Customize Toolbox dialog will appear. Click its Browse button and navigate to the Apress.Toolkit assembly. Click on the Namespace column and look out for the Apress.Toolkit namespace (see Figure 1-3).

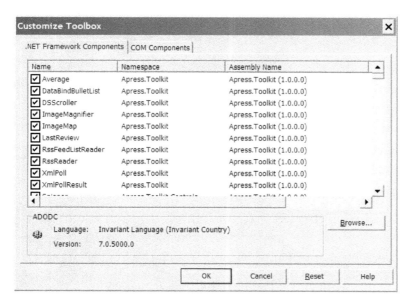

Figure 1-3. Adding new controls

If you're using ASP.NET Web Matrix, the procedure is almost the same: select the Custom Controls tab in the Toolbox window, right-click it, and select Add Local Toolbox Component. In the dialog that appears, select Browse to locate the `Apress.Toolkit.dll` assembly and click OK. Just as in VS .NET, the controls are added to the toolbox.

CHAPTER 2

■ ■ ■

Spinner Control

A very nice control available to Windows Forms developers is the `NumericUpDown` control. It allows the user to increment or decrement a value in steps within a defined range by the application developer. It's useful when you need to keep a value within a range, but want to offer the user the advantage of incrementing it with a simple click of an up or down arrow.

Such a control is not available to Web Forms developers, so we decided to create one. This control is a self-contained custom control that takes care of producing the appropriate client-side JavaScript code to handle the user interaction. This greatly improves the user experience when compared to a server-side only implementation (which is also possible) because it avoids the unnecessary postbacks, which are painful for dialup users.

Scenario

This control is useful in many situations. For example, in a percentage selection we could use it to allow the user to click the up and down arrows and select a percentage between 0 and 100% in steps of 20%.

Another typical usage would be to select a month in a form, from 1 through 12, or an hour or minute of time. Of course, the control will allow manual insertion of the value, but will keep track of valid ranges automatically, and will do so on the client side without the need for a postback.

Most importantly, the control must be cross-browser compatible, at least with the most common and newer browsers, such as Mozilla FireFox and Internet Explorer (IE) 5.5 or higher.

We will create a control that will have the following appearance in a Web page (see Figure 2-1):

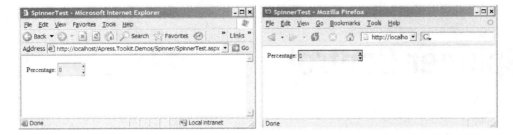

Figure 2-1. *The* Spinner *control rendered in different browsers*

Technology

Usually, even with ASP.NET's own validation controls, there's a need to deploy the JavaScript library used by the controls. This adds complexity to the control's deployment, and certainly allows the developer to modify the JavaScript code it uses, thus increasing the possibility of malfunctioning if it is tampered with. .NET offers the possibility of embedding arbitrary resources, such as images or any other files within an assembly. At run time, these resources can be extracted using classes found in the System.Reflection namespace. We will follow this path to embed the client-side resources used by our control within our control's assembly.

ASP.NET provides the concept of *registering* scripts within a page. Registration is needed if our control uses a client-side library, and the control user drops several controls on a page that could cause duplicate script registrations. Also, we will want to avoid the process of building the script several times, especially if it requires lengthy string manipulation, such as concatenating strings containing the JavaScript code to emit, for every control on the page. If we were directly writing the script to the output at render time from the control, there would be no way to know if other controls on the page had already created and emitted the JavaScript code. Potentially, we can end up with several versions of the same functions. That's why the Page class provides methods to register scripts (e.g., RegisterClientScriptBlock) and associate them with a key. The last chance to use any of these methods is the PreRender stage, however. Along with these methods for registering script, Page also provides a corresponding method for checking if a script has already been registered (i.e., IsClientScriptBlockRegistered). We will use registration-related methods to ensure common script is emitted only once for the whole page.

JavaScript allows us to add arbitrary properties to objects at run time. It is very useful to place temporary values inside an element itself, which can later be used as properties of the element. The effect is similar to that achieved if the object had a new property defined and set, but this is done at run time from our code. We will use this technique to place values in the textbox element itself at run time, so that the common methods can modify its content based on them. This makes the generic methods much cleaner and easy to understand.

Note Object-Oriented (OO) JavaScript is an advanced topic. You can learn more about it in *JavaScript Bible, 5th Edition* by Danny Goodman and Michael Morrison (John Wiley & Sons, Inc., 2004).

The most common approach to rendering graphics to the client browser is to use images. We could have followed this path to render the up and down arrows, but this increases the page's rendered size, and additionally adds the problem of deploying the images. The problems that arise with this approach are similar to what we face with the JavaScript library. Several third-party controls (including Microsoft's free IE WebControls—`http://msdn.microsoft.com/workshop/webcontrols/overview/overview.asp`) distribute image files that have to be placed in a specific folder, which the control has to know in order to display appropriately.

Unicode (`http://www.unicode.org`) is a widely supported standard that extends the ASCII character set, and has the potential to support almost the complete set of characters used in the whole world. Thus, it has a lot of graphic characters that can be used to replace corresponding graphic files, such as the up and down arrows we need to display. .NET supports Unicode natively, and we will take advantage of this feature to render the appropriate interface without using graphic files at all.

Design

The interface design of our control uses an HTML table to distribute the different parts of the user interface (UI). It will contain two rows, one for each graphic arrow, and the cell containing the textbox with the value that will span the two rows. As we just learned from the previous chapter, we are creating all these child controls in the `CreateChildControls()` override method. Without the appropriate table format, the control would look like the image in Figure 2-2.

Figure 2-2. *UI layout for the* Spinner *control*

The JavaScript library will be kept in a separate file to make it easy to design and change while we create it; but to overcome the limitation we stated previously about deployment and unwanted modifications of the library, we will use .NET's ability to embed the script file as a resource into the assembly itself at compile time. The `System.Reflection.Assembly` class contains the `GetManifestResourceStream()` method that allows us to retrieve a resource from the manifest at run time. To do so only the first time the control is used, and to keep the library in a shared variable, we will use the static class constructor, which is called only once. This way we avoid the impact of using reflection for every instance of our control that might be placed on a Web page.

Deployment, then, becomes extremely simple—just copy and use the assembly. Additionally, our control's users can't modify the JavaScript code, and they can't even see it, unless they look at the rendered page's output. But we don't lose the flexibility of having a separate file while we develop the custom control, which gives us the best of both worlds.

To render the arrows, we will use special Unicode characters that look exactly like the up and down arrows we need. A great benefit of this approach is that the characters don't increase the control's weight, and the "images" are automatically resizable just by changing the font size for them at design time. However, we won't allow the control user to change the font, which would hinder the display of the Unicode characters. Again, we also gain in self-containment and deployment ease. To create the special Unicode character programmatically, we will use the ChrW() method, which receives the character's code independently of the current user's culture or code page. This allows our control to render identically whichever culture the user has.

ASP.NET defines four kinds of registerable scripts: client script blocks, startup script, array declarations, and submit statements. In a sample page, the location of these scripts would be the following:

```
<!DOCTYPE HTML PUBLIC "-//W3C//DTD HTML 4.0 Transitional//EN" >
<html>
  ...
  <body>
    <form id="WebForm1" method="post" runat="server"
          onsubmit="alert('This is a submit statement!');">
      <input type="hidden" name="__VIEWSTATE" value="..." />

      <script language=JavaScript>//Client Script Block</script>
        <!-- Here go the page controls -->

      <script language="JavaScript">
        <!-- Here go all the array variable declarations, i.e.:
          var myVars =  new Array("23", "28");  -->
      </script>

      <script language=JavaScript>//Startup Script</script>
    </form>
    <!-- Here go potentially more controls outside the form -->
  </body>
</html>
```

We will use a client script block for the common methods, which will be used by all the Spinner controls on the page. A startup script block will create and assign properties to the textbox element for use inside the common methods, such as the current value, minimum and maximum values, etc.

Implementation

Create a new class file. Give the new class the name Spinner.vb, and add the following Imports we will be using throughout the code:

```
Imports Microsoft.VisualBasic
Imports System
Imports System.ComponentModel
Imports System.Drawing
Imports System.IO
Imports System.Reflection
Imports System.Text
Imports System.Web.UI
Imports System.Web.UI.WebControls
```

Our control will allow the arrows to be placed at either the left or the right of the textbox containing the actual value, so we will add an enumeration for that.

```
Public Enum SpinnerAlign
   Left
   Right
End Enum
```

The text inside the textbox can also be aligned, so we will add another enumeration for that.

```
Public Enum ValueAlign
   Left
   Right
   Center
End Enum
```

Now, we get to the actual control's class definition. Our control will inherit from the base WebControl class because we want to provide visual properties such as Font, ForeColor, etc. We will also implement the marker interface INamingContainer to avoid naming conflicts with other controls on the page.

```
<ToolboxData("<{0}:Spinner runat=""server"" width=""80px""
             buttonsize=""XX-Small"" />")> _
Public Class Spinner
  Inherits WebControl
  Implements INamingContainer
```

We are using the ToolboxData attribute to specify the preferred tag name that the Web Forms designer should use. We have specified a default width and button size (more on this later).

Now, we will add the code that deals with extracting a previously embedded resource. We will use a private Shared variable that will hold the complete JavaScript library code as a single string.

```
Shared Scripts As String
```

The Shared constructor for the class is called the first time any instance tries to access a Shared member, so that's the place we will put the code to extract the resource.

```
Shared Sub New()
  Dim asm As System.Reflection.Assembly = _
      System.Reflection.Assembly.GetExecutingAssembly()

  'We check for null just in case the variable is called at
  'design time.
  If Not asm Is Nothing Then
    Dim resource As String = "SpinnerLib.js"
    Dim stm As Stream = asm.GetManifestResourceStream(resource)
    If stm Is Nothing Then Return

    Try
      Dim reader As StreamReader = New StreamReader(stm)
      Scripts = reader.ReadToEnd()
      reader.Close()
    Finally
      If Not stm Is Nothing Then stm.Close()
    End Try
  End If
End Sub
```

The GetExecutingAssembly() method retrieves an instance of the Assembly class that the current code is running from. This is the assembly where our control's code resides, not the assembly of the calling Web application. Before using this object, we check to see if it's Nothing, which will be the case if the method is called at design time. With this reference, we can call GetManifestResourceStream() with the name of the resource to retrieve, and get a Stream object pointing to it. Saving it to the private variable is just a matter of using a StreamReader to read it until the end.

We expose several properties for our control: ButtonSize, Value, Increment, Maximum, Minimum, ButtonAlign, and TextAlign. The code for all of them is almost the same, basically providing a public property that accesses a private class-level variable of the same type. So, for brevity, we will only take a look at the Increment property, as follows:

```
Dim _inc As Integer = 0

<Bindable(True), Category("Data"), DefaultValue(0)> _
Property Increment() As Integer
  Get
    Return _inc
  End Get

  Set(ByVal Value As Integer)
    _inc = Value
  End Set
End Property
```

There's nothing strange happening here; we just use the Bindable, Category, and DefaultValue attributes to customize our control's appearance at design time. The following property is a little more complex, in order to enforce the control's redraw and also to ensure that the value being assigned is valid:

```
Dim _align As SpinnerAlign = SpinnerAlign.Right

<Bindable(True), Category("Layout"), _
    DefaultValue(SpinnerAlign.Right), _
    Description("Alignment of the Up/Down button controls.")> _
Property ButtonAlign() As SpinnerAlign
  Get
    Return _align
  End Get

  Set(ByVal Value As SpinnerAlign)
    If Not [Enum].IsDefined(GetType(SpinnerAlign), Value) Then
      Throw New ArgumentException()
    End If
```

```
      ChildControlsCreated = False
      _align = Value
    End Set
  End Property
```

In the Set accessor, we check that the value passed is defined in the corresponding enumeration using the Enum.IsDefined() method. This is always good practice and avoids invalid values from being assigned to our property, which is something that can't be ensured just by making the property an Enum.

Finally, we set the base class's ChildControlsCreated property to False, indicating that the current tree of child controls is invalid and should be reconstructed next time it is needed. When this happens, the overridden CreatedChildControls will run again, this time with updated property values, and will generate proper child controls that make up our display.

```
Protected Overrides Sub CreateChildControls()
  Dim tb As New Table()
  Dim tc As TableCell

  'Clear the previous layout.
  MyBase.Controls.Clear()

  tb.CellPadding = 0
  tb.CellSpacing = 0

  'Create the table hierarchy first.
  tb.Rows.Add(New TableRow())
  tb.Rows.Add(New TableRow())
  tb.Rows(0).Cells.Add(New TableCell())
  tb.Rows(0).Cells.Add(New TableCell())
  tb.Rows(1).Cells.Add(New TableCell())

  MyBase.Controls.Add(tb)
```

Up to now, we have created the table we need. We have cleared existing controls and added the newly created table to the Controls collection. Now, we can move on and create the textbox and assign properties to it.

```
  'Create the textbox and add it to the appropriate cell.
  Dim txt as New TextBox
  txt.ID = "txtValue"
  txt.Attributes.Add("onkeypress", "return KeyPressed(event, this);")
  txt.Attributes.Add("onkeyup", "return KeyUp(this);")
```

```
txt.Attributes.Add("onchange", "return SpinnerChanged(this);")
txt.Attributes.Add("onpaste", "return SpinnerChanged(this);")

'Apply the style set to the control to the textbox.
txt.ApplyStyle(Me.ControlStyle)

'Remove textbox borders, which will appear in the table cell instead.
txt.Style.Add("BORDER-TOP", "none")
txt.Style.Add("BORDER-RIGHT", "none")
txt.Style.Add("BORDER-LEFT", "none")
txt.Style.Add("BORDER-BOTTOM", "none")
txt.Width = New Unit("100%")
txt.Text = Me.Value.ToString()
```

Client-side JavaScript event handlers are added to server controls by means of the Attributes collection. We added event handlers for all the relevant events, and will see the client-side library code shortly. Finally, we added style-related attributes to make it fill the table cell.

Now, depending on the ButtonAlign property, the cell to which we have to add the textbox varies, so we assign the temporary variable tc to the appropriate cell before modifying it.

```
If ButtonAlign = SpinnerAlign.Left Then
  tc = tb.Rows(0).Cells(1)
Else
  tc = tb.Rows(0).Cells(0)
End If

tc.Style.Add("vertical-align", "middle")

'Apply the style defined for the whole control to the cell.
tc.ApplyStyle(Me.ControlStyle)

'Simulate textbox borders on the table cell.
tc.Style.Add("BORDER-TOP", "2px inset")
tc.Style.Add("BORDER-RIGHT", "silver 1px solid")
tc.Style.Add("BORDER-LEFT", "2px inset")
tc.Style.Add("BORDER-BOTTOM", "silver 1px solid")
tc.Controls.Add(txt)
tc.RowSpan = 2
tc.Width = New Unit("100%")
```

We have set the RowSpan property in order to make the textbox fill the two rows that comprise the up and down "buttons." The other lines just apply attributes to the cell containing the textbox to make it appear like one, so that the actual text written to it appears vertically centered in the control.

Before we start working on the buttons, we will detect whether the browser is IE to customize appearance, as there are subtle differences across browsers.

```
Dim isIE As Boolean = True

If Context Is Nothing Then
    isIE = True
ElseIf Not (context.Request Is Nothing) Then
    If context.Request.Browser.Browser <> "IE" Then
        isIE = False
    End If
End If
```

The cell where the first button is placed also depends on the ButtonAlign property.

```
If ButtonAlign = SpinnerAlign.Left Then
  tc = tb.Rows(0).Cells(0)
Else
  tc = tb.Rows(0).Cells(1)
End If
```

As we proposed, the buttons will actually be a special character, rendered as the content of the appropriate cell. We will add style to the cell, such as border and background color, in order to make the cell appear as a button. This makes the "buttons" much lighter at run time.

```
'Up "button"
tc.BackColor = System.Drawing.Color.Gainsboro
tc.BorderStyle = CType(IIf(isIE, BorderStyle.Outset,
    BorderStyle.Solid), BorderStyle)
tc.BorderWidth = New Unit("1px")
tc.Style.Add("cursor", "pointer")
tc.Font.Size = _size

tc.Attributes.Add("onmouseup",
    "this.style.backgroundColor='Gainsboro';" + _
    IIf(isIE, "this.style.borderStyle='outset';", "").ToString())
```

```
tc.Attributes.Add("onmousedown",
    "this.style.backgroundColor='WhiteSmoke';" + _
    IIf(isIE, "this.style.borderStyle='inset';", "").ToString())

tc.Attributes.Add("onmouseout",
    "this.style.backgroundColor='Gainsboro';" + _
    IIf(isIE, "this.style.borderStyle='outset';", "").ToString())

tc.Attributes.Add("onclick", "Increment('" + txt.ClientID + "');")

tc.Text = ChrW(9650) 'represents the "_" character.
```

We have added different style and event handlers depending on the browser. The
onmouse*xxx* event handlers only switch the cell's style to simulate a button being pressed
and released. The onclick handler is the one performing the actual work, calling the
JavaScript Increment() method we will see in a moment. Finally, we set the cell's text to
the graphic Unicode character using the ChrW() method, which receives the Unicode
value of the character.

The code for the down button is the same, except for the last two lines.

```
'Down "button"
tc = tb.Rows(1).Cells(0)
tc.BackColor = System.Drawing.Color.Gainsboro
tc.BorderStyle = CType(IIf(isIE, BorderStyle.Outset, _
        BorderStyle.Solid), BorderStyle)
tc.BorderWidth = New Unit("1px")
tc.Style.Add("cursor", "pointer")
tc.Font.Size = _size

tc.Attributes.Add("onmouseup", _
    "this.style.backgroundColor='Gainsboro';" + _
    IIf(isIE, "this.style.borderStyle='outset';", "").ToString())

tc.Attributes.Add("onmousedown", _
    "this.style.backgroundColor='WhiteSmoke';" + _
    IIf(isIE, "this.style.borderStyle='inset';", "").ToString())

tc.Attributes.Add("onmouseout", _
    "this.style.backgroundColor='Gainsboro';" + _
    IIf(isIE, "this.style.borderStyle='outset';", "").ToString())

tc.Attributes.Add("onclick", "Decrement('" + txt.ClientID + "');")
```

```
    tc.Text = ChrW(9660) 'represents the "_" character.
End Sub
```

Note that the onclick event now calls the Decrement() method. This method will, like the Increment() method, receive the ID of the control to modify. Note that we are using the ClientID property instead of the ID, as we need a valid ID for use at the client side; ClientID will ensure a valid and unique ID is ready to be used at the client side. Because of this, you may notice that the final ID that is rendered to the browser is not actually the one we assigned to the textbox (txtValue), but will be prefixed with the ID of its parent, the Spinner control, as we have properly implemented the marker INamingContainer interface on it.

We will override the AddAttributesToRender() method to force the rendered control width. Note that we set the TextBox control width to 100% previously, as omitting this step would result in a control occupying the whole page width. We can add attributes directly to the control using the following method:

```
Protected Overrides Sub AddAttributesToRender( _
    ByVal writer As System.Web.UI.HtmlTextWriter)

  writer.AddStyleAttribute(HtmlTextWriterStyle.Width, _
      Me.Width.ToString())
End Sub
```

Next, we override Render() to add a call to EnsureChildControls (a method provided by the base Control class); this is needed to make sure child controls are created even when our control is being used at design time.

```
Protected Overrides Sub Render( _
    ByVal writer As System.Web.UI.HtmlTextWriter)
  EnsureChildControls()
  MyBase.Render(writer)
End Sub
```

To emit the client-side JavaScript string we loaded in the Shared constructor, we override the OnLoad() method. As we stated at the beginning, the Page class provides a number of properties and methods to handle JavaScript code. What we need to do is register the loaded script only if hasn't been added already.

```
Protected Overrides Sub OnLoad(ByVal e As EventArgs)
  'Register library.
  If Not Page.IsClientScriptBlockRegistered(Me.GetType().FullName) _
      Then
    Page.RegisterClientScriptBlock(Me.GetType().FullName, Scripts)
  End If
```

When we register a script, the Page class keeps a reference to the string and a key associated with it. At render time, it outputs it at the right place depending on the method called (client script block, submit statement, etc.). Note that we use the control type's full name as the key for registering the common script. This is a good way to ensure key uniqueness with other controls. The method we called registers the common script that is shared by all instances of our control, which is why we want to register it only once. Next, we need to render the following JavaScript statements that are unique to each instance:

```
<script language="JavaScript">
<!--
  t = document.getElementById("[TextBoxID]");
  t.step = [Spinner.Increment];
  t.original = [Spinner.Value];
  t.max = [Spinner.Maximum];
  t.min = [Spinner.Minimum];
//-->
</script>
```

What this code will do is append the relevant properties to the textbox element, which are later used by the common methods that we will see in a moment. We could use a StringBuilder and append the current control values mixed with the nonchanging JavaScript code. However, precisely because, for the most part, the statements don't change among Spinner controls, we will use .NET string formatting features, which make the code much more compact. Add the following Shared variable just below the Scripts one we defined at the beginning of this section:

```
Shared StartupScriptFormat As String = _
"<script language=""JavaScript"">t = document.getElementById(""{0}""); t.step = {1};
t.original = {2}; t.max = {3}; t.min = {4};</script>"
```

Now, we can go back to the OnLoad() method and complete the script registration with the following lines:

```
  Page.RegisterStartupScript(Me.ClientID, _
      String.Format( _
          StartupScriptFormat, Me.FindControl("txtValue").ClientID, _
          Me.Increment, Me.Value, Me.Maximum, Me.Minimum))
  MyBase.OnLoad(e)
End Sub
```

We format the string added at the top of the class with the appropriate values in the current control instance. We use the inherited `FindControl()` method to locate the textbox instance inside our custom control, and use it to provide the client script with the unique identifier of the control on the client side.

We can now move on to the common JavaScript code library. Create a new JavaScript file, name it `SpinnerLib.js` and add the following code to it:

```
<script language="JavaScript">
<!--
  function IsChar(code)
  {
    return /\w/.test(String.fromCharCode(code));
  }
```

We will use this method to ensure that the key pressed while in the textbox is an alphanumeric character, and not a control one, such as Enter, Tab, a function key, or any other. We use a JavaScript literal regular expression (`/\w/`) to test for a match against the received code. This expression checks that the passed string is an alphanumeric character or the underscore character. You can find introductory material about regular expressions in MSDN documentation: `ms-help://MS.VSCC/MS.MSDNVS/cpgenref/html/cpconregularexpressionslanguageelements.htm`.

Next, we will add the code for the key press event handler, as follows:

```
  function KeyPressed(e, src)
  {
    var code;

    if (e.which == undefined)
    {
      //IE
      code = e.keyCode;
    }
    else
    {
      //Mozilla/NS6+
      code = e.which;
    }

    // It's not a character value, leave the function.
    if (!IsChar(code)) return true;

    return !isNaN(String.fromCharCode(code));
  }
```

Recall the attribute we used to call this method when we created the textbox:

```
txt.Attributes.Add("onkeypress", "return KeyPressed(event, this);")
```

We pass to the method the special object event, and a reference to the control that fired the event. Unfortunately, the event object's properties are different between IE and FireFox. That's why we check if the which property is defined in the object. This property contains the key pressed under FireFox. Next, we use the previously defined IsChar() method, and finally check if the string entered is a number by using the isNaN() JavaScript method. If the event handling method returns false, the event is canceled and the key isn't inserted in the textbox. Note that the negative sign will be allowed because it's not an alphanumeric character, according to the regular expression we used, so the method will exit before the isNaN() check is performed. We will take into account this symbol in the handler for the following KeyUp event.

When the user enters numbers manually, we need to check if the resulting value is between the bounds defined for the control. We have already checked that the value entered is actually a number, but to compare the whole number in the textbox against the bounds, we need to react to the onkeyup event, when the key pressed has already been added to the textbox. Later, if we find an invalid value, we restore the last known valid value, which is stored as a property of the textbox element itself: original. On each KeyUp event, if a valid value was entered, we save the value for later use.

```
function KeyUp(src)
{
  // If we have a valid value, we save it for later,
  // else we restore the previously saved value.
  if (src.value <= src.max && src.value >= src.min)
  {
    src.original = src.value;
    return true;
  }
  else
  {
    // Exceptional case: the user is entering a negative number.
    if (src.value == "-") return true;

    src.value = src.original;
    return false;
  }
}
```

Again, the attribute that adds this method call inside the textbox is

```
txt.Attributes.Add("onkeyup", "return KeyUp(this);")
```

This time we don't need the event object. Note that the method makes use of the properties we added to the element in the startup script block:

```
if (src.value <= src.max && src.value >= src.min)
```

We take into account the special case when the user is entering a negative value, and skip validation in that case. Either we store a valid value for later and return true (src.original = src.value) or restore the previous valid value and return false (src.value = src.original).

The onchange handler does pretty much the same work by calling the SpinnerChanged() method.

```
function SpinnerChanged(src)
{
  // If we have a valid value, we save it for later,
  // else we restore the previously saved value.

  if (src.value <= src.max && src.value >= src.min)
  {
    src.original = src.value;
    return true;
  }
  else
  {
    src.value = src.original;
    return false;
  }
}
```

Note that we added a call to this method in the IE-only onpaste event. This event is ignored by browsers that don't support it.

Next, we add the methods to increment and decrement the value, which are almost identical to each other.

```
function Decrement(target)
{
  src = document.getElementById(target);
  src.value = src.value - src.step;
  SpinnerChanged(src);
  src.focus();
}
```

```
  function Increment(target)
  {
    src = document.getElementById(target);
    src.value = parseInt(src.value) + parseInt(src.step);
    SpinnerChanged(src);
    src.focus();
  }
//-->
</script>
```

This time the event is fired in the table cells containing our "buttons." The attributes that added the calls to these methods were

```
tc.Attributes.Add("onclick", "Decrement('" + txt.ClientID + "');")
```

and

```
tc.Attributes.Add("onclick", "Increment('" + txt.ClientID + "');")
```

The method now receives an ID, which we use to locate the corresponding element:

```
src = document.getElementById(target);
```

Next, we set the new value by adding or subtracting the step and calling the SpinnerChanged() method that ensures, again, that the resulting value is between the defined bounds. Finally, we set the focus on the element, just in case the user wants to enter the next number manually.

Demonstration

After properly adding the Spinner control to the toolbox or your favorite IDE (remember, we just saw how to do this for VS.NET and for WebMatrix in Chapter 1), we can now simply drop a Spinner control over a new blank Web form. Then we can use the Properties browser to customize the appearance, bounds, and increment step, as shown in Figure 2-3.

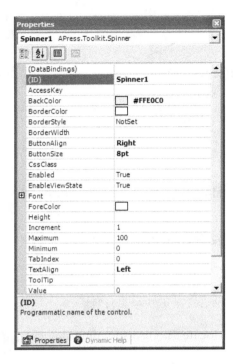

Figure 2-3. *Browsing the* Spinner *control properties*

At run time, each click of the up or down arrows will change the value in steps of 10 (see Figure 2-4).

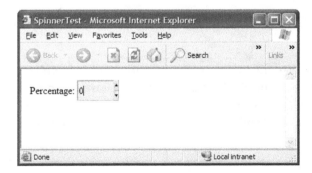

Figure 2-4. *The* Spinner *control in action*

Limitations

One limitation is related to number format. In some countries, the negative symbol may be located in a different place (at the end of the number, for example), or may even be represented with another symbol. This is not allowed in our control, which only accepts the negative sign at the beginning of the value.

In order for the control's attributes to be rendered appropriately under FireFox and Netscape 6 or higher, a "patch" has to be applied to the `machine.config` file. Inside the `browserCaps` section, locate the following element (all in one line):

```
<case match="^Mozilla/5\.0 \([^)]*\) (Gecko/[-\d]+ ➥
)?Netscape6/(?'version'(?'major'\d+)(?'minor'\.\d+)(?'letters'\w*)).*">
```

This element defines the features those browsers support. Add the following below it:

```
<!-- Patch to output attributes for NS6+/Mozilla1.x -->
tagwriter=System.Web.UI.HtmlTextWriter
```

What this attribute tells ASP.NET is that FireFox and Netscape support tags written in the same way as IE. According to Microsoft's comments, this patch, and future ones, will be available from a third party: cyScape, Inc. (`http://www.cyscape.com/browsercaps`).

Extensions

The most obvious extension to this class is to allow other values rather than integers to be entered and incremented or decremented, such as currency values, date/time, even predefined lists like month names, as well as support for a culture-aware or even custom negative number format.

The `NumericUpDown` control available to Windows Forms developers has a sister control called `DomainUpDown` that performs a similar function to the `NumericUpDown` control, except it uses text instead of numbers. We could develop a version of our `Spinner` control similar to this control.

We could also allow the developer to choose a custom Unicode character to display in the buttons, or even a custom picture.

■ ■ ■

CHAPTER 3

Bindable Bullet List

Most Web applications require the listing of data. When particular information in a Web page is provided best in a list, you may find that a bulleted list is useful. ASP.NET provides a good collection of controls that can be used for displaying lists, but most of these controls require much intervention to have the list display in the desired way. In some controls, you may have to define templates for the items, while in others you do not have that degree of flexibility.

In this chapter, you will create a custom control used to bind a list of data to, and then have it presented in a Web page as a bulleted list.

Scenario

The scenario is simple. You might want to list your most impressive skills for your résumé, or list your fourth quarter financial highlights for your organization. Alternatively, you could list the top five items purchased by customers who also bought the item that they are currently viewing on a commerce Web site. The various possible scenarios for listing data and information on Web pages are endless. The key is how you want to display that information. Do you want to manually enter the HTML and hardcode each item in the list using standard bullet tags? On the other hand, is the data too dynamic to be hardcoded in that fashion? You may want a repeater control that will require a template to be defined for how you'd like the user-provided data to be displayed.

The easiest approach to save time is to create a custom control that will easily display the data well—code once, use everywhere.

Technology

While this particular control does not expose any particularly advanced technologies, it will take advantage of some very important object-oriented (OO) programming concepts. In addition, since the control should be as useful and flexible as it can be, we need to ensure that it can bind to data from many different formats. The .NET Framework provides us with several different classes that can hold a list of data: `ArrayList`, `SortedList`, and `Hashtable` are a few examples of them. However, all that these classes have in common is that they are all types of collections. This means that each one of these classes implements the `IEnumerable` interface.

The `IEnumerable` interface serves as a contract for all of a certain class of object. Each of the classes that the control will be able to work with will implement this interface. This will make it very easy to accept many different types of data sources with a minimal amount of code. You will see the solution in action when the control is implemented. Nothing more complicated than the good use of the `IEnumerable` interface occurs in this control.

Design

For the control to be useful, it is designed in such a way so that it is compatible with many of the collection object types in the .NET Framework.

When programmers first learn OO programming, the power of inheritance is often overemphasized. However, inheritance does provide code reuse across related objects, and the functional power of OO programming comes from its related technology, polymorphism. Although a full discussion of OO programming is far beyond the scope of this book, we should elaborate on how the power of polymorphism increases the usability and effectiveness of the bulleted list control.

Polymorphism is an OO programming concept that can be summarized as the ability of objects to act depending on their run-time type. For example, we can call a method on a class and the reference to the class will not care what specific type of object it is, as long as the method is supported in one of the base classes (from `System.Object` upwards). This scenario occurs often in classes that use inheritance or object models that use interfaces. Such a scenario involving interfaces is what we are going to use in our control. As you have seen, the `IEnumerable` interface is implemented in a variety of .NET classes used for maintaining lists of information. See Figure 3-1 to assist you in your understanding of this (to keep the diagram simple, only a few of the derived classes are listed).

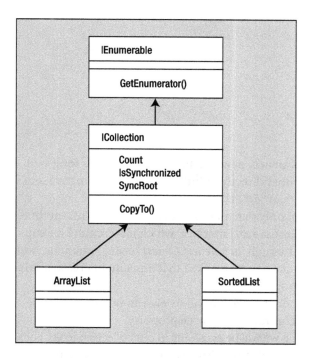

Figure 3-1. *Some classes implementing* IEnumerable

In this diagram, we are showing that the two classes (ArrayList and Sortedlist) both implement the ICollection interface. The ICollection interface derives from IEnumerable and so any class that implements ICollection also indirectly implements IEnumerable. This means that each class must have its own implementation of the GetEnumerator() method, as well as the method and properties of the ICollection interface. In any code written, we will not have to concern ourselves with which class is received, because we know that each class must provide an implementation for each of these methods and properties. This means you only need to specify a parameter or object of type IEnumerable in your code.

In order to make the control easy to understand, we will expose a property with the name DataSource. All bindable controls have a property called DataSource. When this property is present, it is assumed that the data to be bound to this control is passed as an object to this DataSource property. Next, we need to make sure our control is as useful as it can be. We will accomplish this by making the data type of our DataSource property that of IEnumerable. With this data type, the control will be able to bind to several intrinsic types that implement the IEnumerable interface as the following:

- Hashtable

- SortedList

- ArrayList

- BitArray

- Queue

- Stack

- Array

In addition to this list, our control can accept any other custom type as long as it implements the IEnumerable interface, either directly or indirectly. In addition, DataSets can be supported via the DataSet's IListSource.GetList() method.

The IEnumerable interface consists of only one method: GetEnumerator. This method returns an object that implements the IEnumerator interface, which is a contract for supporting simple iteration over a collection through its MoveNext() and Reset() methods, and the Current property. This means, for instance, that an object that implements IEnumerable may be used as the object in a For Each loop.

So far, this is all straightforward for our control. We will receive an object that implements the IEnumerable interface for the control's DataSource property.

However, the IEnumerable interface that we will be accessing in our collection to get back an enumerator object also uses the concept of polymorphism because there are different types of enumerator objects. There is the base enumerator as well as the IDictionaryEnumerator, which inherits from IEnumerator. This allows the GetEnumerator() method to return a base enumerator object or a derived object, in this case an IDictionaryEnumerator object. The difference between these two is that the IDictionaryEnumerator supports the ability to iterate through the collection objects that support the key-value pair structure, such as Hashtable and SortedList. You will see during the "Implementation" section how we work with each type of enumerator.

In order to enhance the design-time support of the control so that users will be able to hook up the control as quickly as possible, we will ensure that our control sets up all of its default values and paints itself appropriately in the designer (for developers using some form of IDE). The control will also allow an image field to be specified for a custom bullet. To make this easier, we will provide the consumer with the ImageURLEditor from the property browser.

Many properties in the property explorer provide a button to launch a custom user interface in order to make editing the property simpler. An example is the Font property. There are a few built-in user interface (UI) editors provided by the framework; in this case, we will use the URL Editor that will provide a file browser interface to locate the image file to be used.

Implementation

Create a new class named `DataBindBulletList` and make it part of the `Apress.Toolkit` namespace. Begin by importing all the required namespaces for the class.

```
Imports System
Imports System.ComponentModel
Imports System.Web.UI
Imports System.Drawing.Design
Imports System.Web.UI.HTMLControls
Imports System.Web.UI.WebControls
Imports System.Web.UI.Design
Imports System.Collections
```

You will need to add references to `System.Design.dll`, `System.Web.dll`, and `System.Drawing.dll` to make use of these namespaces. Now define the class as follows:

```
Namespace Apress.Toolkit
  <ToolboxData("<{0}: DataBindBulletList
runat=""server"" ColumnCount=""1"" DisplayOrientation=""Vertical""/>")>
  Public Class DataBindBulletList
    Inherits WebControl
    Implements INamingContainer
```

Here we have defined a class that will inherit from `WebControl`. Implementing `INamingContainer`—as we saw in Chapter 2—ensures a unique name is assigned to our control.

Now, remember that in the "Design" section we mentioned that there were two types of enumerators: `IEnumerator` and `IDictionaryEnumerator`. We want to be able to deal with both without duplicating much code, so in the next code snippet we define a new subclass, `GenericEnumerator`, that will act as a wrapper accepting both types of enumerator at construction time, while behaving like a standard `IEnumerator` object. This means the control does not need to worry about what kind of enumerator it is dealing with.

```
  Private Class GenericEnumerator
    Implements IEnumerator

    Private _enumerator As IEnumerator
    Private sync As New Object()
```

This class implements `IEnumerator`, which includes a private field of the same type to hold the wrapped enumerator instance (given at construction time), and an object used for thread synchronization. The following is the constructor overload for an IDictionaryEnumerator object:

```
Sub New(enumerator As IDictionaryEnumerator)
  Dim newCollection As New ArrayList()
  While enumerator.MoveNext()
    newCollection.Add(enumerator.Value)
  End While
  Me._enumerator = newCollection.GetEnumerator()
End Sub
```

This creates a new ArrayList object and puts the values in the IDictionaryEnumerator into it (discarding the keys). While MoveNext() returns True, it will add the current enumerator.Value to the ArrayList. It then calls GetEnumerator() on the ArrayList and stores the returned IEnumerator object into the private _enumerator field. The second overload requires no explanation.

```
Sub New(enumerator As IEnumerator)
  Me._enumerator = enumerator
End Sub
```

Now, we're ready to define the property and methods necessary for the IEnumerator object. These are mostly straightforward as well.

```
Public ReadOnly Property Current As Object _
    Implements IEnumerator.Current
  Get
    SyncLock sync
      Return _enumerator.Current
    End SyncLock
  End Get
End Property
```

This property implements IEnumerator.Current, and it uses a SyncLock statement. No code in any other SyncLock statement with a reference to the same object (sync) can execute simultaneously. It has to wait until the first block of code has finished. This makes the enumerator thread-safe so one call cannot call MoveNext() at the same time another is calling Current, for instance. The methods are coded in a similar way, as follows:

```
Public Function MoveNext() As Boolean _
    Implements IEnumerator.MoveNext
  SyncLock sync
    Return _enumerator.MoveNext()
```

```
    End SyncLock
  End Function

  Public Sub Reset() Implements IEnumerator.Reset
    SyncLock sync
      _enumerator.Reset()
    End SyncLock
  End Sub
End Class
```

The methods and property of this object are now thread-safe, which may be useful in certain kinds of applications. Now we can describe the rest of the control.

To increase the customizability of our control, we will expose some properties for consumer access. Of course, we need to preserve the state of these properties across postbacks so their implementation will consist of storing and retrieving them from ViewState; this is what the ImageForBullet property looks like:

```
Public Property ImageForBullet As String
  Get
    Dim obj as Object
        Obj = Me.ViewState ("ImageForBullet")
        If (Not obj is Nothing) Then
                          Return CType (obj,String)
        End If
        Return String.Empty
  End Get
  Set(ByVal value As String)
    Me.ViewState ("ImageForBullet") = value
    Me.ChildControlsCreated = False
  End Set
End Property
```

What we're doing in the Get accessor is first checking if there was any value previously stored into ViewState for that property. If one is found, we just return it, otherwise the default value for the property type is returned: String.Empty in this case. The Set accessor is simpler, consisting of just feeding into ViewState the received value.

The first method we override is CreateChildControls(). In this method, we will be creating our child controls whose rendering will compose the main UI. Our approach will consist of rendering an HTML table with a number of rows and cells that will depend on how many bullets and columns were specified by the user. This method is important because most of the processing will occur here. Every time the state of the control changes, this method should be called in order to allow for the child controls to re-create themselves showing the new changes.

```
Protected Overrides Sub CreateChildControls()
  Controls.Clear()
```

Note that, as specified in Chapter 1, the first thing we're doing in CreateChildControls is clearing any previous children that may exist. Then, we declare variables to hold the HtmlTable objects we will need.

```
Dim _htmltable As New HtmlTable()
Dim tr As HtmlTableRow
Dim tc As HtmlTableCell
Dim Counter As Integer
Dim ColumnCounter As Integer
```

The variable names should be quite self-explanatory. Next, we try to get the current bullets that should be rendered.

```
'If there are bullets to show
If Not (Bullets = Nothing) Then
    'get them by splitting the original string using
    '^ as a separator char
    items = Bullets.Split(sep)
Else
    'at run time the control will produce no output
    If Not (Me.Context Is Nothing) Then
        Return
        'at design time, get a design-time set of bullets
    Else
        items = GetDesignTimeItems()
    End If
End If
```

In the case that there are no bullets to show, we check if the control is running at run time, in which case we just return and no child controls are created; if, instead, we detect the control is running at design time, we call the GetDesignTimeBullets method, which returns a set of design-time bullets.

Bullets is a private property of type String (intended to be used only by the control) that is persisted into ViewState and it's used to hold the list of bullets to be rendered. All bullets are stored into a single string, so we're using a delimiter character (^) for separating them. But if this is a private property, how are you supposed to set the bullets to show? You use the DataSource property by assigning to it any type that implements IEnumerable.

As our control is overriding the OnDataBinding method, it gets a chance to be notified when databinding occurs. When this happens it will iterate through the data provided in the DataSource property and create our custom string containing all the bullets. Here is where our GenericEnumerator enters the scene: to allow us to enumerate the data source without caring about the specific type of enumerator it may implement.

```
Protected Overrides Sub OnDataBinding(ByVal e As EventArgs)

Dim Enumerator As IEnumerator = _
        New GenericEnumerator(_DataSource.GetEnumerator())
Dim items() As String
While Enumerator.MoveNext()
    items = items + CType(Enumerator.Current, String) + "^"
End While
```

Let's continue with the code that creates the child controls.

```
If Me.ColumnCount = 1 Then
    If Me.DisplayOrientation = _
            DisplayOrientationType.Horizontal Then
        tr = New HtmlTableRow
        Dim c As Integer
        For c = 0 To items.Length - 1
            tc = BuildTableCell(items(c))
            tr.Controls.Add(tc)
        Next
        _htmltable.Rows.Add(tr)
```

If ColumnCount is 1, and the orientation is Horizontal, then the code steps through each bullet in a For loop.

If the orientation is Vertical, then there will be several rows and just one column.

```
    Else
        Dim c As Integer
        For c = 0 To items.Length - 1
            tr = New HtmlTableRow
            tc = BuildTableCell(items(c))
            tr.Cells.Add(tc)
            _htmltable.Rows.Add(tr)
        Next
    End If
```

The previous code is straightforward. Now, if ColumnCount is greater than 1, we will ignore the Display Orientation property and display the table as follows:

```
        Else
            Dim Enumerator As IEnumerator = items.GetEnumerator()
            For Counter = 0 To CInt(items.Length / ColumnCount)
                tr = New HtmlTableRow
                For ColumnCounter = 1 To ColumnCount
                    If Enumerator.MoveNext() Then
                        tc = BuildTableCell(Enumerator.Current.ToString())
                        tr.Cells.Add(tc)
                    Else
                        Exit For
                    End If
                Next
                If tr.Cells.Count > 0 Then _htmltable.Rows.Add(tr)
            Next
        End If
```

We start by getting an enumerator for the items array that is holding the bullets to render. We then define a For loop that iterates a number of times equal to the number of items to render divided by three (fractional parts truncated/rounded towards zero) plus one. After creating a new row, we then have another For loop that iterates the number of specified columns. In this inner For loop, a new cell is created and added to the row as long as MoveNext() returns True. If it ever returns False, then the code exits the inner For loop. If the row previously created has any members, then they are added to the table. This stops a blank row from being created if the number of enumerator members is an exact multiple of the number of columns.

Now we can finish the method by adding the HtmlTable to the Control's collection of controls (there should only be one control).

```
    Controls.Add(_htmltable)
End Sub
```

The previous method contains most of the processing for this control. You will now see the code for the helper method, which builds the table cells.

```
Private Function BuildTableCell(ByVal text As String) _
    As HtmlTableCell
  Dim listTag As String
  If Not Me.ImageForBullet = String.Empty Then
    listTag = "<ul><li style='list-style-image:url(" & _
        Me.ImageForBullet & ");'>"
  Else
    listTag = "<ul><li>"
  End If
```

```
Dim tc As HtmlTableCell = New HtmlTableCell()
tc.NoWrap = True
Dim cellLabel As Label = New Label()
cellLabel.ForeColor = MyBase.ForeColor
cellLabel.Text = listTag & (text & "</li></ul>")
tc.Controls.Add(cellLabel)

Return tc
End Function
```

This is a straightforward routine. This method accepts the value of an item from the collection passed into the control and builds up a table cell, which is added into the base HtmlTable control. It checks to see if ImageForBullet has been set, and also if a custom bullet was specified. If so, it modifies the <li> tag to incorporate the Cascading Style Sheets (CSS) style tag for a custom bullet image. This style attribute allows the control to use a custom image for the bullet instead of the default.

Once the control knows what <li> tag to use, it builds a Label control to show the text. The Label control makes it easier to apply the base WebControls properties to the text. In this case, we are only concerned with the ForeColor property; however, we could easily apply any property we see fit. The method then adds the label to the table cell's Controls collection and returns the table cell to the caller, where it will be added to the collection of the HtmlTableRow, and, in turn, to the Rows collection of the HtmlTable.

At this point, the control is in a workable condition. All the code to implement the functionality is in place and we can now compile it and start using it. However, one more thing should occur. This does not affect the behavior of the control, but can make using the control much easier for developers. We will now add some design-time support so the control is configurable without too much code typing. At the end of this section, the only aspect of the control that will have to be coded is the setting of the data source.

Attributes are added to the properties. These attributes define specific design-time behavior. There are a large number of attributes available for use. For an explanation about each of them, consult the MSDN documentation. We will only concern ourselves with the few that will help us out. Modify the property declarations with the following code:

```
<Category("ApressToolkit"), _
 Description("The relative path to an image file within the" + _
 "virtual directory to use for the bullet."), _
 Editor(GetType(System.Web.UI.Design.ImageUrlEditor), _
 GetType(UITypeEditor))> _
Public Property ImageForBullet() As String
    Get
        Dim obj As Object
        obj = Me.ViewState("ImageForBullet")
```

```vb
            If (Not obj Is Nothing) Then
                Return CType(obj, String)
            End If
            Return String.Empty
        End Get
        Set(ByVal value As String)
            Me.ViewState("ImageForBullet") = value
          Me.ChildControlsCreated = False
            Me.EnsureChildControls()
      End Set
    End Property


    <Category("ApressToolkit"), _
     Description("The Data source to display in the list.")> _
    Public Property DataSource() As IEnumerable
      Get
        Return _DataSource
      End Get
      Set(ByVal value As IEnumerable)
        _DataSource = value
        Me.ChildControlsCreated = False
        Me.EnsureChildControls()
      End Set
    End Property


        <Category("ApressToolkit"), _
        Description("States whether the list will be displayed Horizontally or ➡
Vertically")>_
        Public Property DisplayOrientation() As DisplayOrientationType
            Get
                Dim obj As Object = ViewState.Item("DisplayOrientation")
                If Not (obj Is Nothing) Then
                    Return CType(obj, DisplayOrientationType)
                Else
                    Return DisplayOrientationType.Vertical
                End If
            End Get
            Set(ByVal value As DisplayOrientationType)
                ViewState.Item("DisplayOrientation") = value
                Me.ChildControlsCreated = False
                Me.EnsureChildControls()
            End Set
        End Property
```

```
    <Category("ApressToolkit"), _
     Description("The number of columns to be displayed in the list.")> _
    Public Property ColumnCount() As Integer
        Get
            Dim obj As Object = ViewState.Item("ColumnCount")
            If Not (obj Is Nothing) Then
                Return CType(obj, Integer)
            Else
                Return 1
            End If
        End Get
        Set(ByVal value As Integer)
            If value < 1 Then
                Throw New ArgumentException("Value must be 1 or greater")
            End If
            ViewState.Item("ColumnCount") = value
            Me.ChildControlsCreated = False
            Me.EnsureChildControls()
        End Set
    End Property
```

In each property Set method, we have added code to make sure that the control redraws itself. This will give instant visible feedback to the developers in the designer as they change the properties of the control in the property viewer that is available to them. To better organize the properties on the Properties viewer, we specify a category. In this case, all of our properties are listed under the ApressToolkit category in the property viewer. We also add a description so that the developer can select the properties and see a brief description as to what they are supposed to do.

Another attribute of interest is on the ImageForBullet property, called Editor. This attribute allows us to define a Property Editor user interface to correspond with our property. This results in an ellipsis button for the property in the Properties window in Visual Studio .NET. Though it is possible to create your own custom editors for your controls, we can use one already provided by the framework. In this case, we specify an ImageURLEditor. This will make it easier for the developer to point and click to the image file, and just simply click OK to have the URL applied. This user interface is common and looks like what you see in Figure 3-2.

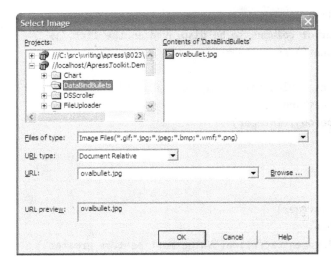

Figure 3-2. *The built-in* ImageURLEditor

Now the control is fully functional and easy to use. Compile the control to an assembly and you're ready to see the bindable bullet list in action.

Demonstration

Once we have compiled our control, added it to the toolbox, and dragged it onto to the designer, it should look like what you see in Figure 3-3.

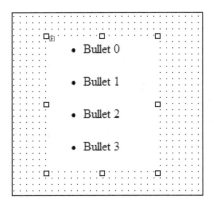

Figure 3-3. Vertical *design-time view*

The code in the CreateChildControls() method generates this default bullet list if the data source is nothing. By doing this, we are able to give visual feedback at design time as to what the control will look like when databound and rendered to the client at run time. Now, alter the property settings and watch the control change in appearance at design time.

Figure 3-4 shows the control with the DisplayOrientation set to Horizontal.

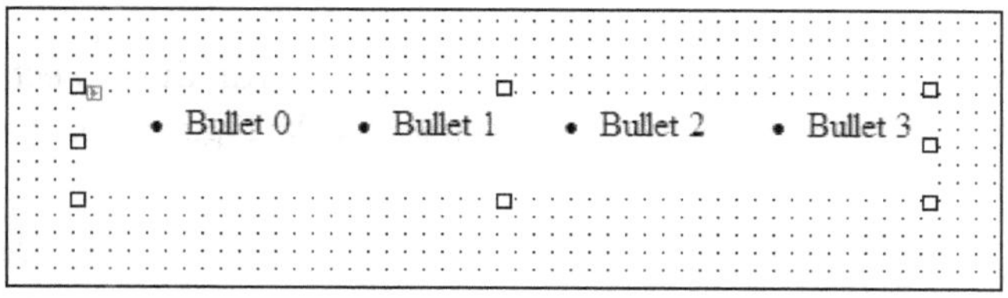

Figure 3-4. Horizontal *design-time view*

In addition, if we change the column count to three, we see our control change dynamically to what is shown in Figure 3-5.

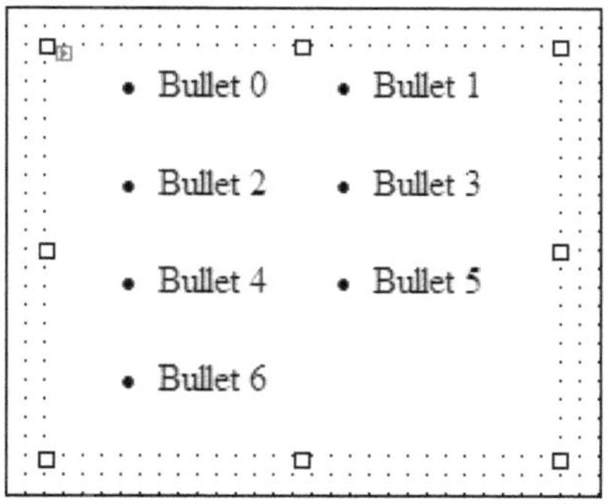

Figure 3-5. Vertical *design-time view with two columns set*

Let's take one more look at our control at run time. You will need some code in the Page_Load event to set up the data source. For this example, let's use the custom bullet property. Set the ImageForBullet property to OvalBullet.jpg in the property explorer, and add the following code:

```vb
Private Sub Page_Load(ByVal sender As System.Object, _
                      ByVal e As System.EventArgs) Handles MyBase.Load
  If Not IsPostBack Then
    Dim source As New ArrayList()
```

```
    source.Add("More pay")
    source.Add("Less working hours")
    source.Add("Longer vacations")
    DataBindBulletList1.DataSource = source
    DataBindBulletList1.DataBind()
  End If
End Sub
```

You can try this out with any of the collection objects listed earlier. If you run the project and add a heading before the bulleted list, you will get a page that looks like Figure 3-6.

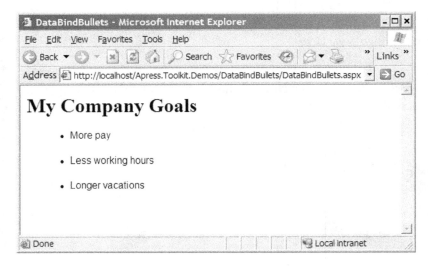

Figure 3-6. *A run-time view of our* DataBindBulletList *control*

Limitations

Our control does not allow the user to set different styles on each list item. It is an all-or-nothing scenario where each item in the list gets the same attributes and styles as every other list item. In addition, the list is limited to showing the data in a tabular format of columns and rows with no special display capabilities. Although we could pass in a collection of tables, the current implementation does not facilitate binding to fields in a data table. We would not be able to do more than list the names of the table that are in the collection.

Extensions

The control as implemented offers some useful possibilities for extensibility or features. This simple control solves a simple problem, but does offer the potential to save developers a lot of time in displaying lists. To extend the functionality of this control, it could offer a custom bullet property that offers a choice of bullets, like those present in Microsoft Word. This could be implemented using a custom `UIEditor` class that displays the bullet styles so that the developer can easily visualize what each one would look like. As another option, the control could expose an enumeration for the CSS list-style-type, such as disc, circles, etc. Also, this control could expose a wide variety of text formatting properties for the data item. In addition, it could offer the ability to display a bullet list of images. When it comes to building custom controls, imagination is the only true limiting factor. Where we are accustomed to databound controls easily binding to backend data stores such as SQL Server via ADO.NET, this would be a handy extension. Additional properties such as `DataValueField` and `DataTextField` could be exposed to indicate what field from a table should be written out to the list.

CHAPTER 4

■ ■ ■

Data Navigator

In business applications today, we usually have the ability to navigate and manipulate sets of data through a comprehensive user interface. The user interface usually provides a data entry field for each relevant element of a table in a database. For example, when working with employee records in a company database, we might provide all the fields necessary for editing and updating information such as employee name or employee date of birth. In addition, we can scroll through the records by using buttons that provide functionality for moving to the next record or the previous record, as well as the ability to apply any changes that have been made.

In Windows applications, this functionality is typically easy to provide (for example, bindable forms). With ASP.NET, we are provided with a nice repertoire of bindable controls, such as the DataGrid and the Repeater. However, the Repeater is not editable and the DataGrid has limitations with respect to how far you can go with editing the data. We will examine these limitations in the next section and explain how a custom control can be used to give functionality that is difficult, if not impossible, to achieve with the standard databinding controls provided with ASP.NET.

Scenario

The requirement for this control is to provide functionality to scroll and update a given DataSet. We need our control to be well encapsulated in order to ensure solid reusability. In addition, the control must be very dynamic in order to handle all different types and amounts of data in our DataSet (like the number of columns and their data types).

With this Control we will be able to navigate a set of data in a user friendly manner while allowing for updates, deletions, additions, and, of course, cancellations to pending modifications.

Let's review the technology required to build our control.

Technology

When working with data over a medium such as the Internet, we are immediately faced with the challenge of maintaining the state of our objects. Typically, the lifetime of an object in a Web application is very short. The objects we use are created, used, and destroyed all before the client is able to see the information they have requested. This concept is especially important for the control we will be creating shortly. We will need to maintain the state of the data passed into it for each click of each button we provide in the user interface. The control will have to know precisely which record of data to present, how many records are available, and be able to hold on to any changes made to the data until the Save button is pressed. We will see how ASP.NET provides us with the tools to accomplish this task rather easily.

Design

Our control will be built completely from controls already provided by the ASP.NET framework, as this will make its rendering and management much simpler. We will be able to take advantage of the interfaces provided by these controls and will not need to re-invent the wheel to achieve some of the simple functionality that they already provide. Also, all the logic is built into the intrinsic controls for maintaining the state of their values. All we need to be concerned with is maintaining the state of the DataSet itself and any other properties that we offer in our control.

We will also be making use of the data-access technology provided by ADO.NET. We will accept a DataSet consisting of one DataTable and then iterate through the columns of the DataTable to generate our user interface.

The basic element for the layout of objects most commonly used in Web pages is the table. It is very easy to use and can assist in providing a simple, easy-to-use interface. Needless to say, we will leverage this element as the basis for our control. The control will build the HTML table dynamically based on the data it receives.

For our control to be versatile, we will have to build and add controls to the table at run time once it receives the data, which is when we will know how many rows the table should have. In our design, the table will always consist of two columns. The first one will hold the name of the DataColumn and the second one will display its value.

Implementation

Now that we have finished discussing the reasoning and design behind the DataNavigator control, we can get to the fun part and start coding it. Let's begin by firing up our favorite editor for working with ASP.NET. We will need to import the following namespaces into our .vb file:

```
Imports System
Imports System.ComponentModel
Imports System.Web.UI
Imports System.Web.UI.HtmlControls
Imports System.Web.UI.WebControls
Imports System.Data.SqlClient
Imports System.Data
```

We will be using intrinsic controls, such as the textbox, and adding them to an HTML table for proper alignment, and we will also be using other classes provided to us by the System.Web.UI.HtmlControls and the System.Web.UI.WebControls namespaces. All the ADO.NET functionality that we will need is made available through the System.Data and System.Data.SqlClient namespaces. We will be using the System.ComponentModel namespace for one specific class that will be explained later.

Once we have declared the namespaces that we will need, we can provide a class definition.

```
<ToolboxData("<{0}:DataNavigator runat=server></{0}:DataNavigator>")> _
Public Class DataNavigator

    Inherits System.Web.UI.WebControls.WebControl
    Implements INamingContainer
```

We have applied an attribute to our class. This attribute, called ToolboxData, as you may recall from Chapter 1, will provide the default markup that should be used when an instance of the control is dragged onto a Web form or user control.

Next, we will define our class members; add the following declaration to the class:

```
Private WithEvents PreviousButton As Button
Private WithEvents NextButton As Button
Private WithEvents SaveButton As Button
Private WithEvents CancelButton As Button
```

These first four declarations will provide a reference to the four buttons that will be displayed to the user. Then we will define two properties that will be backed up into ViewState: DataSet and CurrentIndex; each one of them will be coded using the ViewState-pattern we saw in Chapter 1.

```
    Public Property CurrentIndex As Integer
      Get
        Dim obj as Object
        Obj = Me.ViewState ("CurrentIndex")
```

```
        If (Not obj is Nothing) Then
                Return CType (obj,Integer)
        End If
        Return 0
    End Get
    Set(ByVal value As Integer)
        Me.ViewState ("CurrentIndex") = value
    End Set
End Property
```

The reason for these properties will become more obvious as we continue.

DataSource accepts a DataSet containing a DataTable with the data we want to navigate, and CurrentIndex keeps track of the current position (record) in the Table.

As well as this, our class will also use a few internal utility methods. The SetDataTableValues() method will be used to save the data from the UI to our DataTable for each click of the buttons on the UI. This method will be implemented as follows:

```
Private Sub SetDataTableValues()
    Dim htmltable As htmltable = CType(Controls(0), htmltable)
    Dim tr As HtmlTableRow
    Dim datacol As DataColumn
    Dim colidx As Integer = 0

    For Each tr In htmltable.Rows
        datacol = DataSource.Tables(0).Columns(colidx)
        Dim coltype As Type = DataSource.Tables(0).Columns(colidx).DataType
        If (coltype Is GetType(Boolean)) Then
            DataSource.Tables(0).Rows(CurrentIndex)( colidx) = _
                Math.Abs(CType(CType(tr.Cells(1).Controls(0), _
                CheckBox).Checked, Integer))
        ElseIf (coltype Is GetType(DateTime)) Then
            DataSource.Tables(0).Rows(CurrentIndex)( colidx) = _
                CType(tr.Cells(1).Controls(0), Calendar).SelectedDate
        Else
            DataSource.Tables(0).Rows(CurrentIndex)( colidx) = _
                CType(tr.Cells(1).Controls(0), TextBox).Text
        End If
        colidx = colidx + 1
    Next
End Sub
```

In this method, we iterate over the rows of the `HtmlTable` that we have rendered. We extract the data column based on the index of the column and set the value of that column from the control that corresponds with that column. We also have to check the data type of the column here to know what type of control to insert into the corresponding cell. The SQL data types that we could expect to see are bit fields (boolean) and character fields such as `varchar` or `nvarchar` (string).

The next utility function we will provide for our internal use is the `GetControl()` method, which will be used to determine what data type the column is and return the appropriate type of control. Enter the following code into your class:

```
Private Function GetControl(ByVal Index As Integer) As WebControl
    Dim colType As Type = DataSource.Tables(0).Columns(Index).DataType

    If (colType Is GetType(Boolean)) Then
        Dim chkBox As CheckBox = New CheckBox
        chkBox.Checked = _
            CType(DataSource.Tables(0).Rows(CurrentIndex) _
            (DataSource.Tables(0).Columns(Index)), Boolean)
        chkBox.ApplyStyle(ControlStyle)
        Return chkBox
    ElseIf (colType Is GetType(Decimal) Or colType Is GetType(Double) _
            Or colType Is GetType(Int16) Or colType Is GetType(Int32) _
            Or colType Is GetType(Int64) Or colType Is GetType(Single) _
            Or colType Is GetType(UInt16) Or colType Is GetType(UInt32) _
            Or colType Is GetType(UInt64) Or colType Is GetType(Char) _
            Or colType Is GetType(String)) Then
        Dim txtBox As TextBox = New TextBox
        If (DataSource.Tables(0).Columns(Index).MaxLength <> -1) Then
            txtBox.MaxLength = DataSource.Tables(0).Columns(Index).MaxLength
        End If
        txtBox.Text = _
            DataSource.Tables(0).Rows(CurrentIndex) _
            (DataSource.Tables(0).Columns(Index)).ToString()
        txtBox.ApplyStyle(ControlStyle)
        Return txtBox
    Else
        'At this point we're handling with a nonsupported type
        'add code to return a control for such types
    End If
End Function
```

In this method, given a column index, we check its type against our supported types and return an appropriate control: a TextBox for numeric and string types or a CheckBox for the Boolean type. Note that you could easily add support for other different types by extending the previous code; for example, you could return a Calendar control for DateTime types.

Now that we have our utility methods in place, let's begin to add the code that will create all our controls. As we already learned from Chapter 1, the proper method to accomplish this is the CreateChildControls() provided by the base class. First, define the method as follows:

```
Protected Overrides Sub CreateChildControls()
```

Now that we have our method signature in place, begin by adding the code to retrieve a reference to the DataTable.

```
If DataSource.Tables(0) Is Nothing Then
     Return
End If

If DataSource.Tables(0).Rows.Count = 0 Then
     Return
End If
```

In this code segment, we ensure that the DataSet does actually contain a DataTable and that there is, indeed, data in this table by using the Rows collection's Count property. Now that we know we have some data to work with, we can begin to add the code necessary to create all our child controls that will make up our data navigation UI.

Remember that before beginning to add child controls, we should always ensure that the Controls collection is empty, as follows:

```
Controls.Clear()
```

Next, we will create an HtmlTable, HtmlTableCell, and HtmlTableRow. Using these objects, we will iterate through the DataTable columns and add the appropriate controls to the HtmlTable. Add the following code:

```
Dim htmltable As HtmlControls.HtmlTable = _
    New HtmlControls.HtmlTable()
Dim tr As HtmlTableRow
Dim tc As HtmlTableCell
Dim WebControl As WebControl
Dim ColumnCounter As Integer
```

```
For ColumnCounter = 0 To DataSource.Tables(0).Columns.Count - 1
    tr = New HtmlTableRow
    htmltable.Rows.Add(tr)
    tc = New HtmlTableCell
    tc.InnerHtml = _
        DataSource.Tables(0).Columns(ColumnCounter).ColumnName
    tr.Cells.Add(tc)
    tc = New HtmlTableCell
    tr.Cells.Add(tc)
    WebControl = GetControl(ColumnCounter)
    tc.Controls.Add(WebControl)
Next


Controls.Add(htmltable)
```

In this segment of code, we instantiate the `HtmlTable` that will contain all of the controls that we will need in order to display the data from the `DataTable`. For each column in the `DataTable`, we instantiate an `HtmlTableRow` and two `HtmlTableCell` objects. We add the name of the column as text to the first table cell and we add the control to display the data for the column to the second table cell. Both of these cells are added to the `HtmlTableRow` and, finally, the `HtmlTableRow` is added to the `HtmlTable`. We will use a new `HtmlTable` to hold the four buttons as well as add four cells to one row for this table. Let's do that now.

```
htmltable = New HtmlTable()
tr = New HtmlTableRow()
tc = New HtmlTableCell()


htmltable.Rows.Add(tr)
```

We declare only one `HtmlTableCell` because we will "refresh" the instance after each button. Now, we will add the code to create the buttons and add them to the `HtmlTable`.

```
PreviousButton = New Button()
With PreviousButton
  .Text = "Previous"
  .ApplyStyle(ControlStyle)
  .CommandArgument = CurrentIndex
End With
tc.Controls.Add(PreviousButton)


tr.Cells.Add(tc)
```

```
    tc = New HtmlTableCell()
    NextButton = New Button()
    With NextButton
      .Text = "Next"
      .ApplyStyle(ControlStyle)
      .CommandArgument = CurrentIndex
    End With
    tc.Controls.Add(NextButton)

    tr.Cells.Add(tc)

    tc = New HtmlTableCell()
    CancelButton = New Button()
    With CancelButton
      .Text = "Cancel"
      .ApplyStyle(ControlStyle)
      .CommandArgument = CurrentIndex
      .Attributes.Add("onclick", _
        "window.returnValue=window.confirm" + _
        "('Are you sure you want to cancel?');" + _
        "alert(window.returnValue);void(0);")
    End With
    tc.Controls.Add(CancelButton)

    tr.Cells.Add(tc)

    tc = New HtmlTableCell()
    SaveButton = New Button()
    With SaveButton
      .Text = "Save"
      .ApplyStyle(ControlStyle)
      .CommandArgument = CurrentIndex
    End With

    tc.Controls.Add(SaveButton)

    tr.Cells.Add(tc)

    Controls.Add(htmltable)

  End Sub
```

The only items from this code segment that might warrant further explanation are the `Attributes.Add()` method for the Cancel button and the `CommandArgument` property of each button. The `Attributes.Add()` method allows us to add client-side attributes to our button. In this case, we will use JavaScript to prompt the client for confirmation before letting them cancel what could be a lot of work that they have done. Clients can get very angry if we just let them wipe out hours of work without any confirmation.

The `CommandArgument` property is provided by the `Button` class and is used so that we can provide a custom piece of data to their event handlers. In our case, we will use this property to pass the `CurrentIndex` of the data that we are working with. Let's examine the event handlers that need to be implemented for the four buttons.

The interface for our control will provide four buttons for data navigation: Previous and Next buttons that will allow the user to iterate back and forth through the records; a Cancel button that will undo any changes that have been made to the data; and, finally, a Save button that will allow the user to commit his/her changes to the data store.

Our control will require a way to receive the messages when these buttons are clicked on the client computer. We also want to give the consumer of the class an opportunity to handle the click events for the buttons, as they may want to override our event handlers and provide their own implementation. To provide that ability, we will have to define our own event that we can use to propagate the button click events to the client. Add the following line of code near the top of your class:

```
Public Event ButtonClick(ByVal sender As Object, _
    ByVal e As DataNavigatorButtonEventArgs)
Private WithEvents PreviousButton As Button
Private WithEvents NextButton As Button
Private WithEvents SaveButton As Button
Private WithEvents CancelButton As Button
```

You may notice, in the signature for our event handler, we are referencing a class called `DataNavigatorButtonEventArgs`. This is a custom class that we will create shortly. We will see its implementation in detail following the implementation of our event handlers for the four buttons.

Let's add in that code now. First, the Previous button:

```
Private Sub PreviousButton_Click(ByVal sender As Object, _
    ByVal e As System.EventArgs) Handles PreviousButton.Click

    If PreviousButton.CommandArgument <= 0 Then
        Return
    End If
```

```
    Dim ButtonEventArgs As New DataNavigatorButtonEventArgs(DataSource, _
        DataNavigatorButtonEventArgs.ButtonType.PrevButton)
    RaiseEvent ButtonClick(Me, ButtonEventArgs)

    If Not ButtonEventArgs.Cancel Then
      SetDataTableValues()
      CurrentIndex -= 1
      MyBase.ChildControlsCreated = False
    End If
  End Sub
```

In this event handler, first we get a reference to our `DataTable`. Then, we ensure that we are not already at the first record. If we are at the first record, we simply exit the method and leave the client with the first record's data. Otherwise, we proceed through the event handler. First, we instantiate a `ButtonEventArgs` object since this is the parameter that our custom event expects to receive, and then we raise our custom event.

After completing any processing that the client wanted to do, we can proceed and see if the event was canceled by the client (more detail on this shortly). If the event was not canceled, we decrement our `CurrentIndex` and tell the base class that `ChildControlsCreated` is `False`, so that the `CreateChildControls()` method is invoked next time it is needed, putting the data for the previous record into the fields.

Our code for the Next button looks similar, except we check to make sure we are not at the last record already; if we are not, we proceed and increment the `CurrentIndex`.

Next, we need to handle the events for our Save button, which is straightforward; we will simply pass on the `DataSet` to the consumer of our control. They will be responsible for extracting the `DataSet` and saving it to the data store. They will receive the `DataSet` as part of the `DataNavigatorButtonEventArgs` object. If this event is not canceled by the consumer, we will accept the changes on the `DataSet` object.

By letting consumers get into the middle of the process, we allow them to apply any custom business rules or logic to the data before the changes are committed. While they will have to write the changes to the database, they will save requerying the database to refresh the data. We handle that here by committing the changes up to the point in time the button is pressed. Add the following event handler to the class:

```
  Private Sub SaveButton_Click(ByVal sender As Object, _
      ByVal e As System.EventArgs) Handles SaveButton.Click

    Dim ButtonClickEventArgs As New _
        DataNavigatorButtonEventArgs(DataSource, _
      DataNavigatorButtonEventArgs.ButtonType.SaveButton)

    SetDataTableValues()
    RaiseEvent ButtonClick(Me, ButtonClickEventArgs)
```

```
      If Not ButtonClickEventArgs.Cancel Then
        DataSet.AcceptChanges()
      End If
    End Sub
```

In the case of the Save button, we need to call our utility method to set the `DataTable` fields prior to raising the event. This is to ensure that in the event of the consumer deciding to save the data to the table, they get the latest values.

The Cancel button event handler is also relatively straightforward.

```
  Private Sub CancelButton_Click(ByVal sender As Object, _
      ByVal e As System.EventArgs) Handles CancelButton.Click

    DataSet.RejectChanges()
    MyBase.ChildControlsCreated = False
    RaiseEvent ButtonClick(Me, _
        New DataNavigatorButtonEventArgs(DataSource, _
        DataNavigatorButtonEventArgs.ButtonType.CancelButton))
  End Sub
```

Now that we have our control fully coded, we will code one supporting class. This class inherits from the base `CancelEventArgs` class provided in the `System.ComponentModel` namespace. This provides a `Cancel` property, which is the property that consumers of the class, if they choose to implement our control with events, will use to tell us that they want to cancel the processing of that event.

In addition to this property, we want to be able to give consumers access to some other properties, such as a description of the button that was clicked. We will provide this in the form of an `Enum`. We also want to give them the `DataSet` in the current state that we have it in. As we alluded to earlier, it will give consumers the ability to validate the data after each button click. Let's take a look now at the code to implement this class.

```
Public Class DataNavigatorButtonEventArgs
  Inherits CancelEventArgs

  Public Enum ButtonType
    NextButton
    PrevButton
    SaveButton
    CancelButton
  End Enum

  Private _DataSet As DataSet
  Private _ButtonType As ButtonType
```

```
Friend Sub New(ByVal ds As DataSet, ByVal buttontype As ButtonType)
  _DataSet = ds
  _ButtonType = buttontype
End Sub

Public ReadOnly Property ButtonClickType() As ButtonType
  Get
    Return _ButtonType
  End Get
End Property

Public Property DataSet() As DataSet
  Get
    Return _DataSet
  End Get

  Set(ByVal Value As DataSet)
    _DataSet = Value
  End Set
End Property
End Class
```

Since this class needs to be visible to consumers, we must declare it as a Public class. But, because it is never necessary for consumers to instantiate this class directly, we declare the constructor as a Friend. This means that only classes found in the same assembly as DataNavigatorButtonEventArgs will be able to instantiate this one.

Now that we have our control fully functional, let's create a client application and hook up to the sample Northwind database provided by SQL Server to demonstrate the control's functionality.

Demonstration

The first thing required to be done is to compile all our code into an assembly. Next, in whichever development environment we are working in, we need to reference our assembly and add the control to an .aspx page. The client application will be responsible for creating the DataSet and passing it into our control.

In your test client application, add the following code:

```
Private Sub Page_Load(ByVal sender As System.Object, _
    ByVal e As System.EventArgs) Handles MyBase.Load
```

```
Dim cnn As New SqlConnection("User ID=sa;" & _
    "Password=;" & "Initial Catalog=Northwind;" & _
    "Data Source=(local);")
Dim sql As String = "SELECT ProductName, UnitPrice, " & _
    "Discontinued FROM Products"
Dim da As New SqlDataAdapter()
Dim cmd As New SqlCommand()
Dim ds As New DataSet()
Dim tbl As New DataTable()

With cmd
  .CommandText = sql
  .CommandType = CommandType.Text
  .Connection = cnn
End With

Try
  da.MissingSchemaAction = MissingSchemaAction.Add
  da.SelectCommand = cmd
  da.Fill(tbl)
  da.FillSchema(tbl, SchemaType.Mapped)
  ds.Tables.Add(tbl)

Finally
  If cnn.State <> ConnectionState.Closed Then
    cnn.Close()
  End If
  cmd.Dispose()
  cmd = Nothing
  da.Dispose()
  da = Nothing
End Try

With DataNavigator1
  .DataSource = ds
End With
End Sub
```

Now that we have established the DataSet and set up the properties on an instance of our DataNavigator, we can run our application and begin to navigate through the product's data and edit any we choose. When our application opens in the Web browser, you should see the interface shown in Figure 4-1.

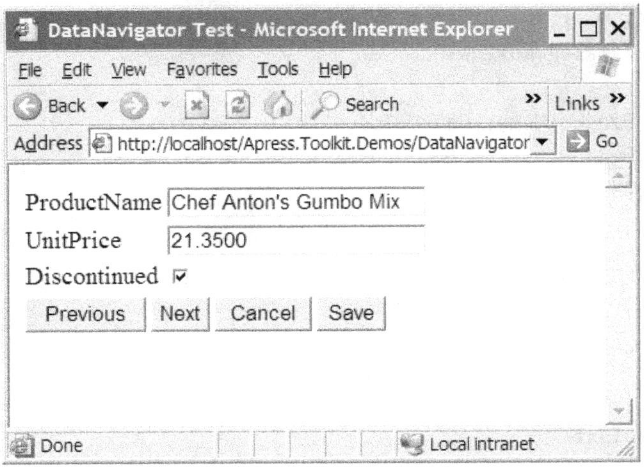

Figure 4-1. *The* DataNavigator *control in action*

Now, we can scroll through the products using the Previous and Next buttons, all of which will raise our custom event. To see the custom event handled, add the following code to the application:

```
Private Sub DataNavigator1_ButtonClick(ByVal sender As Object, _
    ByVal e As DataNavigator.DataNavigatorButtonEventArgs) _
    Handles DataNavigator1.ButtonClick

  Select Case e.ButtonClickType
    Case DataNavigator.DataNavigatorButtonEventArgs.ButtonType.CancelButton
      'The user clicked Cancel button

    Case DataNavigator.DataNavigatorButtonEventArgs.ButtonType.NextButton
      'The user clicked Next

    Case DataNavigator.DataNavigatorButtonEventArgs.ButtonType.PrevButton
      'The user clicked Previous button

    Case DataNavigator.DataNavigatorButtonEventArgs.ButtonType.SaveButton
      'The user clicked Save button

  End Select
End Sub
```

In this code segment, we are able to determine easily which button was clicked. Then, we can do what we need to do with the DataSet exposed by our custom DataNavigatorButtonEventArgs object.

Limitations

Our control's main limitation is caused by the way we are preserving the DataSource property between postbacks. We are just storing the value for this property (a DataSet instance) into ViewState. As you may remember from Chapter 1, the ViewState serializer is optimized to handle just a few bunches of types, and DataSet is definitively not one of them. Because of this, the ViewState footprint can get very large depending on the number of records stored into the DataTable contained in the DataSet. In the example given throughout this chapter, the DataTable has 3 columns and 77 records, which accounts for about 25kb of the ViewState's size. Handling hundreds or even thousands of records will generate such a large ViewState that it would make the page almost unusable. Of course, there should be no need to really send a thousand records down to the client; in the event of this possibility, other approaches—in addition to improving the ViewState's size—are necessary first, like implementing data-pagination.

In order to modify this control so that it makes an improved use of ViewState, you could start by defining a new simple class that models a record containing fields (i.e., Record class) and a strongly typed collection to easily handle instances of it (i.e., RecordCollection class). Then our control would need a new public property (i.e., Records) that will serve to access an instance of the RecordCollection class. Both Record and RecordCollection classes could implement the IStateManager interface with their own code to serialize themselves into ViewState: as long as they make sure they are not using any nonsupported type by the ViewState serializer, the footprint should be much smaller as there would be no need to invoke the BinaryFormatter at all. You may want to go over Chapter 1 again to refresh key points about ViewState serialization.

Extensions

There are many ways to extend this control. For example, it could be extended to include both client-side and server-side validations by adding the validation controls that are provided by the .NET Framework. With these controls, we would be able to ensure that numeric fields in the DataTable only receive numeric values using the RegularExpressionValidator, as well as ensure that all columns that do not allow null values have a value specified using the RequiredFieldValidator. Also, all of these checks could be added at the client side, thus avoiding an unnecessary postback when invalid data is entered.

In addition, we could extend this control by providing additional functionality to the user. We could add two more buttons that provide the ability to add new records and delete records from the DataTable.

We could also extend the look and feel of this control by providing additional properties for control alignment (e.g., two columns of data or four HtmlTable cells). Plus, we could add the ability to work with master-detail records. As you can see, there are a number of ways this control could be extended to suit your needs.

CHAPTER 5

■ ■ ■

File Uploader

Uploading files to a Web site is becoming more popular as people wish to share photographs on sites such as those designed to meet up with old schoolmates, for various online file sharing tools, and for Web-based e-mail providers. These are not the only scenarios, but the ability to upload a file and either store it on a server, in a database, or even send it by e-mail is becoming a more common practice. The control discussed in this chapter provides us with such ability.

Scenario

The general purpose of the control is to upload a stream of information and then manipulate it in different methods that are common on several of today's Web sites. Uploading images and storing them is perhaps the most common practice; however, there is no need to stop there.

The aim is to have a control that can both present the HTML necessary to provide a user interface for uploading a file to the server, and provide for different ways of dealing with the file once received. The three different methods covered here are saving, adding to a database, and e-mailing. The control should also handle exceptions well and be thread-safe.

Technology

Due to the flexibility of the control, which allows three different actions to take place, there are three different technologies we need to discuss. These are *SMTP*, *ADO.NET*, and *File Streams*. The technology used at the client side makes use of the `<input type="file">` tag, and uses a form that sends multipart MIME data. This is part of the HTTP specification and allows us to upload a file via HTTP with no complicated client-side code.

SMTP

SMTP is a mail transfer protocol that is used for sending e-mails over the Internet. We will make use of SMTP to send an uploaded file by mail. The file upload has to be initiated by the user and, for obvious security reasons, this can't be done automatically without user approval.

Within the .NET Framework there is the `System.Web.Mail.SmtpMail` class, which can be used to talk to an SMTP service and send e-mails out from a .NET application. By simply specifying the name of the SMTP server, allowing the SMTP class to default to the inbuilt SMTP server, we can send e-mails with attachments just as we would do from any mail client, such as Microsoft Outlook.

SMTP itself often has to be explicitly installed as it isn't usually installed by default. In many instances, the name of the server will be `localhost` or the local IP address `127.0.0.1`. If you have to use an external SMTP server, such as a Microsoft Exchange server, you need to find its name or IP address.

From the Control Panel, select Administrative Tools ➤ Internet Information Services or Internet Services Manager; the name may differ depending on your operating system. Find the Default SMTP Virtual Server node and click Domains. The right-hand side panel will alter and define the name of the SMTP server to use, ensuring that it is running. It is also necessary for the Relay Restrictions to be removed so that mail can be sent. To accomplish this, move to the Default SMTP Virtual Server node, right-click Select Properties, and select the Access tab. Click the Relay button near the bottom of the screen and ensure that the radio option button "All except the list below" is chosen.

ADO.NET

Connecting to a database is a straightforward task. Many of you will have worked on SQL Server or on another database for storing information within Web sites you designed. The technology that drives database access has changed in ADO.NET and there is now a specific provider with optimized methods to use for SQL Server. In addition, you can add third-party providers for speedy access to other databases, such as the Oracle and MySQL ADO.NET providers.

When accessing a database, it is still necessary to create a connection as well as a SQL command to execute. However, the way you work with parameters has been redesigned, as well as the way you actually execute the SQL itself. It is not necessary to see all the different methods that exist for SQL execution, and there are many different Apress books (http://www.apress.com) that can help you out. The method we will be working with in this example will revolve around passing SQL code to the SQL Server database and not worrying about any information being returned. We achieve this through the `ExecuteNonQuery()` method.

If you are going to do more than simply insert data into a table in SQL Server, which is what is happening in this control, then you could always use different methods. For example, you may wish to use stored procedures to execute multiple SQL statements.

File Streams

The third technology we will be dealing with is the use of `FileStream` to upload our file and reference it from a variable. The control we will demonstrate contains a `PostedFile` property of type `HTTPPostedFile`, which has an `InputStream` property to get access to the stream.

Once the `FileStream` object has a pointer to the file, then we can read the file *asynchronously* or *synchronously* using the appropriate methods. As we want processing to suspend while we read in the file, we will use the synchronous method.

Design

The first thing to point out is that, unlike some of the controls in this book, this one has been implemented as a `User Control`. Recall that when we talked—back in Chapter 1—about the differences between User Controls and Custom Controls, we highlighted the UI as being a determining factor of when to choose one over the other. On the *pro* side, our `FileUploader` control has a static UI that can be easily "designed" by dragging a few existing controls; this is the reason why we decided to implement it as a User Control. On the *con* side, this means we cannot embed it into the toolbox, nor amend its properties in the Properties browser of an IDE.

Other design considerations surround the flexibility of the control. As three different ways of using an uploaded file are permitted, should they remain within the control or form separate DLLs in their own right? There is not really enough code to warrant moving these outside our Web control as such, but if they could be used elsewhere then perhaps the code should be separate. For clarity, all of the code has remained within the `User Control` itself.

Implementation

Create a new ASP.NET User Control and call it `FileUploader.ascx`. Then import the namespaces required for our e-mail, file, and SQL Server data manipulation, as well as the `System.Text.RegularExpressions` namespace necessary for some of the validation logic of the properties, as shown here:

```
Imports System.Web.Mail
Imports System.Web.Mail.SmtpMail
Imports System.Data
Imports System.Data.SqlClient
Imports System.IO
Imports System.Text
Imports System.Text.RegularExpressions
```

Before we see the Visual Basic .NET code, we will first look at the HTML elements and ASP.NET controls placed within the control. The element is a `File Upload` control, and the control is a `Button`. The screen layout should look similar to the screenshot in Figure 5-1.

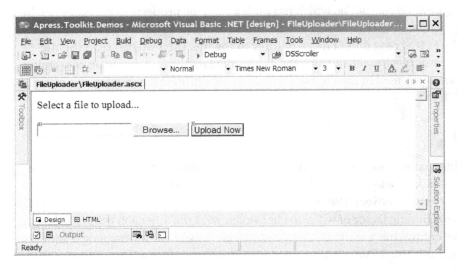

Figure 5-1. *Design-time view of the* `FileUploader` *control*

Next, we are listing the HTML that will make up the UI for our control. The element with id FileToUpload is a simple folder browser-type control, which will allow for the search of a specific file and, as a feature of the `<input>` tag, is standard in HTML.

In addition, you can see the various properties and Visual Basic `onclick` event handler definition added here:

```
<p>
  Select a file to upload...
</p>
<p>
  <input id="FileToUpload" style="WIDTH: 281px; HEIGHT: 26px"
         type="file" size="24" runat="server" />
  <asp:Button id="UploadNow" onclick="UploadNow_Click" runat="server"
              Height="24px" Width="97px" Text="Upload Now">
  </asp:Button>
</p>
```

Now we can move on and look at the VB .NET code within the ASP.NET User Control. As the file may be used to save to a database, to a physical location on the server, or to send an e-mail message, various properties and settings need to be provided. For this design, we will use an enumeration to specify the action to be performed when uploading a file. This is defined as follows:

```
Public Enum Save
  ToFile
  ToDB
  ViaEmail
End Enum
```

This will be used in the UploadAction property later. We need to define another Enum, called AuthType, as well.

```
Public Enum AuthType
  Windows
  SQLServer
End Enum
```

This specifies how the user will be authorized when saving to a SQL Server database. There is another value to include here, the MAXFILESIZE, which, in this implementation, will define the maximum file size allowed to be saved, e-mailed, or added to a database. It is implemented as a constant, as follows:

```
Private Const MAXFILESIZE = 2097152
```

In this case, we have set the limit as 2MB (2048*1024). There is one other constant used in this control, as follows:

```
Private Const SMTPSERVER As String = "localhost"
```

This contains the address of the SMTP server used for mailing. There is one more method to show before we go into our class level declarations and properties—a page load event handler.

```
Protected Sub FileUploader_Load(sender As Object, _
                         e As EventArgs)
  If Page.Application("FileUploaderLock") Is Nothing Then
    Page.Application.Add("FileUploaderLock", New Object())
  End If
End Sub
```

This method listens for the Load event on the control's Page. We will use some thread synchronization in part of this control, and by declaring an object in the application-level variables, we can be sure that all sessions that may access this control can only access the specified code block once. Here we ensure that the application-level variable (FileUploaderLock) is set.

Now we can move on to our class-level variable declarations and properties. First, here are properties that contain the enumerated values.

```
Dim _uploadAction As Save
Public Property UploadAction As Save
  Get
    Return _uploadAction
  End Get

  Set(value As Save)
    _uploadAction = value
  End Set
End Property

Dim _authenticationType As AuthType
Public Property AuthenticationType As AuthType
  Get
    Return _authenticationType
  End Get

  Set(value As AuthType)
    _authenticationType = value
  End Set
End Property
```

These properties are just Get and Set methods for their corresponding private variables. Their values determine how the file is to be saved, and if saved to a database, how we should authenticate against it. The first property we will cover is the one that sets the path name of the file to upload.

```
Dim _pathForFile As String
Public Property PathForFile As String
  Get
    Return _pathForFile
  End Get

  Set(value As String)
    If value.IndexOfAny(Path.InvalidPathChars) = -1 Then
      _pathForFile = value
    Else
      Throw New ArgumentException("Invalid path name")
    End If
  End Set
End Property
```

In the Set method, this property checks to see if the path specified for the file name contains any of the characters contained in the System.IO.Path.InvalidPathChars Char array. These are some characters not permitted in a path name and so this property just provides some early validation of the value entered. It throws an ArgumentException if the value does contain one of these characters. Otherwise, the property value is changed.

We use a similar pattern for the properties that specify the database name and its authentication properties.

```
Dim _serverName As String
Public Property ServerName As String
  Get
    Return _serverName
  End Get

  Set(value As String)
    If value.IndexOf(" ") = -1 Then
        _serverName = value
    Else
      Throw New ArgumentException( _
          "ServerName cannot contain any spaces")
    End If
  End Set
End Property

Dim _databaseName As String
Public Property DatabaseName As String
  Get
    Return _databaseName
  End Get

  Set(value As String)
    If value.IndexOf(" ") = -1 Then
      _databaseName = value
    Else
      Throw New ArgumentException( _
          "DatabaseName cannot contain any spaces")
    End If
  End Set
End Property
```

The ServerName and DatabaseName properties will each throw exceptions if, when set, their values contain spaces.

```vbnet
Dim _userId As String
Public Property UserId As String
  Get
    Return _userId
  End Get

  Set(value As String)
    If value.IndexOf(" ") = -1
      _userId = value
    Else
      Throw New ArgumentException( _
          "UserId cannot contain any spaces")
    End If
  End Set
End Property

Dim _password As String
Public Property Password As String
  Get
    Return _password
  End Get

  Set(value As String)
    If value.IndexOf(" ") = -1
      _password = value
    Else
      Throw New ArgumentException( _
          "Password cannot contain any spaces")
    End If
  End Set
End Property
```

The UserName and Password properties work in an identical way to the previous properties. Now we can look at those properties necessary for sending a file via e-mail.

```vbnet
Private Const EMAILPATTERN As String = _
    "[^@()<>;, \x00-\x20]+@[a-z]([a-z0-9-]+\.)+[a-z]{2,4}"
```

The constant defined here forms the majority of a regular expression we will be using to ensure that the e-mail addresses given appear to be valid before passing them to the SmtpMail object used for sending the mail. It isn't an all-encompassing expression because it doesn't, for instance, ensure that the text entered is only in the ASCII range of values, or that any of the domain name parts don't end with a hyphen, but the SmtpMail.Send()

method will throw an exception if those rules are broken (and we can handle that later). This just prevents simple mistakes from occurring in the property Set methods, like multiple @ signs and using commas or semicolons. Additionally, this particular pattern does not allow the optional name surrounded by parentheses as is often specified in e-mail addresses. This kind of address isn't necessary for this control.

Now let's look at the EmailFromAddress property.

```
Dim _emailFromAddress As String
Public Property EMailFromAddress As String
  Get
    Return _emailFromAddress
  End Get

  Set(value As String)
    If Regex.IsMatch( _
        value, "^" & EMAILPATTERN &"$", _
        RegexOptions.IgnoreCase Or _
        RegexOptions.ExplicitCapture) Then
      _emailFromAddress = value
    Else
      Throw New ArgumentException("Not a valid e-mail address")
    End If
  End Set
End Property
```

In the Set method, we use the IsMatch() method of the Regex object to ensure the value given appears to be a valid e-mail address. This will prevent accidentally entering an incorrect address, although it doesn't quite prevent all kinds of invalid e-mail addresses. The ^ and $ characters anchor the pattern to the beginning and the end of the string, respectively. This prevents invalid characters, including whitespace, from appearing at the start or end of the pattern.

The RegexOptions.ExplicitCapture option helps the performance of the regular expression by not attempting to explicitly capture and store any of the groups in the expression (those items surrounded by parentheses).

Now let's see the EmailToAddress property, as follows:

```
Dim _emailToAddress As String
Public Property EmailToAddress As String
  Get
    Return _emailToAddress
  End Get
```

```
  Set(value As String)
    If Regex.IsMatch( _
        value, "^(" & EMAILPATTERN & "(;\s*" & _
        EMAILPATTERN & ")*)$", RegexOptions.IgnoreCase Or _
        RegexOptions.ExplicitCapture) Then
      _emailToAddress = value
    Else
      Throw New ArgumentException("Must be an (optionally) " & _
          "semicolon separated list of valid addresses")
    End If
  End Set
End Property
```

This is very similar to the previous property. The difference is that it allows multiple recipients of the e-mail, separated by semicolons and zero or more whitespace characters. There can be one or more e-mail addresses specified in this way. If the value does not match this pattern, then an ArgumentException is thrown.

Now let's see the EmailSubjectLine property, as shown here:

```
Dim _emailSubjectLine As String
Public Property EmailSubjectLine As String
  Get
    Return _emailSubjectLine
  End Get

  Set(value As String)
    _emailSubjectLine = value.TrimEnd()
  End Set
End Property
```

This property contains no validation. There are restrictions in the SMTP specification, such as it must contain only ASCII values, but we ignore them in this case and rather than complain about them, we just remove any whitespace characters from the end of the value entered into the property Set method. This handles the case where a carriage return is entered at the end of the subject line. This is not permitted. Each header of the e-mail is delimited by a single carriage return, so these are not allowed as part of the content of the subject line. TrimEnd() just removes all whitespace from the end of the value string.

Finally, let's see the EmailBodyContent property.

```
Dim _emailBodyContent As String
Public Property EmailBodyContent As String
  Get
    Return _emailBodyContent
  End Get
```

```
      Set(value As String)
        _emailBodyContent = value
      End Set
    End Property
```

Because of the various content permitted in the body of the e-mail, we perform no validation at all. There is little reason to do so, considering any ASCII character is permitted. If we wished to disallow all non-ASCII characters in this and the previous properties, then we'd use [^\u0080-\uFFFF]+ as part of the validation regular expression.

This completes the property definitions. Now we can look at the uploading of the file. The Browse button within the FileUploader control is simply there to browse for the files and form part of that control, so a separate method is required to start the upload process. We do this with the Click event handler for the UploadNow button.

```
Sub UploadNow_Click(sender as Object, e As EventArgs)
  If Not FileToUpload.PostedFile Is Nothing Then
    Dim fileLen As Integer = FileToUpload.PostedFile.ContentLength
    If fileLen > 0  And fileLen < MAXFILESIZE Then
```

The FileToUpload HTML control appears in our ASP.NET page as an HtmlInputFile control. This control contains a PostedFile property that returns an HttpPostedFile property, which is only set if one or more files have been posted. If an object is set, we check to ensure that its length is greater than zero, to avoid saving an empty file stream, and less than MAXFIILESIZE.

The next thing we want to do is declare the Select Case statement that will inspect the value of the UploadAction enumeration and respond accordingly.

```
      Select Case Me.UploadAction
```

We'll start with Save.ToFile to save the file; rather than using another stream to do this with the complexity involved, it is much simpler to use the HttpPostedFile.SaveAs() method. This handles the entire stream processing for us.

```
      Case Save.ToFile
        Try
            FileToUpload.PostedFile.SaveAs(Me.PathForFile + "\" + _
path.GetFileName(FileToUpload.Value))
        Catch ex As Exception
            ReportErrorMessage(ex)
        End Try
```

The call to HttpPostedFile.SaveAs() method is contained within a Try block, so if an exception is thrown during the save operation, then it will be handled by the Catch block that passes it to the private ReportErrorMessage() method. This will be defined shortly and it merely presents the error to the reader in a JavaScript alert box. Now let's see the case where the file is to be saved to a database.

```
Case Save.ToDB
  Try
    Dim uploadFileStream As Stream
    uploadFileStream = FileToUpload.PostedFile.InputStream
    Dim incomingFile(fileLen) As Byte
    uploadFileStream.Read(incomingFile, 0, fileLen)
    SaveToDB(incomingFile, FileToUpload.PostedFile.FileName)
  Catch ex As Exception
    ReportErrorMessage(ex)
  End Try
```

This Case statement retrieves a stream object from the InputStream property of the HttpPostedFile object returned from the FileToUpload.PostedFile property, and stores it in a local variable. It then refers to the length of the file from the previously declared fileLen variable, and declares a new byte array of this size, large enough to hold the file stream. It then calls the Read() method of the stream object.

Read() accepts three arguments. The first is the byte array to store the file stream in. The second is where in the array to start storing the stream (in this case, the start). The third contains the total number of bytes to read in (the length of the file). It then passes the new byte array to the private SaveToDB() method, which will be detailed shortly.

Now we can move on to the largest case to be dealt with, that of Save.ViaEmail.

```
Case Save.ViaEmail
  Dim isLocked As Boolean
  Dim fileName As String
  Try
    Dim path As String = FileToUpload.PostedFile.FileName
    Dim index As Integer
    index = path.LastIndexOf("\"c)
    If index = -1 Then
      index = path.LastIndexOf("/"c)
    End If
    fileName = path.Substring(index + 1)
```

The first part of this case is straightforward. It retrieves the full path of the uploaded file from the client's machine (transmitted in the HTTP header) and finds the location of the last \ character inside this string. If LastIndexOf() returns -1, then there are no \ characters in the path and either the path is relative, or it doesn't use that character as a directory separator. We, therefore, handle the case where the file could have been sent from a Unix OS and check for the last index of the / character. We, then, return the file name, disregarding any path information, by returning the substring of the path variable, starting from index+1. This excludes the last path separator, and if the return value from the last LastIndexOf() call was -1, then it returns the whole string.

This method of determining the file name will work with most operating systems (Windows, Unix, and Macintosh), and if some other OS is used, as long as the directory separator isn't an invalid character for a file name (invalid as defined by Windows), then that would work too. In the following snippet, you'll see how we use fileName:

```
SyncLock Application("FileUploaderLock")
  isLocked = True
  If File.Exists(fileName) Then
    index = 1
    While File.Exists(index.ToString("D3") & fileName)
      index += 1
    End While
    fileName = index.ToString("D3") & fileName
  End If
  File.Create(fileName).Close()

End SyncLock
isLocked = False
FileToUpload.PostedFile.SaveAs(fileName)
SendEmail(fileName)
```

In this code, we have started a SyncLock on the FileUploaderLock object stored in the Application collection after the control's Load event has been fired. This provides an exclusive lock on this object, which means that only one SyncLock block on any thread will execute at any given time. If two people upload files with the same name via e-mail at the same time without this SyncLock block, an IO exception could be thrown. We also define a boolean, isLocked, that is set to True on entering the SyncLock, and False on leaving.

Inside the block, we check to see if a file already exists with the name fileName, and if so, then we use the same index variable as used before and set it to 1. Then we use the ToString() method to specify that the index should be written as three digits, and prefix that to the beginning of the file name. While this file exists, it increments the index and tries again, until the file does not exist. This ensures that the same extension and similar name is kept for the file name.

Once we have a unique file name, we create the file and immediately close the file stream returned on creation, end the SyncLock block, save the file uploaded into this file (the SaveAs() method will just write over the existing file), and call the private helper method SendEmail() with the name of this file passed as an argument. Now for the last part of the block:

```
        Catch ex As Exception
          ReportErrorMessage(ex)
          If isLocked Then
            System.Threading.Monitor.Exit( _
                Application("FileUploaderLock"))
          End If
        Finally
          If Not fileName Is Nothing
            File.Delete(fileName)
          End If
        End Try
    End Select
```

If an exception is caught during execution of this block, then it calls the
ReportErrorMessage() method with the exception passed as an argument. It then makes
use of the Monitor.Exit() method. When you start a SyncLock block, it calls Monitor.Enter()
on the object passed in. If the exception was thrown inside the SyncLock block, then the
End SyncLock statement would never be reached and so no further executing code could
obtain an exclusive lock on the Application("FileUploaderLock") object. What we do,
therefore, is check to see if the isLocked variable is True. If it is, then we have a lock and
so we release it by using the Monitor.Exit() method.

In the Finally block, if fileName was set when the exception was thrown, then we
remove the file, if it exists. File.Delete() does not throw an exception if the file does not
exist. This tidies up this method before we reach the End Select statement. We can now
move on to the last parts of this method block.

```
    Else
      If fileLen = 0 Then
        ReportErrorMessage(New ApplicationException( _
            "File is empty"))
      Else
        ReportErrorMessage(New ApplicationException( _
            "File is larger than " & _
            (MAXFILESIZE-1).ToString() & " bytes long"))
      End If
    End If
  Else
    ReportErrorMessage(New ApplicationException( _
        "No File specified to upload"))
  End If
End Sub
```

This handles the cases where the file was too large or small, or no file was uploaded. An error message is given via the ReportErrorMessage() method in each case. We can now look at the ReportErrorMessage() method.

```
Private Sub ReportErrorMessage(ByVal ex As Exception)
       Dim str As String
       Dim exMsg As String
       exMsg = ex.Message.Replace("'", """")
       str = String.Format("<script language='javascript'>{0}</script>", _
"alert ('An error has been reported:\n" & exMsg & "');")
       Page.RegisterStartupScript(Me.UniqueID, str)
End Sub
```

First, we make sure to replace any single quote characters in the exception message with double quote characters, this is necessary so the following JavaScript code doesn't break. Then we create a string containing a <script> tag with just an alert message to the user; after that, we use one of the available methods in Page to properly register the formed script code, the RegisterStartupScript. This reports the message contained within the exception. When the page is rendered again following the form post, the alert box will appear in the user's browser.

The following SaveToDB() method deals with saving the information to a SQL Server table. It is possible to use Windows Authentication or SQL Server Authentication within this example. This covers usage of the control in-house where Windows Authentication can be used to tie a specific user to a table or stored procedure. Alternatively, you can use SQL Server Authentication. So the setting of the property dealing with authentication types defines what information needs to be placed within the connection string.

```
Private Sub SaveToDB(fileContents() As Byte, fileName As String)
  Dim ConnString As New StringBuilder
  ConnString.Append("Data Source=" & ServerName)
  ConnString.Append(";initial catalog=" & DatabaseName)
  ConnString.Append(";")
  If AuthenticationType=AuthType.Windows Then
    ConnString.Append("Integrated Security=SSPI;")
  Else
    ConnString.Append("uid=" & UserId)
    ConnString.Append(";pwd=" & Password & ";")
  End If
```

The first part of this method creates a connection string using a StringBuilder object. It builds up the initial details about the server and database name first, and then it adds the security settings depending on the value of the AuthenticationType property.

```vb
    Dim Conn As SqlConnection
    Dim SqlQuery As New StringBuilder
        SqlQuery.Append("INSERT INTO Categories _
 (CategoryName, Description, Picture) ")
        SqlQuery.Append("VALUES('")
        SqlQuery.Append(HttpUtility.UrlEncode(fileName))
        SqlQuery.Append("','Testing ASP.NET FileUploader', @ImageFile)")

        Dim SqlCmd As SqlCommand
```

The next part declares the SqlConnection and SqlCmd objects to be used in the following block. It also builds the SQL query, which contains a URL-encoded version of the
file name (to remove and encode any values that may cause problems as part of a SQL
query—like apostrophes). It also contains the @ImageFile parameter, which will be populated
using the command object in the following block of code:

```vb
    Try
       Conn = New SqlConnection(ConnString.ToString())
       SqlCmd = New SqlCommand(SqlQuery.ToString(), Conn)
       SqlCmd.Parameters.Add(New SqlParameter("@ImageFile", _
           SqlDbType.Image)).Value = fileContents
       Conn.Open()
       SqlCmd.ExecuteNonQuery()
    Finally
       If Not Conn Is Nothing
         Conn.Close()
         Conn.Dispose()
       End If
       If Not SqlCmd Is Nothing
         SqlCmd.Dispose()
       End If
    End Try
  End Sub
```

The code is placed into a Try...Finally block. We first define the SqlConnection object
and then the SqlCommand object, using the SQL query built up earlier. Then we set the value
of the @ImageFile parameter to be the contents of the byte array passed into the method
as an argument. Lastly, the connection is opened and the ExecuteNonQuery() method is
called, which is used whenever a result isn't expected from the SQL statement.

In the Finally block, which will execute even in the event of an exception being thrown,
we close the connection object and call the Dispose() methods on both the SqlConnection
and SqlCommand objects. This ensures all resources are freed before exiting this method.
Remember that the Try...Catch block that wrapped this method call catches any thrown
exception.

Sending an e-mail with the file as an attachment is a straightforward process. Let's look at the SendEmail() method.

```
Private Sub SendEmail(fileName As String)
  Dim emailMessage As New MailMessage()
  With emailMessage
    .From = Me.EmailFromAddress
    .To = Me.EmailToAddress
    .Subject = Me.EmailSubjectLine
    .Body = Me.EmailBodyContent

    Dim MailAttach As New MailAttachment(fileName)

    .Attachments.Add(MailAttach)
  End With
```

Here, we create a new MailMessage object and use the values stored in the properties to populate its From, To, Subject, and Body properties. Then we create a new MailAttachment object and attach the file specified in the argument passed to the method. This attachment is then added to the MailMessage object, via the Attachments property's IList collection.

In the next Try...Finally block, a SyncLock is started using the Monitor.Enter() call, which we saw previously, while the SmtpMail object's SmtpServer field is set and the MailMessage object is sent.

```
  Try
    System.Threading.Monitor.Enter(GetType(SmtpMail))
    SmtpMail.SmtpServer = SMTPSERVER
    SmtpMail.Send(emailMessage)
  Finally
    System.Threading.Monitor.Exit(GetType(SmtpMail))
  End Try
End Sub
```

We use the type of the SmtpMail object as the object to provide an exclusive lock on, because you cannot use a shared object for the lock. In the Finally block, we release the lock on the object.

If you use similar code whenever you access the mail server object, then you can be certain that the SmtpServer field won't change before sending the mail. You must ensure that you use the code exactly as shown previously, however; because if some code elsewhere in your application obtained a lock on this object and never released it, then all other code that attempted to obtain a lock would block indefinitely. This is known as a *deadlock* and must be avoided.

Tip If there was more than one attachment, then you could iterate through the collection using a For Each...Next loop.

The coding of our control is now complete.

Demonstration

Once the control is complete, we can see it in action. The following page will reference the control we have just created, and allow you to upload a file to the server. Create an ASP.NET Web page and enter the following code (call it FileUploadPage.aspx). In the Page_Load() method, we will set the properties ready for when the control is used.

```
Sub Page_Load(sender As Object, e As EventArgs) Handles MyBase.Load
  With FileUploader
    .UploadAction = .Save.ToFile
```

The previous code just defines Page_Load as the event handler for the page's Load event and sets the UploadAction to Save.ToFile (which is the default value for this property anyway).

Within the following code, the location to which the file will be saved is hardcoded, as you can see. Use of a simple textbox could replace this if you desired; this was not done here so we can keep the demonstration clear of any outside interference.

```
.PathForFile = "C:\Test"
.AuthenticationType = .AuthType.SQLServer
.UserId = "sa"
.Password = String.Empty
.ServerName = "(local)"
.DatabaseName = "Northwind"
```

If you have SQL Server running as a named instance or on a remote server, you would need to alter (local) to show its exact location. Another way would be to use a Web.Config file to define the details; but, again, for clarity, we have simply defined the details here.

Tip Keep in mind that the account under which ASP.NET is running should have write privileges to the folder specified in the PathForFile property.

In the following code, the e-mail's To and From are defined:

```
      .EmailFromAddress = "postmaster@Apress.com"
      .EmailToAddress = "nonexistent@Apress.com"
      .EmailSubjectLine = "New file"
      .EmailBodyContent = "Look at this new file"
   End With
End Sub
```

The details, although going to the same domain, do still have to travel through the SMTP mail server so this code still provides an adequate test. Semicolons can separate recipients if there is more than one name to be defined.

Now let's look at our HTML.

```
<html>
<head>
  <title>
    Demonstration of uploading a file using the FileUploader control
  </title>
</head>
<body>
  <form enctype="multipart/form-data" runat="server">
```

For the FileUploader control to work properly, the form has to be of multipart/form-data type. This is a World Wide Web Consortium (W3C) standard and is also a more efficient method of transporting binary data across the Internet. For more on content types, check out the W3C site and relevant link found at http://www.w3.org/TR/1998/REC-html40-19980424/ interact/forms.html#form-content-type. Luckily, we don't have to worry about the case of the page developer forgetting to properly set the form's enctype attribute as one of the children of our control, the HtmlInputFile control already has the code to properly set this.

Here you can see a declaration for the FileUploader control.

```
  <p>
    <Apress:Fupl id="FileUploader" runat="server"></Apress:Fupl>
  </p>
  </form>
</body>
</html>
```

That is all the code, so save the file and execute it. You can change the UploadAction in the Page_Load() method to see all the other actions working. For example:

```
.UploadAction = .Save.ToDB
```

and

```
.UploadAction = .Save.ViaEmail
```

Limitations

By allowing the control to e-mail the uploaded file, we are limiting ourselves to using the inbuilt SMTP mail server, which, as you read earlier, has specific operating system limitations. There are no limitations to the type of file used.

Of course, we did not allow for different types of databases to be used with this control, too. This is easily rectified since connecting to different databases through ADO.NET is a simple procedure. We could, for instance, alter this control to access different databases using an `OleDbConnection`, or the Oracle ADO.NET connection object.

Also, for ease of demonstration, we hardcoded values and did not add further buttons or textboxes to our control to allow choices. These can be added easily to the control if you don't wish to have to change the upload action each time you want to use a different aspect of the file uploader. In addition, we also hardcoded some of the values used when saving a file to a database; in order to allow the control to work against different tables, some new properties should be added so the page developer could specify that.

Extensions

One of the best extensions this control could have is to test the `ContentType` of the file uploaded and, based on it, perform different tasks. For example, if it detects that it's dealing with an image file, it could convert it to another format or maybe resize it to a required size.

In addition, we could add some code to render only if a server-side form is present in the page, as this is vital for the proper functioning of our control. This could be achieved by overriding the `Render` method, calling `Page.VerifyRenderingInServerForm`, which will throw an exception if a server-side form can't be found, and finally call the `Render` base class implementation.

CHAPTER 6

■■■

Globalizable Page

In any customer-focused application, it's important to speak to customers in their own language, and when we're doing business on the Web, we could be talking to people anywhere in the world. In this chapter, we'll develop a component that will help us speak to Web clients in their own language wherever possible.

The process of constructing an application so that it can support user interaction in a number of languages is called *internationalization*. The process of taking an internationalized application and adapting it to a particular language or culture is called *localization*. Because they're such long words, internationalization and localization are usually abbreviated as I18N and L10N respectively, after their first and last letters and the number of letters in between.

What we'll be developing is a Page-derived base class that can be used to choose the best language from those available, and then use it to deliver localized content to a client.

Scenario

Suppose you run a flight booking service, selling seats on planes throughout the world. Your clients are likely to be geographically distributed and they probably speak other languages besides your own, but they would all happily use your service if they could properly interact with it. To accomplish this, you'll need to print the dates and times in a format they understand, as well as provide localized translations of your descriptive text; the rewards will make the effort worthwhile if you can broaden your customer base.

So, having identified that your biggest market opportunities are in Latin America and Europe, and commissioned translations into Spanish, Portuguese, and Italian, how do you decide which version of your interface to show to each particular user?

This is where our custom page class comes in. Rather than forcing the user to choose the most appropriate language, it detects their preference and delivers the most appropriate version of the content available.

Technology

The HTTP protocol supports a facility called *content negotiation.* In content negotiated requests, the client tells the server what kinds of content it supports or prefers, and the server selects the most appropriate form to return. HTTP defines content negotiation headers for file types, character encodings, and human languages. This last item is what we'll be using here.

In Internet Explorer, at the bottom of the Options dialog is a Languages button, which brings up the dialog shown in Figure 6-1.

Figure 6-1. *IE's Language Preference dialog box*

This allows you to specify which languages you understand and provide an order of preference. The codes to the right of the language names in brackets are International Organization for Standardization (ISO) language codes; the first has two parts, a language identifier (en) and a region identifier (us), and specifies the variant of English spoken in the United States. The second provides only a language identifier, with no region code.

What do browsers do with these preferences? They include a header in all the outgoing HTTP requests that looks like the following:

```
Accept-Language: en-us,es;q=0.5
```

This is a content negotiation header, and it tells the Web server the user's language preferences. In this case, it says the user prefers U.S. English, but will accept Spanish. The q=0.5 suffix represents the relative degradation in desired quality, and it says the user likes Spanish about half as much as he likes U.S. English. This is an arbitrary value, provided by the browser to ensure that the Web server understands what order the user's preferred languages should be considered in.

So, if a Web site receives a request from this browser, including this header, and it has content available in Spanish, Portuguese, and Italian, but not in English, it should send the Spanish version, even though it isn't the user's preferred choice, because it doesn't have English content available.

We can access the content of the `Accept-Language` HTTP header in an ASP.NET page by querying the `Page.Request.UserLanguages` property.

Our base class will identify the best-fitting language available and, having done so, will then set the default culture of the executing thread, where page processing takes place, to a .NET `System.Globalization.CultureInfo` object representing the specified language. This culture object is used by the string formatting and resource loading facilities of .NET to obtain localized dates, times, currencies, and translated strings; so having set it, it becomes easy to localize all of the elements on a page to the correct language and culture.

Design

It's important that the appropriate culture is chosen early enough during page processing so that it is available for all of the elements of the page. For this reason, we have elected to put our cultural decision-making logic in the page's `OnInit()` method.

We'll code a class that inherits from `System.Web.UI.Page`, and overrides the `OnInit()` method. Then, to make any other page globalizable, we simply make that page inherit, not from `Page`, but from our custom `Page`-derived class instead, which we will name `GlobalizablePage`.

A page that inherits from our `GlobalizablePage` class can specify what languages it supports, and then the inherited initialization logic will ensure that the thread's culture will be set to one of our supported languages—the one most appropriate for the client making a particular request.

Implementation

Our base class, which is contained in a single file, may be compiled into its own class library or you may want to opt for directly including it in the project for your Web application.

Let's step through the code.

```
Imports System
Imports System.Web.UI
Imports System.Globalization
Imports System.Threading
Imports System.Text.RegularExpressions
```

We need to import the `System.Web.UI` namespace, and you'll have to add a reference to the `System.Web.dll` assembly to ensure it's made available.

Now, we declare the Apress.Toolkit namespace and begin to define the GlobalizablePage class. As we have said before, it inherits from Page.

```
Namespace Apress.Toolkit

    Public Class GlobalizablePage
        Inherits Page
```

We're going to keep track of the culture we've selected for the page in the private field _culture. We need to remember what the culture settings were before we changed them so we can restore the thread to its original state (after all, we can't assume the Web server won't reuse the thread to handle another request). And finally, we initialize an array of strings identifying the languages the page supports with a call to the InitSupportedCultures() method, which we'll come to shortly.

```
        Private _culture As CultureInfo = CultureInfo.CurrentUICulture
        Private _underlyingUICulture As CultureInfo _
                            = CultureInfo.CurrentUICulture
        Private _underlyingCulture As CultureInfo _
                            = CultureInfo.CurrentCulture
        Private _supportedCultures As String() _
                            = InitSupportedCultures()
```

We also need to use a regular expression to pull out the language specifiers from the Accept-Language header (remember, it may also contain a short floating point number representing the relative degradation in desired quality). We'll see how this is used later, but basically this string of characters will match and help us extract any sequence of two or three letters (a language specifier), followed optionally by a hyphen and two more letters (a region specifier).

```
        Private ReadOnly cultureSpecRegEx As String _
                            = "[a-zA-Z]{2,3}(-[a-zA-Z]{2})?"
```

We provide two read-only properties to allow code in the page to access the culture that has been selected and the original list of cultures the page supports.

```
        Public ReadOnly Property SelectedCulture() As CultureInfo
            Get
                Return _culture
            End Get
        End Property
```

```
Public ReadOnly Property SupportedCultures() As String()
    Get
        Return _supportedCultures
    End Get
End Property
```

Next, we get to the heart of the methods that are used to choose a culture. The first, IsCultureSupported, takes a CultureInfo object as an argument and returns True if the page supports the culture, and False otherwise. This method is made overridable so that pages inheriting from our class can provide their own logic for deciding if they support a culture or not.

The default implementation looks into the array of supported cultures to see if the specified culture's language name is there.

```
Public Overridable Function IsCultureSupported( _
                ByVal culture As CultureInfo) As Boolean
    Return Array.IndexOf(SupportedCultures, _
                culture.TwoLetterISOLanguageName) >= 0
End Function
```

The InitSupportedCultures() method is called before the page's Init event is fired to obtain the array of language name strings that the page supports. It is also overridable, so that a page extending this can return its own array of supported language codes. Overriding this method provides the simplest way to specify the languages a page supports—overriding IsCultureSupported() requires the overrider to include more complex logic.

```
Public Overridable Function InitSupportedCultures() _
                                            As String()
    Dim a() As String _
            = {_underlyingCulture.TwoLetterISOLanguageName}
    Return a
End Function
```

Next, we override the OnInit() method. Note that we are preventing further overriding of OnInit; this is to ensure that other classes deriving from our GlobalizablePage can't break it by overriding OnInit() and by failing to call the base class implementation. It's important to the event handling mechanism of ASP.NET that we include a call somewhere in this method to MyBase.OnInit(), since it is the parent class's implementation and the one in charge of finally firing the Init event.

The approach of this method is simply to iterate through the languages in the UserLanguages property, in order, and ask the IsCultureSupported() method whether or not each language is supported by the page. The first one we find that is supported we set as the page culture.

```
        Protected NotOverridable Overrides Sub OnInit( _
                                ByVal e As System.EventArgs)
            Dim requestedLang As String
            Dim cultureFinder As New Regex(cultureSpecRegEx)

            For Each requestedLang In Request.UserLanguages
                Try
                    Dim requestedCulture As CultureInfo
                    Dim cultureSpec As String _
        = cultureFinder.Match(requestedLang).Captures(0).Value
                    requestedCulture _
        = CultureInfo.CreateSpecificCulture(cultureSpec)
                    If IsCultureSupported(requestedCulture) Then
                        _culture = requestedCulture
                        Thread.CurrentThread.CurrentUICulture _
                                        = requestedCulture
                        Thread.CurrentThread.CurrentCulture _
                                        = requestedCulture

                        Exit For
                    End If
                Catch ex As Exception
                End Try
            Next

            MyBase.OnInit(e)
        End Sub
```

Note that we have set two separate properties on the current thread—the CurrentCulture and the CurrentUICulture. The former is the culture used to format dates and numbers while the latter is the culture used by .NET to load culture-specific resources. We have changed both.

Having fooled around with the thread, it's important to tidy up afterwards. We override OnUnload() and call MyBase.OnUnload(), ensuring that all of the page control's OnUnload() methods are called and any registered Unload event handlers run before we reset the thread's culture.

```
        Protected Overrides Sub OnUnload(ByVal e As System.EventArgs)
            MyBase.OnUnload(e)
            Thread.CurrentThread.CurrentCulture = _underlyingCulture
            Thread.CurrentThread.CurrentUICulture _
                = _underlyingUICulture
        End Sub
    End Class
End Namespace
```

That's our complete class. As we said before, you may choose to compile it into its own assembly, which you may reference later from your Web application or, better yet, add it directly in your Web application project and get it compiled into the application assembly.

Handling Localizable Resources

What we have seen so far is how to make a page aware of the user language preferences and properly set the cultures for the current thread. Given this, any I18N-aware control, like the built-in Calendar, will properly render a localized UI without any additional effort on our part.

But we haven't seen yet how we can implement such an I18N-aware control. We will do this right now, focusing exclusively on the handling of string resources.

Resources, the .NET Way

The .NET Framework offers support for reading resources by means of the ResourceManager class found in the System.Resources namespace; note that this class is not specific to ASP.NET and you can use it from any type of application.

You define your resources in a resource file, which is an XML file with a particular schema and an extension of .resx. In the companion download, you will find two resource files: SR.resx, which contains the resources in English, and SR.es.resx, which contains the resources in Spanish. (You can find the code samples for this chapter in the Downloads section of the Apress Web site at http://www.apress.com.) Let's take a look at the specific portion of SR.resx where we define two string resources.

```
<data name="WelcomeText">
        <value>Welcome to our site.</value>
</data>
<data name="GoodbyeText">
        <value>Goodbye! Thanks for visiting.</value>
</data>
```

As you can see, the format for defining strings is pretty simple. The name attribute of the <data> tag serves as the resource key and the content of the <value> tag represents the resource value.

In addition, you could specify placeholders in a string and replace them later at run time by defining the string as follows:

```
<data name="FileNotFound">
        <value>The specified file {0} can not be found.</value>
</data>
```

Later, when you retrieve the previous string, it's just a matter of using the String.Format method to customize it with any run-time specific value.

A Little Help from Visual Studio .NET

What happens to resource files? If you are using Visual Studio .NET, it will compile the .resx files into .resources files (binary format) and embed them into the assembly. Moreover, if it finds a .resx file whose name contains a culture specifier, like the SR.es.resx mentioned previously, this .resx file will be compiled, too, and embedded, but this time to a *satellite assembly* (an assembly containing only resources and no code at all). This *satellite assembly* will be named after the main assembly, but contained in a subfolder named after the culture identifier.

If you are not using Visual Studio .NET as your IDE, you are not totally out of luck. You will just need to do some more work that includes compiling and embedding the .resx file by using the command line compiler vbc.exe.

Note that although it is possible to use resource files without actually embedding them to an assembly, this is not recommended for ASP.NET applications as it breaks XCOPY deployment.

The SR Pattern

The .NET Framework itself and most applications running on it follow what is unofficially known as the "SR pattern" for handling resources. This consists of a helper class usually named SR which implements the *singleton* pattern. Let's take a look at it in detail, beginning with the class declaration.

```
Friend NotInheritable Class SR

    Private resources As ResourceManager
    Private Shared singleton As SR
    Private Shared SyncRoot As New Object
```

As you can see, it is declared as NotInheritable and Friend, because it should not be inherited and, also, it should only be accessible from the assembly where it's being declared, as no other code from any other assembly should be interested in any of our localizable resources.

What follows is the implementation of two constructors, one for each instance and one for the type itself. The first one will just make sure the private member field singleton is set to Nothing. The second shared one will create an instance of the ResourceManager type passing "SR" as the root name of the resources and the assembly containing the SR type as the main assembly for the resources.

```
Shared Sub New()
    SR.singleton = Nothing
End Sub

Friend Sub New()
    Me.resources = New ResourceManager("SR", MyBase.GetType.Module.Assembly)
End Sub
```

We've just said that we were going to implement the *singleton* pattern and that is done in the following function:

```
Private Shared Function GetSingleton() As SR
    If SR.singleton Is Nothing Then
        SyncLock (SyncRoot)
            If SR.singleton Is Nothing Then
                SR.singleton = New SR
            End If
        End SyncLock
    End If
    Return SR.singleton
End Function
```

This function ensures that each time we call it we get the very same instance of SR. An if statement and proper locking code has been added to avoid multiple instances being created.

Then we have a utility function that, given a key, will return an associated string using the GetString method of the ResourcesManager class accessed through the private member field named resources.

```
Public Shared Function GetString(ByVal name As String) As String
    Dim res As SR = SR.GetSingleton
    If (res Is Nothing) Then
        Return Nothing
    End If
    Return res.resources.GetString(name)
End Function
```

To make things even easier, we can have as many properties for accessing the localized strings as we may need; the following code offers quick access to two strings using the keys WelcomeText and GoodByeText:

```vb
    Public Shared ReadOnly Property WelcomeText() As String
        Get
            Return SR.GetString("WelcomeText")
        End Get
    End Property

    Public Shared ReadOnly Property GoodbyeText() As String
        Get
            Return SR.GetString("GoodbyeText")
        End Get
    End Property
End Class
```

These properties are very simple and do not need much further explanation. They will allow us to access the localized strings in the following fashion:

```vb
Dim str As String
str = SR.WelcomeText
```

instead of the more error-prone and "untyped" one, as follows:

```vb
Dim str As String
str = SR.GetString("WelcomeText")
```

It's important to note that not every single string should go into a resource file, but only strings that need to be localized. Strings that won't benefit from localization (e.g., a well-known registry key) are much better candidates to appear as constants of a type rather than to go into a resource file.

Demonstration

We'll provide a quick example showing how using this class as a base for our pages, they are automatically localizable. We'll use the ASP.NET Calendar control and code to access the two previously defined resource strings from a page and to show globalization in action.

We'll show how to use the base class from a page with a code-behind file. Here's the TestGlobalizablePage.aspx page:

```
<%@ Page Language="vb" AutoEventWireup="false" ➡
Codebehind="TestGlobalizablePage.aspx.vb" Inherits="TestGlobalizablePage" %>
<!DOCTYPE HTML PUBLIC "-//W3C//DTD HTML 4.0 Transitional//EN">
```

```html
<html>
    <head>
            <title>Test Globalizable Page</title>
    </head>
    <body>
            <form id="Form1" method="post" runat="server">
                <P><asp:Label id="Label1"
runat="server">Label</asp:Label></P>
                <P><asp:calendar id="Calendar1"
runat="server"></asp:calendar></P>
                <asp:Label id="Label2" runat="server">Label</asp:Label>
            </form>
    </body>
</html>
```

and here's the code-behind file, testI18N.aspx.vb:

```vb
Imports System.Resources

Public Class TestGlobalizablePage
    Inherits Apress.Toolkit.GlobalizablePage
    Protected WithEvents Label1 As System.Web.UI.WebControls.Label
    Protected WithEvents Label2 As System.Web.UI.WebControls.Label
    Protected WithEvents Calendar1 As System.Web.UI.WebControls.Calendar

    Public Overrides Function InitSupportedCultures() As String()
        Dim langs() As String = {"it", "pt", "es"}
        Return langs
    End Function

    Private Sub InitializeComponent()

    End Sub

    Private Sub Page_Load(ByVal sender As System.Object, _
ByVal e As System.EventArgs) Handles MyBase.Load
        Label1.Text = SR.WelcomeText
        Label2.Text = SR.GoodbyeText
    End Sub
End Class
```

As you can see, all we've done in the code-behind file is declare that the class inherits from `GlobalizablePage`, and then override the `InitSupportedCultures()` method to return the languages our site supports. In this case, we've elected to provide our calendar in Spanish (es), Portuguese (pt), and Italian (it).

Now, with the browser configured as shown previously (to prefer U.S. English, but to allow Spanish), when we view the page we see the window in Figure 6-2 in our browser.

Figure 6-2. *Serving resources in Spanish*

As you can see, the `Calendar` control is, and the two defined resource strings are, displaying in Spanish—our second-choice language, but just one of the many supported by the Web site.

Now, if we add support for the English culture by modifying the `InitSupportedCultures` like this:

```
Public Overrides Function InitSupportedCultures() As String()
    Dim langs() As String = {"en", "it", "pt", "es"}
    Return langs
End Function
```

after compiling and browsing the page again, we will get its output in English, as shown in Figure 6-3.

Figure 6-3. *Serving resources in English*

Limitations

One subtle limitation of this class that you need to be aware of is that the logic for setting up the current thread culture is running in the Page.OnInit method. This particular method—unlike the other OnXXX methods, such as OnLoad and OnPreRender—runs only after all children-corresponding OnInit methods have run. This means that any code we may have in any control OnInit method will run *before* the appropriate culture is set for the running thread. Although this is not a big limitation—as you can almost always move any depending code to OnLoad—it's one you should be well aware of.

A bigger limitation is that our approach (that of a Page-derived base class) requires that your pages all inherit from a custom class. Because .NET only supports single inheritance, this means you can't incorporate this feature into a page that has to inherit from any other source. Moreover, we're also assuming that you only want to make pages aware of globalization and just ignore any other handler that may exist. For instance, you may have a custom handler that serves images files; with our current approach, this handler (which just implements the IHttpHandler interface and does not derive from our custom class) won't benefit from the features you saw previously. If this is your case, then you could abandon the Page-derived class approach and move the relevant code to application-wide events, like Application_BeginRequest and Application_EndRequest, that will always execute regardless of the handler type (be it Page or any custom one you may have).

Extensions

If your Web site visitor's first language is French, but she also speaks English (and your site is natively in English, but makes a French translation available), which language should you use? In our implementation, the user will get her first choice—French. But if the French translation is incomplete or patchy, wouldn't it be better to offer her the English version, since she'll probably understand it?

To improve our service in these circumstances, we could label the quality of each version of the site that we publish—just like a browser rates each of the client's preferences with a relative degradation in desired quality. So, our site's English version might have a quality level of 1.0, but our French translation (some features missing, only some content available) only merits a 0.3. Now, when a request arrives from a browser with French labeled at 1.0 and English at 0.5, we can assess both combinations by multiplying the quality of our version in that language by the quality of the user's preference for the language. In this case, French scores 0.3 overall (0.3×1.0) and English scores 0.5 (1.0×0.5), so we should send them the English version.

CHAPTER 7

Validation Control

For any Web developer building forms that take user input, validating them quickly and efficiently (with minimum disruption to the user if they make a mistake) while ensuring strict integrity of the entered data is not a simple task.

Now that Microsoft has taken over the validation of Web Forms input controls with a set of built-in validation controls, it may appear that the battle is over. However, there are a number of issues that make them unsuited for every possible need. One very important aspect is that they only offer client-side JavaScript validation for the IE browser. Other browsers will always require a postback to execute server-side validation code. The built-in extensibility mechanism involves creating a new validation control and overriding methods, which can become quite complex. Also, the provided validation controls are not culture-aware, limiting their application in international contexts.

For a form's validation architecture to be extensible, it has to provide good design-time aids to the developer, but, at the same time, allow for functional division of work, leaving the validation routines to the people in charge of the business logic, not the Web and control designers. In addition, the controls have to be highly responsive, reacting whenever possible as users type, telling of any mistake they have made, and preventing the entry of invalid data on the form.

We will build a validation system that satisfies all these requirements, which can be easily extended, and which takes advantage of advanced JavaScript facilities to offer a client-side environment as similar as possible to the server-side model of events and classes.

Scenario

Microsoft's validation controls provide very basic functionality, such as required fields, comparison tests, and general data-type constraints. However, extending the functionality with custom validation involves creating code for the server- and client-side validation, without any help on the part of the validation library. The client-side JavaScript objects, functions, and methods may be completely ignored by the VB .NET developer, and may impose a learning curve in order to get highly responsive Web Forms. Clearly, the path is to make a much better JavaScript library to aid the developer, and offer extensibility through the use of custom classes that perform the validation. This way we will significantly increase the developer's productivity, and allow for completely customized validation libraries to be available enterprise-wide.

The library has to support the capture of user errors as the information is entered, but also has to provide a familiar environment for the .NET developer, with classes like Char, String, and CultureInfo, which are absolutely indispensable for non-trivial client-side validation.

Technology

We will create an ASP.NET custom control that will implement a .NET System.Web.UI.IValidator interface. This will allow us to integrate seamlessly with the existing validation controls and the validation summary control. We will use methods at the page level to register our control as a validator, so the page developer doesn't have to deal with a new interface. He can just ask for Page.IsValid and get the right answer.

The validation methods to execute will be implemented in separate classes, which will implement our custom IValidationProvider interface. By using interfaces, we allow third-party libraries to make use of our infrastructure.

Every VB .NET developer will be familiar with .NET classes such as Char or String, but there are significant differences between the VB .NET language and the JavaScript language. The Char type doesn't even exist in JavaScript. We will take advantage of the limited object-oriented (OO) features of JavaScript to re-create these objects and make them available on the client side, thus allowing the .NET developer to work as usual with the classes he already knows. This involves extensive use of the JavaScript prototyping mechanism for building objects.

We will use classes in the System.Globalization namespace to enable validation that is internationalization-aware. The key class for internationalization is CultureInfo, so we will replicate it as a JavaScript object too, bringing some of the power of .NET globalization features to the client side.

Finally, there are major differences between the event model of browsers and that of .NET. Moreover, there are differences between browsers. We will take care of these inconsistencies and re-create an event-handling model to use in custom validation classes that emit JavaScript code that resemble that of .NET event handlers. We will give them the familiar sender and e parameters to work with, with the same properties as the .NET counterparts. Developers of custom validation classes can emit client-side code that will be very similar to their server-side VB .NET code.

Finally, we will make extensive use of regular expressions, which are very useful to validate and match values. Mastering this technique is not easy, but adds an important tool to the developer's toolbox, which is not only a widely implemented feature, but also works almost exactly the same in .NET, JavaScript, Java, Perl, PHP, etc., so it will broaden the developer's knowledge beyond .NET too. VS .NET has good documentation on the topic, and you can find sample regular expressions (including some very complex ones) at http://www.regexplib.com/.

The JavaScript library will be included in our control as an embedded resource.

Design

To avoid the clutter of having multiple validation controls whose only difference is the validation algorithm they use, we separate the validation code from the control's code. So, we will have only one validation control, which is configurable according to the desired validation algorithm to use. This is a significant departure from the approach taken by the ASP.NET built-in validation controls where you have six different controls, each one with its own validation logic embedded within it. The new validation architecture is seen in Figure 7-1.

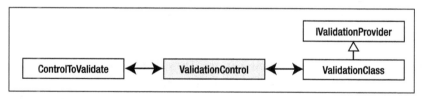

Figure 7-1. *Structure of the new validation architecture*

Each validation algorithm is isolated in a class that implements the IValidationProvider interface. We provide design-time support to make it easy to select the specific validation to use.

Event handling is adjusted to .NET standards. For this purpose, we provide global event handling JavaScript functions that prepare the sender and e arguments to pass to the validation code. The developer can use these variables almost like their .NET equivalents. On the client-side, the processing is as seen in Figure 7-2.

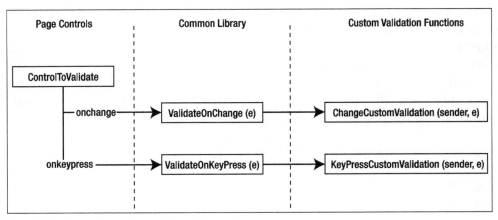

Figure 7-2. *Event handling at the client side*

The common library's ValidateOnChange() and ValidateOnKeyPress() functions prepare the arguments to use in the custom functions, which are optionally emitted by the validation classes implementing the IValidationProvider interface. If the developer decides to emit JavaScript code, he can use the familiar .NET event-handling model. The function even has the same signature and behavior as the CancelEventHandler and KeyPressEventHandler .NET classes, with their corresponding CancelEventArgs and KeyPressEventArgs argument parameter.

We recreate the Char, String, and CultureInfo objects on the client side, so they are readily available for use by the custom validation functions. They use the JavaScript prototyping mechanism to create the objects and, in the case of CultureInfo, its DateTimeFormat, NumberFormat, and TextInfo properties are also created.

Char and String implementations are just JavaScript implementations of the .NET classes. They use JavaScript code to copy their features. They always have the same functionality, so they are placed in the embedded common library.

CultureInfo, on the other hand, is dynamic, because it will depend on the culture that the Web application is running (if the control's CultureAware is set to False) or the culture of the client. Thus, it is implemented as a dump of the relevant properties in the form of a JavaScript object. This way it keeps the same layout as its .NET equivalent.

On the client side, we reconstruct the validator control, too, so we can handle its IsValid, ErrorMessage, and other properties in an OO way. The server control emits the code to create an object of this type, passing the initial values as set in the server side. The common library takes care of initializing the object and saving it in a list of validators for the page.

Microsoft's validation controls show errors not as the user is typing, but only when the focus leaves the current control or when the form is submitted. This fill-everything-then-see-errors approach clearly allows for some improvement. As we stated before, we aim to offer instant feedback. To do so we need to attach our client-side logic to the onchange and onkeypress events of the control whose contents we wish to validate.

One detail we had to take into account here is that the control to validate can be either an HTML server control, a `WebControl`-derived class, or more properly, any class that implements the `ValidationPropertyAttribute` attribute, as defined by the ASP.NET validation infrastructure. But the base `Control` class doesn't have an `Attributes` collection that we can use to add the values, so how do we handle them? The solution is to check in the pre-render handler that the control to validate implements the `IAttributeAccessor`, which both `HtmlControl`- and `WebControl`-derived classes implement. If it does, we add the JavaScript event handlers; otherwise, the control simply won't use `onchange` and `onkeypress` events to offer this improved user experience.

Implementation

Our validator control will be contained in a class library. Create a new class library project and remove the default namespace from the project properties. Add references to `System.Design.dll` and `System.Web.dll`.

First, we will create the `IValidationProvider` interface, which will be implemented by any class that provides client- and server-side validation facilities, and through which our control will interact with custom validation logic. The first member defines the `Validate()` method to be called on the server.

```
Imports System.Web.UI
Imports System.ComponentModel
Imports System.Web.UI.WebControls
Imports System.Globalization
Imports System.ComponentModel.Design
Imports System.Reflection
Imports System.Text
Imports System.IO

Namespace Apress.Toolkit.Validation

  Public Interface IValidationProvider
    Function Validate(ByVal validator As ValidatorControl, _
                  ByVal value As String) As Boolean
```

The following functions tell the validator control whether we provide client scripts:

```
    Function HasScriptForChange() As Boolean
    Function HasScriptForKeyPress() As Boolean
```

The following method outputs client-side script for validating the whole value entered on the textbox. The client-side JavaScript function has the same signature as the `CancelEventHandler` delegate. The `ValidatorControl` class generates the function signature automatically.

```
Function GetScriptForChange(ByVal validator As ValidatorControl) _
        As String
```

The following method outputs client-side script for validating each keystroke entered in the textbox. The client-side JavaScript function has the same signature as the `KeyPressEventHandler` delegate. The `ValidatorControl` class generates the function signature automatically.

```
Function GetScriptForKeyPress( _
            ByVal validator As ValidatorControl) As String
  End Interface
End Namespace
```

We use the `HasXX` approach to avoid emitting empty JavaScript code. This is similar to the .NET implementation of `TypeConverters`, as you will see shortly.

To make it easier for implementers, we'll provide an abstract (`MustInherit`) class with a default implementation of all the methods. Therefore, derived classes only have to override the desired methods. The following is the abstract `BaseValidationProvider` class:

```
Namespace Apress.Toolkit.Validation
  Public MustInherit Class BaseValidationProvider
    Implements IValidationProvider

    Public Overridable Function Validate( _
          ByVal validator As ValidatorControl, _
          ByVal value As String) As Boolean _
          Implements IValidationProvider.Validate
      Return True
    End Function

    Public Overridable Function HasScriptForChange() As Boolean _
          Implements IValidationProvider.HasScriptForChange
      Return False
    End Function

    Public Overridable Function HasScriptForKeyPress() As Boolean _
          Implements IValidationProvider.HasScriptForKeyPress
      Return False
    End Function
```

```vbnet
    Public Overridable Function GetScriptForChange( _
            ByVal validator As ValidatorControl) As String _
            Implements IValidationProvider.GetScriptForChange
        Return String.Empty
    End Function

    Public Overridable Function GetScriptForKeyPress( _
            ByVal validator As ValidatorControl) As String _
            Implements IValidationProvider.GetScriptForKeyPress
        Return String.Empty
    End Function
End Class
```

It just provides an empty skeleton, which always returns True to the server-side Validate method, and doesn't return JavaScript code. We will see concrete implementations later. Let's see the validation control that uses these classes.

The control inherits from Label and implements the .NET's IValidator interface in order to integrate with the built-in validation infrastructure.

```vbnet
<DefaultProperty("ErrorMessage"), ➡
ToolboxData("<{0}:ValidatorControl runat=server></{0}:ValidatorControl>")> _
    Public Class ValidatorControl
        Inherits Label
        Implements IValidator
```

Integration with ASP.NET validation is achieved by registering and unregistering our control at the proper stages of control initialization, as follows:

```vbnet
    Protected Overrides Sub OnInit(ByVal e As System.EventArgs)
        MyBase.OnInit(e)
        'Add this validator to the collection on the page.
        Page.Validators.Add(Me)

        ...

    End Sub

    Protected Overrides Sub OnUnload(ByVal e As System.EventArgs)
        'Remove ourselves from the collection.
        Page.Validators.Remove(Me)
        MyBase.OnUnload(e)
    End Sub
```

We'll be adding more code to the OnInit() method later on.

By adding the control to the page Validators collection, the page framework will automatically use it to determine the page validation state, fill any ValidationSummary controls available, and so on. The System.Web.UI.IValidator interface is the bridge between ASP.NET and our control. It has the following members:

```
Public Interface IValidator
  Public Property ErrorMessage() As String
  Public Property IsValid() As Boolean
  Public Sub Validate()
End Interface
```

When the Validate method is called, the IsValid property has to be updated accordingly. The ASP.NET page will then add the ErrorMessage to any ValidationSummary present on the page, and set the Page.IsValid property accordingly.

Our implementation of the properties is straightforward.

```
Dim _isvalid As Boolean = True
Dim _assembly As String = String.Empty
Dim _type As String = String.Empty
Dim _control As String
Dim _display As ValidatorDisplay = ValidatorDisplay.Static
Dim _cultureaware As Boolean = True
Dim _info As CultureInfo


<Browsable(False)> _
Public Property ErrorMessage() As String _
              Implements IValidator.ErrorMessage
  Get
    Return MyBase.Text
  End Get
  Set(ByVal value As String)
    MyBase.Text = value
  End Set
End Property


<Browsable(False), DesignerSerializationVisibility( _
DesignerSerializationVisibility.Hidden)> _
Public Property IsValid() As Boolean Implements IValidator.IsValid
  Get
    Return _isvalid
  End Get
  Set(ByVal value As Boolean)
```

```
      _isvalid = value
    End Set
End Property
```

We make the ErrorMessage property map to the control's Text inherited property, and we hide it from the property browser to avoid confusion for the developer; by doing this, we believe we're simplifying the design provided by Microsoft by offering just one single error message (the label or the summary message) regardless of the location it may be shown. The IsValid property is hidden both from the property browser and from the serialization process (generation of the HTML source code tags), and returns the value of a private variable updated in the Validate method, like so:

```
Public Sub Validate() Implements IValidator.Validate
  Dim val As IValidationProvider
  Me.IsValid = True
  val = Me.GetValidator()
  Try
    Me.IsValid = val.Validate(Me, GetControlValue())
  Catch e As Exception
    Page.Trace.Warn("Apress.Toolkit.Validation", _
        String.Format("Validator {0}.{1} threw an exception.", _
        Me.AssemblyName, Me.TypeName), e)
    Me.IsValid = False
  End Try
End Sub
```

Note that we update the property according to the result of calling the Validate method in the IValidationProvider object retrieved by the helper GetValidator() method that we'll see in a moment. We pass it the control itself (Me) and the value set on the control to validate, which is retrieved by the GetControlValue() helper method, which we'll see shortly, too.

The Catch block provides a hint on how the validation class implementation is assigned to the validation control. We expose AssemblyName and TypeName properties, which define the class to use to perform validation for this control. The GetValidator() method uses them to instantiate and return the corresponding class.

```
Private Shared LoadedValidators As New Hashtable()

Private Function GetValidator() As IValidationProvider
  If Me.AssemblyName = String.Empty Then
    Throw New ArgumentException("AssemblyName property not set.")
  End If
```

```
    Dim val As IValidationProvider

    If Not LoadedValidators.ContainsKey(Me.TypeName) Then
      val = CType(Activator.CreateInstance(Me.AssemblyName, _
          Me.TypeName).Unwrap(), IValidationProvider)
      LoadedValidators.Add(Me.TypeName, val)
    Else
      val = CType(LoadedValidators(Me.TypeName), _
          IValidationProvider)
    End If

    Return val
End Function
```

We keep a static list of instantiated validators to avoid creating multiple validator instances. This should help with performance. The key for each item is the TypeName property, which contains the fully qualified name of the class. If the class isn't found in the preloaded list, we create an instance using the Activator class.

Before we look at the GetControlValue() method, we have to see the ControlToValidate property we expose, which allows the developer to select a control on the page to validate. This property is simply the ID of the target control, but to offer the drop-down control that built-in validators do, we take advantage of attributes on the property definition.

```
<DefaultValue(""), _
Description("The ID of the control to validate."), _
TypeConverter(GetType(ValidatedControlConverter)), _
Category("Behavior")> _
Public Property ControlToValidate As String
  Get
    Return _control
  End Get
  Set(ByVal value As String)
    _control = value
  End Set
End Property
```

The TypeConverter attribute is the one that allows the feature shown in Figure 7-3 at design time.

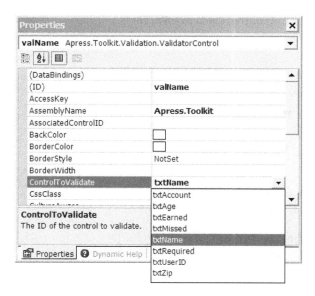

Figure 7-3. *Browsing the properties of the* ValidatorControl

But how, for example, does the converter know that a textbox can be used for the ControlToValidate property and not a HyperLink control? And how does the validator know which property of the target control to use? The secret is in an attribute that is applied to the textbox and other controls that want to be the source for validation. Here's the attribute as it is applied to the TextBox control:

```
<ValidationProperty("Text")>
Public Class TextBox Inherits WebControl, IPostBackDataHandler
```

The ValidatedControlConverter looks at the controls on the page and only shows on the list those with this attribute in place. So the GetControlValue() method will also need to retrieve this attribute in order to know which property to get the value from. This method uses the helper method to locate the control first, prior to retrieving of property value.

```
Private Function GetControlToValidate() As Control
  If Me.ControlToValidate = String.Empty Then
    Throw New ArgumentException( _
        Me.ID & ".ControlToValidate not set.")
  End If
```

```
    Dim ctl As Control = Page.FindControl(Me.ControlToValidate)
    If ctl Is Nothing Then
      Throw New ArgumentException( _
          String.Format("Control to validate {0} wasn't found.", _
            Me.ControlToValidate))
    End If

    Return ctl
  End Function
```

We use the page's FindControl() method to locate the proper control instance and return it. Let's now look at the GetControlValue() method, as follows:

```
    Private Function GetControlValue() As String
      Dim ctl As Control = Me.GetControlToValidate()

      Dim val As ValidationPropertyAttribute
      val = CType(TypeDescriptor.GetAttributes( _
          ctl).Item(GetType(ValidationPropertyAttribute)), _
          ValidationPropertyAttribute)

      If val Is Nothing Then
        Throw New ArgumentException( _
            "Control to validate " & Me.ControlToValidate & _
            "isn't a valid source for validation.")
      End If

      Dim prop As PropertyDescriptor = _
          TypeDescriptor.GetProperties(ctl).Item(val.Name)
      Return CType(prop.GetValue(ctl), String)
    End Function
```

The TypeDescriptor class provides a way to retrieve attributes from an object, and returns an AttributeCollection instance. We use this class's Item indexer property passing the attribute type we are looking for, which is returned if it exists in the object. After we have retrieved it, we use the ValidationPropertyAttribute.Name property with the TypeDescriptor object to retrieve the PropertyDescriptor, which allows access to the property value by means of the GetValue() method.

Forcing the developer to remember and enter the exact fully qualified type name of the class to use wouldn't be good. So we use a mechanism similar to that provided by the ValidatedControlConverter to preload and filter types to show in a drop-down list. We first have to create the custom TypeConverter, like so:

```
Public Class ValidatorTypeConverter
  Inherits TypeConverter

  Public Overloads Overrides Function _
        GetStandardValuesSupported( _
        ByVal context As ITypeDescriptorContext) As Boolean
    Return True
  End Function

  Public Overloads Overrides Function _
        GetStandardValuesExclusive( _
        ByVal context As ITypeDescriptorContext) As Boolean
    Return True
  End Function

  Public Overloads Overrides Function GetStandardValues( _
        ByVal context As ITypeDescriptorContext) _
        As StandardValuesCollection
    Dim val As ValidatorControl = _
        CType(context.Instance, ValidatorControl)
    If val.AssemblyName = String.Empty Then Return Nothing
    Dim svc As ITypeResolutionService = _
        CType(context.GetService( _
        GetType(ITypeResolutionService)), _
        ITypeResolutionService)
    If svc Is Nothing Then Return Nothing
```

First, we use the context parameter to cast the Instance property currently in use to the ValidatorControl type. The service retrieved from the host is used to check for an existing reference to the specified assembly. This works under ASP.NET Web Matrix, too. With the service available, we can ask it for the assembly object, as follows:

```
Dim name As New AssemblyName()
name.Name = val.AssemblyName
Dim asm As [Assembly] = svc.GetAssembly(name)
If asm Is Nothing Then Return Nothing
```

What we do next is iterate through all the types in the assembly, looking for those implementing our IValidationProvider interface and which aren't abstract (MustInherit).

```
Dim list As System.Collections.ArrayList = _
    New System.Collections.ArrayList()
Dim types() As Type = asm.GetTypes()
```

```
      Dim t As Type
      For Each t In types
        If Not t.IsAbstract And _
            t.FindInterfaces([Module].FilterTypeName, _
            "IValidationProvider").Length <> 0 Then
          list.Add(t.FullName)
        End If
      Next


      Return New StandardValuesCollection(list)
    End Function
  End Class
```

Finally, we just return the collection of valid values. This converter has to be associated with the TypeName property through an attribute.

```
< TypeConverter(GetType(ValidatorTypeConverter)), _
Description("The class implementing the validation code."), _
Category("Validator"), DefaultValue("")> _
Property TypeName() As String
  Get
    Return _type
  End Get
  Set(ByVal value As String)
    _type = value
  End Set
End Property
```

The AssemblyName property has to be entered manually, as, unfortunately, the ITypeResolutionService doesn't provide a way to retrieve all the referenced assemblies for the current project.

```
<Description("The name of the assembly with the classes " + _
"implementing the validation code. Use the name as it appears " _
& "in the References folder."), _
Category("Validator"), DefaultValue("")> _
Property AssemblyName() As String
  Get
    Return _assembly
  End Get
  Set(ByVal value As String)
    _assembly = value
  End Set
End Property
```

Our control supports a CultureAware property to specify whether it should assume the culture of the client browser or of the application.

```
<Description("Make the control aware of client culture when " & _
"validating values."), Category("Appearance")> _
Public Property CultureAware() As Boolean
  Get
    Return _cultureaware
  End Get
  Set(ByVal value As Boolean)
    _cultureaware = value
  End Set
End Property
```

Based on this property, the following code initializes the other property, Culture:

```
Protected Overrides Sub OnInit(ByVal e As System.EventArgs)
  MyBase.OnInit(e)
  Page.Validators.Add(Me)
  If Not CultureAware Then
    Me.Culture = CultureInfo.CurrentCulture
  Else
    Me.Culture = CultureInfo.CreateSpecificCulture( _
        context.Request.UserLanguages(0))
  End If
End Sub
```

The Culture property then holds the CultureInfo object to use in validation code, as follows:

```
<Browsable(False)> _
Public Property Culture() As CultureInfo
  Get
    Return _info
  End Get
  Set(ByVal value As CultureInfo)
    _info = value
  End Set
End Property
```

As we said, this object will be dumped as a JavaScript object for the client code to use. But before we move on to the script handling and the library, let's look at the rendering process.

Our control, just like the built-in ones, provides a `Display` property that allows customizing the control's appearance when errors are found. Look at the .NET documentation for the different settings this property supports.

```
<Description("How the validator is displayed."), _
Category("Appearance"), DefaultValue(ValidatorDisplay.Static)> _
Public Property Display() As ValidatorDisplay
  Get
    Return _display
  End Get
  Set(ByVal value As ValidatorDisplay)
    _display = value
  End Set
End Property
```

This value causes different attributes to be placed on the control at render time. That's performed in the `AddAttributesToRender()` method override, like so:

```
Protected Overrides Sub AddAttributesToRender( _
        ByVal writer As System.Web.UI.HtmlTextWriter)
  If CType(Me, IComponent).Site Is Nothing Then
    Select Case Me.Display
      Case ValidatorDisplay.None
        Me.Style.Add("display", "none")
      Case ValidatorDisplay.Dynamic
        If Not IsValid Then
          Me.Style.Add("display", "inline")
        Else
          Me.Style.Add("display", "none")
        End If
      Case ValidatorDisplay.Static
        If Not IsValid Then
          Me.Style.Add("visibility", "visible")
        Else
          Me.Style.Add("visibility", "hidden")
        End If
    End Select
  End If

  MyBase.AddAttributesToRender(writer)
End Sub
```

Casting the control to IComponent allows us to check the Site property, which is only set if the control is being used at design time. That way we avoid the control becoming invisible at design time. The final bit about rendering is how we add the validation event handlers to the control to validate. First, we add our handler for its PreRender event in our OnLoad() override.

```
Protected Overrides Sub OnLoad(ByVal e As System.EventArgs)
  InitializeScripts()
  MyBase.OnLoad(e)
  AddHandler GetControlToValidate().PreRender, _
      New EventHandler(AddressOf OnTargetPreRender)
End Sub
```

Note that the events only have to be added if the validation class emits code for them. We check that in the event handler, as follows:

```
Private Sub OnTargetPreRender(ByVal sender As Object, _
                             ByVal e As EventArgs)
  Dim val As IValidationProvider = Me.GetValidator()
  Dim ctl As IAttributeAccessor

  If (TypeOf sender Is IAttributeAccessor) Then
    ctl = CType(sender, IAttributeAccessor)

    If val.HasScriptForChange() Then
      ctl.SetAttribute("onchange", _
          "return ValidateOnChange(event);")
    End If

    If val.HasScriptForKeyPress() Then
      ctl.SetAttribute("onkeypress", _
          "return ValidateOnKeyPress(event);")
    End If
  End If
End Sub
```

We use the System.Web.UI.IAttributeAccessor interface to be compatible with any control that implements it, adding flexibility to our implementation. We use the methods provided by the IValidationProvider to determine whether to add the attributes or not. Note that our processing is similar to that of the TypeConverter we saw earlier, which uses the GetStandardValuesSupported method to determine if the GetStandardValues method has to be called or not.

We'll see what the ValidateOnChange and ValidateOnKeyPress functions do in a moment.

Embedding scripts as resources in an assembly was covered in Chapter 2, so we'll just show the code that extracts the library prior to rendering. For an explanation of this code and the script registering mechanism, take a look at the Spinner control.

```
Shared ValidatorLibScript As String

Shared GlobalKey As String = GetType(ValidatorControl).FullName
Shared CultureKey As String = GlobalKey + "Culture"

Shared Sub New()
  Dim asm As [Assembly] = [Assembly].GetExecutingAssembly()

  If Not asm Is Nothing Then
    Dim resource As String = "ValidatorLib.js"
    Dim stm As Stream = asm.GetManifestResourceStream(resource)
    If Not stm Is Nothing Then
      Try
        Dim reader As StreamReader = New StreamReader(stm)
        ValidatorLibScript = reader.ReadToEnd()
        reader.Close()
      Catch e As Exception
        Throw New ApplicationException( _
            String.Format("Couldn't extract {0} for {1}.", _
            resource, GlobalKey), e)
      Finally
        CType(stm, IDisposable).Dispose()
      End Try
    End If
  End If
End Sub
```

As we saw previously, the main script-handling routine is InitializeScripts, which is called inside the OnLoad() method override. The first thing that the method does is check whether scripts should be rendered at all, that is, if the client browser supports it, which is encapsulated in the following RenderScripts method:

```
Private Function RenderScripts() As Boolean
  Return (Context.Request.Browser.EcmaScriptVersion.Major >= 1 _
      And Context.Request.Browser.EcmaScriptVersion.Minor >= 2 _
      And Context.Request.Browser.W3CDomVersion.Major >= 1)
End Function
```

Now let's look at the inside of the InitializeScripts() method. It's fairly lengthy, so we'll see each logic block in turn.

```
Private Sub InitializeScripts()
  If Not RenderScripts() Then Return

  Dim sb As StringBuilder

  If Not Page.IsClientScriptBlockRegistered(CultureKey) Then
    sb = New StringBuilder()
    sb.Append("<script language=""javascript"">")
    sb.Append(ControlChars.NewLine)
    CreateStartupCurrentInfo(sb)
    sb.Append("</script>")
    Page.RegisterClientScriptBlock(CultureKey, sb.ToString())
  End If
```

The CreateStartupCurrentInfo() helper method will be shown shortly. Briefly, it dumps all the relevant properties of the Culture property as a JavaScript object, as we said. We use the CultureKey string as the key for registering it, as we don't need to emit it more than once per page. Also, the IsClientScriptBlockRegistered check saves us from repeatedly performing the same string concatenations.

```
If Not Page.IsClientScriptBlockRegistered(GlobalKey) Then
  Page.RegisterClientScriptBlock(GlobalKey, ValidatorLibScript)
End If
```

This line registers the common library we will be using. The library is held in the Shared ValidatorLibScript variable we loaded in the Shared constructor. The following code deals with emitting the code provided by the validator class selected. The code emits JavaScript functions with the following structure:

```
<script language="javascript">
  function Change[key](sender, e)
  {
    [IValidationProvider.GetScriptForChange]
  }
  ApressToolkitValidator.prototype.Change[key] = Change[key];

  function KeyPress[key](sender, e)
  {
    [IValidationProvider.GetScriptForKeyPress]
  }
  ApressToolkitValidator.prototype.KeyPress[key] = KeyPress[key];
</script>
```

The key value is the control's TypeName (the qualified name of the validation class) without the dots. Note that the functions are added to a special object type defined in the common library. For now, let's say it's the client-side representation of a validation control. The prototyping mechanism allows the methods to be called directly on an instance of the ApressToolkitValidator JavaScript object. Because of this, the code generated by the IValidationProvider implementation can use the this keyword to refer to the current validator being executed. This way it can query for its IsValid, ErrorMessage, and other properties, should it want to.

What follows is the code to produce the output:

```
Dim val As IValidationProvider = GetValidator()
Dim key As String = Me.TypeName.Replace(".", "")

If Not Page.IsStartupScriptRegistered(key) Then
  sb = New StringBuilder()
  sb.Append("<script language=""javascript"">")
  sb.Append(ControlChars.NewLine)

  If val.HasScriptForChange() Then
    sb.Append("function Change").Append(key)
    sb.Append("(sender, e)").Append(ControlChars.NewLine)
    sb.Append("{").Append(ControlChars.NewLine)
    sb.Append(val.GetScriptForChange(Me))
    sb.Append(ControlChars.NewLine).Append("}")
    sb.Append(ControlChars.NewLine)
    sb.Append("ApressToolkitValidator.prototype.Change")
    sb.Append(key).Append(" = Change").Append(key)
    sb.Append(";").Append(ControlChars.NewLine)
    sb.Append(ControlChars.NewLine)
  End If

  If val.HasScriptForKeyPress() Then
    sb.Append("function KeyPress").Append(key)
    sb.Append("(sender, e)").Append(ControlChars.NewLine)
    sb.Append("{").Append(ControlChars.NewLine)
    sb.Append(val.GetScriptForKeyPress(Me))
    sb.Append(ControlChars.NewLine).Append("}")
    sb.Append(ControlChars.NewLine)

    sb.Append("ApressToolkitValidator.prototype.KeyPress")
    sb.Append(key).Append(" = KeyPress").Append(key)
    sb.Append(";").Append(ControlChars.NewLine)
    sb.Append(ControlChars.NewLine)
  End If
```

```
        sb.Append("</script>")

        If (val.HasScriptForChange() Or _
            val.HasScriptForKeyPress()) And _
            TypeOf GetControlToValidate() Is IAttributeAccessor Then
          Page.RegisterStartupScript(key, sb.ToString())
        Else
          Page.RegisterStartupScript(key, String.Empty)
        End If
      End If
```

Note that the functions and the prototype extension are only emitted once per validator type (the key). That's because the type itself doesn't change. Instead, new instances of the validator are added. This is shown in the following code:

```
      sb = New StringBuilder()
      sb.Append("<script language=""javascript"">")
      sb.Append(ControlChars.NewLine)
      sb.Append("AddValidator(")
      sb.Append("""").Append(Me.ControlToValidate).Append(""",")
      sb.Append("""").Append(Me.ErrorMessage).Append(""",")
      sb.Append("""").Append(Me.Display.ToString()).Append(""",")
      sb.Append(Me.IsValid.ToString().ToLower()).Append(",")
      sb.Append( _
        val.HasScriptForKeyPress().ToString().ToLower()).Append(",")
      sb.Append( _
        val.HasScriptForChange().ToString().ToLower()).Append(",")
      sb.Append("""").Append(Me.ClientID).Append(""",")
      sb.Append("""").Append(key).Append(""");")
      sb.Append(ControlChars.NewLine).Append("</script>")
      Page.RegisterStartupScript(Me.ClientID, sb.ToString())
    End Sub
```

We register this as a startup script, which is placed at the bottom of the page. The following output is produced by the code (with some formatting):

```
<script language="javascript">
  AddValidator(
    [ControlToValidate],
    [ErrorMessage],
    [Display],
    [IsValid],
    [IValidationProvider.HasScriptForKeyPress()],
```

```
        [IValidationProvider.HasScriptForKeyPress()],
        [ClientID],
        [key]);
</script>
```

The AddValidator() function is provided in the common library, and is the one responsible for keeping the list of validator controls on the page and their targets.

The last method of our control is the one that dumps the CultureInfo object, called at the beginning of the InitializeScripts method that we just saw.

```
Private Sub CreateStartupCurrentInfo( _
            ByRef builder As StringBuilder)
    Dim n As String = ControlChars.NewLine

    builder.Append(n).Append("var CultureInfo;").Append(n)
    Me.DumpProperties(builder, String.Empty, "CultureInfo", _
                Culture)
    Me.DumpProperties(builder, "CultureInfo", "DateTimeFormat", _
                Culture.DateTimeFormat)
    Me.DumpProperties(builder, "CultureInfo", "NumberFormat", _
                Culture.NumberFormat)
    Me.DumpProperties(builder, "CultureInfo", "TextInfo", _
                Culture.TextInfo)
End Sub
```

This method calls another helper method that performs the actual dump, receiving the StringBuilder, the name of the JavaScript variable to emit, the property to attach code to, and the object to dump, as shown here:

```
Private Sub DumpProperties( _
            ByRef builder As StringBuilder, _
            ByRef varName As String, _
            ByRef propName As String, _
            ByVal value As Object)
    Dim props As PropertyInfo()
    Dim prop As PropertyInfo
    Dim n As String = ControlChars.NewLine
    builder.Append(n).Append("function ").Append(propName)
    builder.Append("() {").Append(n)

    props = value.GetType().GetProperties( _
        BindingFlags.Instance Or BindingFlags.Public)
```

```vbnet
      For Each prop In props
        If prop.PropertyType.IsValueType Then
          If prop.PropertyType Is GetType(Char) Or _
            prop.PropertyType.IsEnum Then
            builder.Append(ControlChars.Tab).Append("this.")
            builder.Append(prop.Name).Append(" = """)
            builder.Append(prop.GetValue(value, Nothing))
            builder.Append(""";").Append(n)
          ElseIf prop.PropertyType Is GetType(Boolean) Then
            builder.Append(ControlChars.Tab).Append("this.")
            builder.Append(prop.Name).Append(" = ")
            builder.Append(prop.GetValue( _
                value, Nothing).ToString().ToLower())
            builder.Append(";").Append(n)
          Else
            builder.Append(ControlChars.Tab).Append("this.")
            builder.Append(prop.Name).Append(" = ")
            builder.Append(prop.GetValue(value, Nothing))
            builder.Append(";").Append(n)
          End If
        ElseIf prop.PropertyType Is GetType(String) Then
          builder.Append(ControlChars.Tab).Append("this.")
          builder.Append(prop.Name).Append(" = """)
          builder.Append(prop.GetValue(value, Nothing))
          builder.Append(""";").Append(n)
        ElseIf prop.PropertyType.IsArray Then
          'Can we output array values? Not critical for now.
        End If
      Next

      builder.Append("}").Append(n)
      If varName <> String.Empty Then _
          builder.Append(varName).Append(".")
      builder.Append(propName)
      builder.Append( _
          " = new ").Append(propName).Append("();").Append(n)
    End Sub
  End Class
End Namespace
```

This code makes extensive use of reflection to iterate through the properties of the object, and to get their names and values. The key line is

```
        props = value.GetType().GetProperties( _
            BindingFlags.Instance Or BindingFlags.Public)
```

It asks for the public instance properties of the object passed in. Then we simply iterate and build the lines that add properties to the this keyword. To better understand what is generated by this method, take a look at the generated dump.

```
<script language="javascript">
var CultureInfo;

function CultureInfo() {
  this.LCID = 1033;
  this.Name = "en-US";
  this.DisplayName = "English (United States)";
  this.NativeName = "English (United States)";
  this.EnglishName = "English (United States)";
  this.TwoLetterISOLanguageName = "en";
  this.ThreeLetterISOLanguageName = "eng";
  this.ThreeLetterWindowsLanguageName = "ENU";
  this.IsNeutralCulture = false;
  this.UseUserOverride = true;
  this.IsReadOnly = false;
}
CultureInfo = new CultureInfo();

function NumberFormat() {
  this.CurrencyDecimalDigits = 2;
  this.CurrencyDecimalSeparator = ".";
  this.IsReadOnly = false;
  this.CurrencyGroupSeparator = ",";
  this.CurrencySymbol = "$";
  this.NaNSymbol = "NaN";
  this.CurrencyNegativePattern = 0;
  this.NumberNegativePattern = 1;
  this.PercentPositivePattern = 0;
  this.PercentNegativePattern = 0;
  this.NegativeInfinitySymbol = "-Infinity";
  this.NegativeSign = "-";
  this.NumberDecimalDigits = 2;
  this.NumberDecimalSeparator = ".";
  this.NumberGroupSeparator = ",";
  this.CurrencyPositivePattern = 0;
  this.PositiveInfinitySymbol = "Infinity";
```

```
    this.PositiveSign = "+";
    this.PercentDecimalDigits = 2;
    this.PercentDecimalSeparator = ".";
    this.PercentGroupSeparator = ",";
    this.PercentSymbol = "%";
    this.PerMilleSymbol = "‰";
}
CultureInfo.NumberFormat = new NumberFormat();
...
</script>
```

Similar code is emitted for the `CultureInfo.DateTimeFormat` and `CultureInfo.TextInfo` properties. Look at the .NET Framework documentation about these objects and how they reflect culture-specific information.

As a result of this code being emitted, any JavaScript code, either the common library or the custom validator implementations, has a globally available `CultureInfo` object, as follows:

```
var CultureInfo;
```

When the object is instantiated, the `CultureInfo` constructor appends all the properties that we saw to the object, making them immediately available to JavaScript code using the variable.

```
function CultureInfo() {
  //Append properties
}
CultureInfo = new CultureInfo();
```

So the following JavaScript code would show the current culture display name:

```
alert(CultureInfo.DisplayName);
```

Next, the same process is performed for the `NumberFormat` function, but this time, instead of creating a new object, it is appended as a property of the `CultureInfo` variable, passed as an argument to the `DumpProperties` method.

```
function NumberFormat() {
  //Append properties
}
CultureInfo.NumberFormat = new NumberFormat();
```

After this call, the following code would show the current currency symbol:

```
alert(CultureInfo.NumberFormat.CurrencySymbol);
```

Note that the object's properties are called and queried in a similar way as they would in .NET. We will see the great benefits of this when we create some sample validator implementations. The server-side code is finished now. Let's move on to the client-side JavaScript code.

JavaScript Library

Take a look at the provided ValidatorLib.js file. The file starts by creating a JavaScript object equivalent to the .NET Char class, which is very useful for validation purposes, as it provides a number of methods to check the type of a single character, used mainly by the onkeypress handlers.

```
<script language="javascript">
<!--
/*************************************************
/*       .NET Char class equivalent.
/*************************************************/
function Char()
{
}
Char.IsDigit = function (c) { return /^\d$/.test(c); };
Char.IsLetter = function (c) { return /^[a-zA-Z_,\s]$/.test(c); };
Char.IsLetterOrDigit = function (c) { return this.IsDigit(c) || this.IsLetter(c);
};
Char.IsLower = function (c)
{
  return c == c.toLowerCase();
};
Char.IsNumber = function (c)
{
  var reg = "^[0-9";
  reg += "\\" + CultureInfo.NumberFormat.NumberDecimalSeparator;
  reg += "\\" + CultureInfo.NumberFormat.NumberGroupSeparator;
  reg += "\\" + CultureInfo.NumberFormat.NegativeSign;
  reg += "\\" + CultureInfo.NumberFormat.PositiveSign;
  reg += "]$";
  return new RegExp(reg).test(c);
};
Char.IsUpper = function (c)
{
  return c == c.toUpperCase();
};
Char.IsWhitespace = function (c) { return c = " "; };
```

```
/**************************************************
/*       End of Char object
/**************************************************/
```

This time we aren't registering the methods with the object's prototype, thus making the methods Shared. All the methods receive a parameter that is the character to check. Note how IsNumber takes advantage of the CultureInfo object emitted by the server control to make the function culture-aware. It also makes extensive use of regular expressions to match characters against a predefined pattern. With this object in place, we can write code like the following:

```
alert(Char.IsDigit("a"));    //Displays 'false'
alert(Char.IsLetter("a") && Char.IsLower("a"));    //Displays 'true'
```

The same approach is followed to re-create the .NET String object. This time, however, we have to give it a different name because String is already a JavaScript type.

```
function NetString(value)
{
  this._value = value;
  this.Intern = value;
  this.Length = value.length;
  this.Empty = "";
  this.Whitespace = " ";
}
function Chars(index)
{
  return new NetString(this.Intern.charAt(index));
}
function EndsWith(value)
{
  return this.Intern.substring(
    this.Intern.length - value.length,
    this.Intern.length) == value;
}
function Equals(value)
{
  return this.Intern == value;
}
function IndexOf(value)
{
  return this.Intern.indexOf(value);
}
```

```
function IndexOfAny(anyOf)
{
  var pos;

  for (i = 0; i < this.Intern.length; i++)
  {
    for (j = 0; j < anyOf.length; j++)
    {
        if (this.Intern.charAt(i) == anyOf[j])
            return i;
    }
  }
  return -1;
}
//Other method definitions.
```

The Intern property provides access to the underlying JavaScript String object. We implemented some of the .NET String methods and properties, so you can take advantage of the framework documentation as well to learn the features of each of them.

To allow the developer to use JavaScript String object methods transparently, we provide passthrough methods, too.

```
function charAt(index) { return this.Intern.charAt(index); }
function charCodeAt(index) {
  return this.Intern.charCodeAt(index);
}
//Other method definitions.
```

All of the methods are added to the prototype later.

```
NetString.prototype.Chars = Chars;
NetString.prototype.EndsWith = EndsWith;
NetString.prototype.Equals = Equals;
NetString.prototype.IndexOf = IndexOf;
NetString.prototype.IndexOfAny = IndexOfAny;
//Other methods prototyping.
//Register String methods passthrough.
NetString.prototype.charAt = charAt;
NetString.prototype.charCodeAt = charCodeAt;
//Other methods prototyping.
```

The NetString object is used, among other things, to build sender and e arguments for the event handlers. This way, the developer of custom validation algorithms can work with the familiar methods of the .NET equivalents.

Next comes the validator object definition, as follows:

```
function ApressToolkitValidator(controlToValidate, errorMessage,
          display, isValid, validateKeyPress, validateChange,
          id, functionName)
{
  this.ControlToValidate = controlToValidate;
  this.ErrorMessage = errorMessage;
  this.Display = display;
  this.IsValid = isValid;
  this.ValidateChange = validateChange;
  this.ValidateKeyPress = validateKeyPress;
  this.Id = id;
  this.FunctionName = functionName;
  this.ValidatorControl = document.getElementById(id);
}
function RefreshState()
{
  //Hide/show label.
  if (this.Display == "None") return;
  if (this.Display == "Dynamic")
    this.ValidatorControl.style.display =
      this.IsValid ? "none" : "inline";
  if (this.Display == "Static")
    this.ValidatorControl.style.visibility =
      this.IsValid ? "hidden" : "visible";
}
ApressToolkitValidator.prototype.RefreshState = RefreshState;
```

Note that it's the validator object itself that keeps a reference to the control it validates. This way, the rest of the code gets much simpler, as shown here:

```
//Global variable to hold validators
var ApressToolkitValidators = new Array();

//Register a new validator in the page
function AddValidator(controlToValidate, errorMessage,
          display, isValid, validateKeyPress, validateChange,
          id, functionName)
```

```
{
  var arr = null;
  //First locate the array of validator for the target control.
  for (i = 0; i < ApressToolkitValidators.length; i++)
  {
    if (ApressToolkitValidators[i] == controlToValidate)
    {
      arr = ApressToolkitValidators[i].Elements;
      break;
    }
  }

  //If we don't find one, create a new array now.
  if (arr == null)
  {
    arr = new Array();
    var t = new String(controlToValidate);
    t.Elements = arr;
    //The key in the array is the control ID itself.
    ApressToolkitValidators.push(t);
  }

  var val = new ApressToolkitValidator(controlToValidate,
          errorMessage, display, isValid, validateKeyPress,
          validateChange, id, functionName);

  //Add the new validator to the array of validators for the
  //target control to validate.
  arr.push(val);
}
```

The global ApressToolkitValidators variable holds a String object for each control that has validators attached. The key line here is where we add an Elements array property to the String object, to hold the actual validator instances:

```
var t = new String(controlToValidate);
t.Elements = arr;
```

From now on, the string object with the control ID additionally has an Elements property with an array of the assigned validators. Here, we can appreciate the flexibility of the JavaScript object model. Recall that the AddValidator function was emitted from the server control, with the parameters corresponding to the control's own properties.

When we added the event handlers to the control to validate, the generated output for a textbox would be similar to the following:

```
<input name="txtAge" type="text" id="txtAge" onchange=➡
"return ValidateOnChange(event);" onkeypress="return ValidateOnKeyPress(event);" />
```

The ValidateOnChange function is defined as follows:

```
//If any one validator returns false, the whole event is canceled.
function ValidateOnChange(e)
{
  var sender = PrepareSender(e);
  var argument = PrepareChangeArgument(e);
  var validators = new Array();
  var cancel = false;

  //Retrieve the list of validators for the current control.
  for (i = 0; i < ApressToolkitValidators.length; i++)
  {
    if (ApressToolkitValidators[i] == sender.id)
    {
      validators = ApressToolkitValidators[i].Elements;
      break;
    }
  }

  //Call the validation method on each validator.
  for (i = 0; i < validators.length; i++)
  {
    var validator = validators[i];
    //Execute the appropriate function.
    if (validator.ValidateChange)
    {
      //Reset Cancel flag.
      argument.Cancel = false;
      //Call: validator.Change[key](sender, argument);
      eval("validator.Change" + validator.FunctionName +
          "(sender, argument);");

      //If the event is canceled, the whole function will be.
      if (argument.Cancel) cancel = true;
          //Update the validator display.
```

```
        validator.RefreshState();
    }
  }

  return !cancel;
}
```

First, we retrieve the array of validator elements for the control being validated. Next, we iterate them and, if they have the ValidateChange property set to true (sent by the server control), we use the eval() JavaScript method to call the validation function (again, sent by the server control on behalf of the IValidationProvider implementation in use). Note that the code checks the status of the argument.Cancel property, which can be set in the function generated on the validator class to cancel the event, just as you would do in VB .NET (it's the e.Cancel inside that handler).

Before we look at the PrepareXXX methods, let's look at the ValidateOnKeyPress function, because it's almost the same as the previous one.

```
//If any one validator returns false, the whole event is canceled.
function ValidateOnKeyPress(e)
{
  var sender = PrepareSender(e);
  var argument = PrepareKeyPressArgument(e);
  var validators = new Array();
  var cancel = false;

  //Retrieve the list of validators for the current control.
  for (i = 0; i < ApressToolkitValidators.length; i++)
  {
    if (ApressToolkitValidators[i] == sender.id)
    {
      validators = ApressToolkitValidators[i].Elements;
      break;
    }
  }

  //Call the validation method on each validator.
  for (i = 0; i < validators.length; i++)
  {
    var validator = validators[i];
    //Execute the appropriate function.
    if (validator.ValidateKeyPress)
    {
      //Reset Handled flag.
      argument.Handled = false;
```

```
        //Call: validator.KeyPress[key](sender, argument);
        eval("validator.KeyPress" + validator.FunctionName +
            "(sender, argument);");

        //If the event is handled, it has to be canceled.
        if (argument.Handled) cancel = true;
          validator.RefreshState();
    }
  }

  return !cancel;
}
```

Note that the only difference is that it now checks for the validator.ValidateKeyPress property, and calls the validator.KeyPress[key] event handler function. It uses the argument.Handled flag instead of the Cancel one now, according to the .NET delegate definition.

Now, let's see the PrepareSender function used by both functions.

```
/*  The sender object will provide access to a Text and   */
/*  (if available in the source element) a Value property */
function PrepareSender(e)
{
  var sender;

  if (!e) var e = window.event;

  if (e.srcElement != undefined)
    sender = e.srcElement;
  else
    sender = e.target;

  //The Value may differ from the Text, as in a Select element.
  if (sender.value != undefined)
    sender.Value = new NetString(sender.value);
  else
    sender.Value = "";

  if (sender.text != undefined)
    sender.Text = new NetString(sender.text);
  else
    sender.Text = sender.Value;

  return sender;
}
```

We take into account the differences between Mozilla FireFox and IE browsers in the implementation of the event object received by an event handler. We add the Text and Value properties for use in custom handlers.

The PrepareChangeArgument initializes the argument to pass to the ChangeXXX custom handler emitted by the IValidationProvider implementation, as follows:

```
/*  The e event argument will provide the Cancel property. */
/*  Look the .NET documentation for CancelEventArgs        */
function PrepareChangeArgument(e)
{
  if (!e) var e = window.event;

  var arg = new Object();
  //By default, the event passes on.
  arg.Cancel = false;
  return arg;
}
```

Note that the value returned is simply an empty object with a single property, Cancel, which is used within a handler to flag the cancellation of an event.

The PrepareKeyPressArgument function is a little more complex.

```
/* The e event argument will provide the .NET equivalents of   */
/* Handled (to cancel the event) and KeyChar properties. Look the */
/* .NET documentation of KeyPressEventArgs. Additionally we provide */
/* a KeyCode property. IsControl is a FireFox workaround.       */
function PrepareKeyPressArgument(e)
{
  if (!e) var e = window.event;

  var arg = e;
  var key;

  //By default, the event should pass over.
  arg.Handled = false;

  //IE doesn't define the which event property.
  if (e.which == undefined)
    key = e.keyCode;
  else
    //In NS6+/Mozilla, charCode is used if its an
    //alphanumeric key and keyCode is used if it is not.
    key = (e.charCode != 0) ? e.charCode : e.keyCode;
```

```
  arg.KeyChar = String.fromCharCode(key);
  arg.KeyCode = key;
  if (e.charCode == 0 || e.altKey || e.ctrlKey)
    arg.IsControl = true;
  else
    arg.IsControl = false;

  return arg;
}
</script>
```

Here the code is more browser-aware. It takes into account the fact that FireFox sends the onkeypress event to controls even if the key is a control key. Therefore, we add an IsControl property to expose that fact to custom validator authors.

If we take a second look at the processing sequence we saw previously, we can now understand how it is achieved by the close interaction between the server control-generated JavaScript and the common library we built. We can now expand the diagram a little, as shown in Figure 7-4.

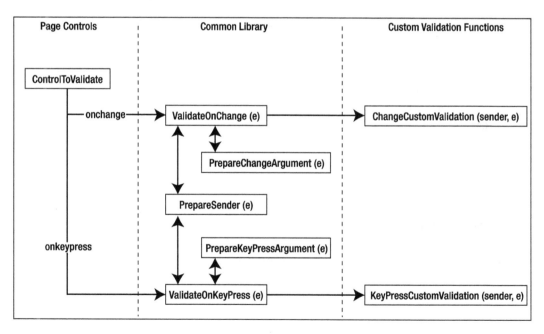

Figure 7-4. *A closer look at event handling at the client side*

Calling the server-side generated validation function on the actual validator is possible because we added it to the `ApressToolkitValidator` prototype itself.

Finally, it's time to build our base validation control. We still have to develop some validation provider classes, but our base validator is complete.

Demonstration

Now that the infrastructure is in place, let's take a look at actual validator implementations, starting with a simple one, the `IntegerValidator` class.

```
Imports Microsoft.VisualBasic
Imports System
Imports System.Text

Namespace Apress.Toolkit.Validation
  Public Class IntegerValidator
    Inherits BaseValidationProvider

    Public Overrides Function Validate( _
        ByVal validator As ValidatorControl, _
        ByVal value As String) As Boolean
      Try
        Convert.ToInt32(value)
        Return True
      Catch
        Return False
      End Try
    End Function
```

The server-side version is pretty simple. It just tries to convert the received value to an `Int32`. Client code requires a little more work, especially because of the string concatenation.

```
    Public Overrides Function HasScriptForChange() As Boolean
      Return True
    End Function

    Public Overrides Function HasScriptForKeyPress() As Boolean
      Return True
    End Function

    Public Overrides Function GetScriptForChange( _
        ByVal validator As ValidatorControl) As String
```

```
'---- Expected output ----
'if (parseInt(sender.Text) != sender.Text) e.Cancel = true;
'if (e.Cancel) this.IsValid = false;
'else this.IsValid = true;
'------------------------
Dim sb As New StringBuilder()
sb.Append(ControlChars.Tab)
sb.Append( _
    "if (parseInt(sender.Text) != sender.Text) e.Cancel = true;")
sb.Append(ControlChars.NewLine).Append(ControlChars.Tab)
sb.Append("if (e.Cancel) this.IsValid = false;")
sb.Append(ControlChars.NewLine)
sb.Append(ControlChars.Tab)
sb.Append("else this.IsValid = true;")
Return sb.ToString()
End Function
```

Note that we use the sender.Text property to get the new value for the control, and note how we can cancel the event by setting the e.Cancel property to true. We also update the validator state by directly calling this.IsValid, as the function is executing in the validator itself.

This is one of those situations where VB .NET programmers might envy C# developers; the same function would look something like this to them:

```
public override string GetScriptForChange(ValidatorControl validator)
{
  return
    @"if (parseInt(sender.Text) != sender.Text) e.Cancel = true;
    if (e.Cancel) this.IsValid = false;
    else this.IsValid = true;";
}
```

That's because C# supports the concept of a string literal, identified by the @ sign preceding a string. The string can then span multiple lines without complaints from the compiler. Hopefully, VB .NET will support this someday. Let's see the remaining method now.

```
Public Overrides Function GetScriptForKeyPress( _
    ByVal validator As ValidatorControl) As String
'---- Expected output ----
'if (!Char.IsDigit(e.KeyChar) && !e.IsControl) e.Handled = true;
'if (e.IsControl) return;
'if (e.Handled) this.IsValid = false;
```

```
        'else this.IsValid = true;
        '-------------------------
        Dim sb As New StringBuilder()
        sb.Append(ControlChars.Tab)
        sb.Append("if (!Char.IsDigit(e.KeyChar) && !e.IsControl) " & _
                            "e.Handled = true;")
        sb.Append(ControlChars.NewLine).Append(ControlChars.Tab)
        'Don't change valid state if it's a control key.
        sb.Append("if (e.IsControl) return;")
        sb.Append(ControlChars.NewLine).Append(ControlChars.Tab)
        'Set the IsValid flag event we are canceling the event.
        'This way the user gets a hint of what's wrong with the key.
        sb.Append("if (e.Handled) this.IsValid = false;")
        sb.Append(ControlChars.NewLine)
        sb.Append(ControlChars.Tab)
        sb.Append("else this.IsValid = true;")
        Return sb.ToString()
    End Function
  End Class
End Namespace
```

Here we take advantage of the Char object we created to ensure the key is a digit, and update the validator state accordingly. That's all that is required to validate for our first validation class.

Let's move on to a validator that only allows letters. The following are the relevant methods of the AlphaValidator:

```
    Public Overrides Function Validate( _
    ByVal validator As ValidatorControl, _
    ByVal value As String) As Boolean
   Return Regex.IsMatch(value, "^[a-zA-Z_,\s]*$")
End Function

Public Overrides Function GetScriptForChange( _
    ByVal validator As ValidatorControl) As String
   '---- Expected output ----
   'if (!/^[a-zA-Z_,\s]*$/.test(sender.Text)) e.Cancel = true;
   'if (e.Cancel) this.IsValid = false;
   'else this.IsValid = true;
   '-------------------------
    Dim sb As New StringBuilder()
    sb.Append(ControlChars.Tab)
```

```vbnet
    sb.Append( _
      "if (!/^[a-zA-Z_,\s]*$/.test(sender.Text)) e.Cancel = true;")
    sb.Append(ControlChars.NewLine).Append(ControlChars.Tab)
    sb.Append("if (e.Cancel) this.IsValid = false;")
    sb.Append(ControlChars.NewLine)
    sb.Append(ControlChars.Tab)
    sb.Append("else this.IsValid = true;")
    Return sb.ToString()
End Function


Public Overrides Function GetScriptForKeyPress( _
    ByVal validator As ValidatorControl) As String
    '---- Expected output ----
    'if (!Char.IsLetter(e.KeyChar) && !e.IsControl) e.Handled = true;
    'if (e.Handled) this.IsValid = false;
    'else this.IsValid = true;
    '------------------------
    Dim sb As New StringBuilder()
    sb.Append(ControlChars.Tab)
    sb.Append( _
      "if (!Char.IsLetter(e.KeyChar) && !e.IsControl) e.Handled = true;")
    'Don't change valid state if it's a control key.
    sb.Append("if (e.IsControl) return;")
    sb.Append(ControlChars.NewLine).Append(ControlChars.Tab)
    'Show the message even if the key isn't output, to provide a hint.
    sb.Append("if (e.Handled) this.IsValid = false;")
    sb.Append(ControlChars.NewLine)
    sb.Append(ControlChars.Tab)
    sb.Append("else this.IsValid = true;")
    Return sb.ToString()
End Function
```

This class takes advantage of regular expressions to ensure certain content in the input string. Note that the expression used for the server-side .NET code is exactly the same as that used for the onchange client-side JavaScript function: ^[a-zA-Z_,\s]*$. Shortly, it means that between the input start (^) and its end ($), any number (*) of lowercase (a-z) or uppercase (A-Z) letters, underscores (_), or whitespaces (\s) are allowed. In JavaScript, the expression is enclosed in forward slashes (/) to represent a literal regular expression.

We have also provided NegativeNumericValidator and PositiveNumericValidator, and a particularly interesting CurrencyValidator, which solves the very common problem of validating localized currency values. This validator uses a separate method to build the regular expression, which reinforces the concept of their language independence; the same regular expression is used in .NET as in the JavaScript environment.

```
Private Function BuildPattern(ByRef val As ValidatorControl) As String
  'Builds the following expression, with culture-aware symbols:
  '"^\$?([0-9]{1,3},([0-9]{3},)*[0-9]{3}|[0-9]+)(\.[0-9][0-9])?$"
  Dim sb As New StringBuilder()
  Dim i As Integer

  With val.Culture.NumberFormat
    sb.Append("^\").Append(.CurrencySymbol)
    sb.Append("?([0-9]{1,3}\").Append(.CurrencyGroupSeparator)
    sb.Append("([0-9]{3}\").Append(.CurrencyGroupSeparator)
    sb.Append(")*[0-9]{3}|[0-9]+)(\")
    If (.CurrencyDecimalDigits > 0) Then _
        sb.Append(.CurrencyDecimalSeparator)
    'Append the number of digits.
    For i = 1 To .CurrencyDecimalDigits
      sb.Append("[0-9]")
    Next
    sb.Append(")?$")
  End With

  Return sb.ToString()
End Function
```

The expression allows an optional currency symbol corresponding to the validator control's culture, a set of numbers optionally separated in groups of three digits by the group separator for the culture, and, finally, a decimal separator follow by the specified number of digits (if it's greater than zero). This method is used both from the server-side and the client-side code.

```
Public Overrides Function Validate( _
    ByVal validator As ValidatorControl, _
    ByVal value As String) As Boolean
  Return Regex.IsMatch(value, BuildPattern(validator))
End Function
Public Overrides Function GetScriptForChange( _
    ByVal validator As ValidatorControl) As String
  '---- Expected output ----
  'if (!/[BuildPattern]/.test(sender.Text)) e.Cancel = true;
  'if (e.Cancel) this.IsValid = false;
  'else this.IsValid = true;
  '------------------------
  Dim sb As New StringBuilder()
  sb.Append(ControlChars.Tab)
```

```
    sb.Append("if (!/").Append(BuildPattern(validator))
    sb.Append("/.test(sender.Text)) e.Cancel = true;")
    sb.Append(ControlChars.NewLine).Append(ControlChars.Tab)
    sb.Append("if (e.Cancel) this.IsValid = false;")
    sb.Append(ControlChars.NewLine)
    sb.Append(ControlChars.Tab)
    sb.Append("else this.IsValid = true;")
    Return sb.ToString()
End Function
```

Again, the client-side code is very similar to what we already saw. The keypress handler is more complicated now, as we have to accept the client culture's group and decimal separator and currency symbol, but only allow the last two to appear once in the control's value.

```
Public Overrides Function GetScriptForKeyPress( _
    ByVal validator As ValidatorControl) As String

    Dim sb As New StringBuilder()
    sb.Append(ControlChars.Tab)
    sb.Append("if (!(Char.IsDigit(e.KeyChar) || ")
    sb.Append( _
 "(e.KeyChar == CultureInfo.NumberFormat.CurrencyGroupSeparator) || ")
    sb.Append("(e.KeyChar == CultureInfo.NumberFormat.CurrencySymbol" _
 & "&& sender.Text.IndexOf(CultureInfo.NumberFormat.CurrencySymbol)" _
 & "== -1) || ")
    sb.Append("(e.KeyChar == CultureInfo.NumberFormat.CurrencyDecimalSeparator" _
 & "&& sender.Text.IndexOf(CultureInfo.NumberFormat" _
 & ".CurrencyDecimalSeparator) == -1)) && ")
    sb.Append("!e.IsControl) e.Handled = true;")
    'Don't change valid state if it's a control key.
    sb.Append("if (e.IsControl) return;")
    sb.Append(ControlChars.NewLine).Append(ControlChars.Tab)
    'Show the message even if the key isn't output, to provide a hint.
    sb.Append("if (e.Handled) this.IsValid = false;")
    sb.Append(ControlChars.NewLine)
    sb.Append(ControlChars.Tab)
    sb.Append("else this.IsValid = true;")
    Return sb.ToString()
End Function
```

Now, the CultureInfo.NumberFormat.* property calls make the code a little difficult to read on paper, but believe me, it looks great in VS .NET or ASP.NET Web Matrix! Note that it invalidates any input that isn't a digit or one of the special symbols defined by the NumberFormat object, and particularly handles the case of the currency and decimal symbols, which are allowed only once by using the IndexOf method on the current control's text: sender.Text.IndexOf([char]).

Building a Test Form

We have built a test form (named Validation\sample.aspx, provided with the download code in the Downloads section of the Apress Web site at http://www.apress.com), which looks like Figure 7-5 in Visual Studio.

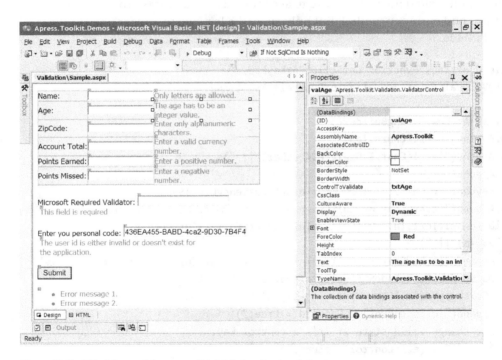

Figure 7-5. *Working with several* ValidatorControl *instances*

We're also making use of an additional custom validation control for the personal ID code. You can examine the code in the download package to see some more client-side validation techniques.

One great feature we offer through the custom ValidatorConverter is showing a dropdown list for the TypeName property in the Properties browser, with all the classes in the selected AssemblyName that are valid classes to use (see Figure 7-6).

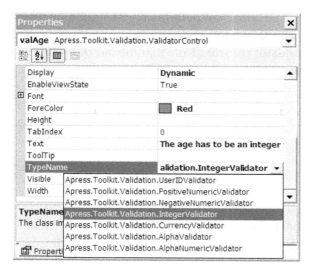

Figure 7-6. *Browsing the* TypeName *property*

At run time, invalid values are intercepted by the keypress handlers, and a message tells the user what's wrong with the key. Figure 7-7 shows that our validation control integrates seamlessly with the built-in ValidationSummary and messages displayed by built-in validation controls, such as the RequiredFieldValidator in this case.

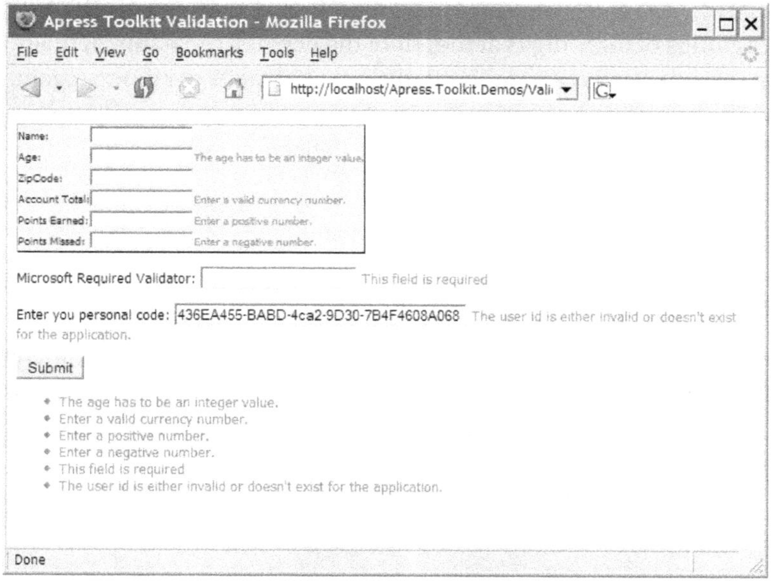

Figure 7-7. *Displaying validation errors*

Here's what happened in Figure 7-7: a postback was performed with invalid values in all fields, except for the Name textbox. The server-side code caught the errors and built the summary, including our custom validator controls. Note that the last one with the personal code wasn't found on the database, thus the message is displayed. Later on, the user tried to enter a number or control code in the Name field, and the label showed up. The Account Total field is validating the currency symbol (only one allowed), the optional group separator (not used in this case), and the decimal separator (only one again). Note that there are only two decimal digits, as defined by the current culture.

Limitations

A limitation of our implementation is that it doesn't actually intercept the submit event, so invalid data may actually be posted to the server. This is not a problem for application logic, as it's always validated on the server side, too. Although invalid values in IE won't allow the user to leave the field, this will be possible in FireFox. As a side effect of this, when built-in validators are used, if the browser is IE, the submit event will be canceled if the validators say so, and the summary will be populated only with the built-in validators messages.

This can be solved by adding the capability of catching the submit event and interacting more closely with ASP.NET built-in validators and the validation summary control. This involves working with the variables declared, building the summary, and appending to the existing one, etc.

Our CurrencyValidator, NegativeNumericValidator, and PositiveNumericValidator classes assume number groups of three digits at the left of the decimal separator. Actually, the CultureInfo.NumberFormat provides an array with the count of digits per group (again, .NET documentation is the best place to start). A way to dump this array as another property of the generated JavaScript object is needed, but .NET Reflection makes it difficult to handle arrays and their enumeration.

Extensions

Besides the natural extensions of new validator classes to handle dates, negative currency values, etc., a great extension would be to implement the String.Format method, receiving the NumberFormatInfo or DateFormatInfo we have already dumped, to display values according to the current locale.

Numbers and currency have additional negative and positive patterns, which may change the value's representation, for example, a negative symbol may have a (n) pattern, meaning that a negative number should be enclosed in parentheses. There's no easy way to apply these patterns, however, because they are not regular expressions, but arbitrary integer values which have to be translated to the corresponding pattern by looking at the pattern format tables provided in .NET documentation.

Finally, a bigger set of .NET objects could be implemented, as they may provide useful features for validation, such as the `DateTime` object, which could work in conjunction with the `DateFormatInfo` object we defined.

CHAPTER 8

Image Magnifier

There are a lot of interactive server controls you can build, and the ImageMagnifier ASP.NET custom control built in this chapter is just one of them. The user is presented with a thumbnail image, perhaps of a map, and then allowed to interactively magnify the section of the image they're most interested in viewing.

Scenario

A typical scenario where you might want to use this control is on any photo-related Web site (those hosting photo albums, photo blogs, etc.). In the case of a photo album, the user might start by browsing an index containing the different categories available for the album, then click on any category and arrive at a page with thumbnails of the available photos. After selecting a particular photo, he could be given the option to zoom in to look at the maximum possible detail.

Another scenario where our ImageMagnifier control could be of use is in a geographic map site. The user might start searching by selecting a country, then drill down into the map looking for cities and streets by simply clicking on the exact point that he wants to examine. Advanced Geographic Information System (GIS) tools, such as Autodesk Map, query a database and retrieve the portion of the selected map stored in it. The ImageMagnifier ASP.NET server control is not that complex at all, but it could serve as a jumpstart to which you could add more GIS-oriented functionality.

Technology

The ImageMagnifier ASP.NET server control uses graphics device interface (GDI+) classes provided in the .NET Framework to dynamically manipulate images. Since we want dynamic interactivity, clips of the original image based on user clicks are generated on the fly. This control really demonstrates how the availability of rich classes from within ASP.NET allows you to perform complex programming without leaving the .NET language of your choice! In addition, you'll learn how inheritance is used to add additional functionality over existing Web controls and to create new controls.

Design

Our design goal is to create a control that shows a zoomed and stretched portion of the image when a user clicks on it. The developer of the page would provide a full-scale image (the maximum zoom possible) and specify a smaller size (thumbnail) in which to display the image to the user (see Figure 8-1).

Figure 8-1. *Thumbnail and zoomed-in views of the same picture*

As you can see from Figure 8-1, a user clicks over a thumbnail image (the image on the left) and the control then displays an image with the same dimensions as the original, but zoomed in to display a more detailed portion of the image (the image on the right). The user is free to keep drilling into the image until the maximum zoom level is reached.

Control Selection

There are a couple of ways you can build ASP.NET custom controls. One way is to use inheritance and extend upon the functionality of the existing controls. The .NET Framework already provides a class that models an image button, the `ImageButton` class (found in the `System.Web.UI.WebControls` namespace). Hence, we will be building our `ImageMagnifier` control by extending the `ImageButton` control. The `ImageButton` control provides the `OnClick()` event handler that can be overridden to customize the control's behavior when the user clicks on it. This event handler provides an `ImageClickEventArgs` parameter containing the exact X and Y pixel coordinates of the user's mouse pointer. Instead of creating a server control from scratch, deriving it from the `WebControl` generic class, we can derive our control from the `ImageButton` class, getting the functionality mentioned earlier, plus other features such as the `ImageUrl` property, which is useful for retrieving either absolute or relative image paths.

Temporary Image Files

One of the design goals of the `ImageMagnifier` control is that it must be able to generate images dynamically. Due to this, the user could click virtually anywhere in the image, so it's not possible to use pre-made images. Hence, for each user session, a new set of images will be created. The approach we will be taking is to store these generated images in a temporary folder on the server. If the site has a large number of visitors, then care should be taken to ensure a scheduled clean up of the files in the temporary folder and also that the server does not run out of disk space. If you can live with the limitation of using only `InProc` session mode, then you may want to try to code the cleanup code in a handler attached to the `Session_End` event. As you may know, this event will only fire when `InProc` session mode is used, so for other session modes you still need to resort to a scheduled cleanup.

Implementation

Let's create an `ImageMagnifier.vb` file and write the following code, starting with all the namespaces needed by the control. Other than standard server control namespaces such as `System.Web.UI`, `System.Web.UI.WebControls`, and `System.ComponentModel`, we have to import the namespaces that contain the GDI+ classes that will be used to manipulate the images.

```
Imports System
Imports System.Web.UI
Imports System.Web.UI.WebControls
Imports System.ComponentModel
Imports System.Drawing
Imports System.Drawing.Imaging
Imports System.Drawing.Drawing2D
```

We modify the ImageMagnifier class definition to make it extend the ImageButton class. Besides a few private member fields, we define a TempPath property. Since the images will be created and saved on the fly, the page developer needs to assign a directory with *write* access where the control will save the temporary image files; the TempPath property contains the relative path to that folder. Another point worth mentioning is the _zoomFactor variable that represents the amount by which magnification is performed. By default, we have set it to 2, so every time the user clicks, the image zooms in by a factor of 2 and the appropriate clip shows.

```
Namespace Apress.Toolkit

    Public Class ImageMagnifier
        Inherits System.Web.UI.WebControls.ImageButton

        Private _tempPath, _thumbPath, _fileName As String
        'Zoom factor
        Private _zoomFactor as integer = 2

        <EditorAttribute(GetType(System.Web.UI.Design.UrlEditor), _
        GetType(System.Drawing.Design.UITypeEditor))> _
        Public Property TempPath() As String
          Get
              Return Me._tempPath
          End Get
          Set
            Me._tempPath = value
          End Set
        End Property
```

The OnLoad() method of the control is called when it's loading; we override this method to perform its initialization. First, the base class's OnLoad() method is called, and then we set up the temporary path and file name that will be used to save the image clips. While setting up the temporary path, we use the MapPath() method of the Page object, which maps a URL into a corresponding file system path. We also use the DirectorySeparatorChar property of the Path class to append the directory separator after the path.

The file name is constructed using the SessionID, which is unique per user, along with the value of the current date and time. This helps us create a unique file name every time a dynamic image is generated.

Next, we check if a value is present for the originalImageURL key in the ViewState's collection. If the value is not present, it indicates that we are loading the control for the first time, so we call the private method ProcessOriginalImage() to perform some initial tasks for loading the ImageMagnifier control for the first time.

```
Protected Overrides Sub OnLoad(e As EventArgs)
'Call the Base classes OnLoad method
        MyBase.OnLoad(e)

        'Set the local path to the temporary directory
        Me._thumbPath = Me.Page.MapPath(Me.TempPath) + _
                System.IO.Path.DirectorySeparatorChar

        'Set a unique file name based on the SessionID
        'and Current time
        Me._fileName = Me.Context.Session.SessionID + _
                DateTime.Now.Ticks.ToString() + ".jpg"

        'If the ViewState value does not exist,
        'we are loading the control for the first time
        If ViewState("originalImageURL") Is Nothing Then
                'Call method to load image for the first time
                Me.ProcessOriginalImage()
        End If
End Sub
```

The `ProcessOriginalImage()` method shown next is called the first time the `ImageMagnifier` control is loaded. First, we save the URL to the image specified by the page developer into `ViewState` so that we can use it later when the control is posted back and the `ImageUrl` property changes. Then, we create a new `Image` object using the `Image` class's shared method, `FromFile()`, passing the path to the file as a parameter.

A new delegate, `myCallback`, to the method `ThumbnailCallback()` (shown at the end of this listing) is created of the type `GetThumbnailImageAbort`. This delegate is passed as a parameter to call the `GetThumbnailImage()` method, along with the page developer-defined `ImageMagnifier` control's width and height and an `IntPtr.Zero` value. The `Image` object's `GetThumbnailImage()` method is used to create a thumbnail image of the specified size. The delegate and `IntPtr.Zero` values have no use as such, but you need to pass them along, since they are required by the .NET Framework while calling the underlying Win32 function.

Once we have the thumbnail for the original image ready, we store its width and height into `ViewState` as well as saving the thumbnail to the temporary folder with a unique file name. As soon as the thumbnail is saved, the `Image` objects are disposed by calling their `Dispose()` method. One important point to remember here is that the .NET Framework provides us with automatic memory management, but as far as resources like `Graphics` objects and file handles are concerned, it's left to the coder's discretion to explicitly release the resources. Hence we use a `Try...Catch...Finally` block to ensure that the `Image` resources are released as soon as they are no longer needed.

Finally, the `ImageUrl` property of the control is updated to point to the newly saved thumbnail image.

Also shown in the next listing is the ThumbnailCallback() function; this is just a dummy function that returns a False value.

```
Protected Overridable Sub ProcessOriginalImage()
        'Save the path to the User specified original image
        ViewState("originalImageURL") = Me.ImageUrl

        Dim orgImage As System.Drawing.Image = Nothing
        Dim thumbImage As System.Drawing.Image = Nothing

        Try
        'Build Image from the user specified path
        orgImage = _
            System.Drawing.Image.FromFile(Me.Page.MapPath(Me.ImageUrl))
        Dim myCallback As New _
        System.Drawing.Image.GetThumbnailImageAbort( _
                AddressOf ThumbnailCallback)
        'Get a Thumbnail of the original image, of the size
        'specified by the user
        thumbImage = _
                orgImage.GetThumbnailImage( _
                Convert.ToInt32(Me.Width.Value), _
                Convert.ToInt32(Me.Height.Value), _
                myCallback, System.IntPtr.Zero)
        'Save the Height and Width of the thumbnail image in
        'ViewState
        ViewState("newWidth") = thumbImage.Width
        ViewState("newHeight") = thumbImage.Height
        'Save the thumbnail to the temporary location
        thumbImage.Save(Me._thumbPath + Me._fileName, _
                ImageFormat.Jpeg)

        Catch e As Exception
                'Rethrow the exception
                Throw New Exception("An exception occurred while " & _
                        "creating the ImageMagnifier Control", e)
        Finally
                'Never forget to release the resources
                orgImage.Dispose()
                thumbImage.Dispose()
        End Try
```

```
                'Set the ImageUrl to the thumbnail image created
                Me.ImageUrl = Me.TempPath + "/" + Me._fileName
    End Sub


    Public Function ThumbnailCallback() As Boolean
                Return False
    End Function
```

Since we have to retrieve mouse pointer coordinates when the user clicks on the control, we have to override the OnClick event handler and use the ImageClickEventArgs parameter. The ShowZoomImage() method helps to zoom and show the correct clip from the original image. We pass the X and Y coordinates found in the ImageClickEventArgs to this method so that it can locate the point where the user clicked.

```
    Protected Overrides Sub OnClick(e As ImageClickEventArgs)
                Me.ShowZoomImage(e.X, e.Y)
    End Sub
```

The ShowZoomImage() method is where the bulk of the processing takes place. The ShowZoomImage() method accepts the X and Y coordinates that will be used to retrieve mouse pointer coordinates. The code starts by defining a few private variables from the GDI+ API; these variables are set to Nothing so that we can use them within our Try...Catch...Finally blocks. We then retrieve the URL of the original image stored in ViewState and load the Image object by calling the shared FromFile() method. The width and height of the previously created thumbnail are also restored back from ViewState and multiplied by the _zoomFactor variable to arrive at the width and height of the new thumbnail to be displayed.

```
    Protected Overridable Sub ShowZoomImage(ByVal coordX_
                        As Integer, ByVal coordY As Integer)
                Dim orgImage As System.Drawing.Image = Nothing
                Dim thumbImage As System.Drawing.Image = Nothing
                Dim clipImage As System.Drawing.Bitmap = Nothing
                Dim clipBrush As System.Drawing.TextureBrush = Nothing
                Dim imgGraphics As System.Drawing.Graphics = Nothing
                Try
                                'Retrieve the Original user specified image
                                'The path of the original Image is stored in ViewState
                                orgImage = _
                                        System.Drawing.Image.FromFile( _
                                        Me.Page.MapPath( _
                                        ViewState("originalImageURL").ToString()))
                                'Create Height and Width for the new thumbnail,
                                'Applying 2x Zoom, based on the current thumbnail image
                                Dim newWidth As Integer = _
```

```
                       Integer.Parse(ViewState("newWidth").ToString())_
                    * Me._zoomFactor
            Dim newHeight As Integer = _
      Integer.Parse(ViewState("newHeight").ToString()) _
                              * Me._zoomFactor
```

Once we have the width and height of the new image, we check whether they exceed the width and height of the original full-size image provided by the page developer. We perform this check since we do not wish to zoom beyond the original image size. If the new image size is less than that of the original image, we, again, call the GetThumbnailImage() method of the Image object holding reference to the original image. The newly calculated width and height, along with the callback delegate and IntPtr.Zero parameters, are passed to the GetThumbnailImage() method. If our new image's size exceeds the original image, we make the thumbImage object reference the original image, so that a clip from the original image will be shown.

```
        If newWidth < orgImage.Width And _
                            newHeight < orgImage.Height Then
            Dim myCallback As New _
System.Drawing.Image.GetThumbnailImageAbort( _
            AddressOf ThumbnailCallback)
            thumbImage = orgImage.GetThumbnailImage( _
            newWidth, _
            newHeight, _
            myCallback, System.IntPtr.Zero)
        Else
            thumbImage = orgImage
        End If
```

The next code listing does the required mathematical calculations for our ImageMagnifier control.

First, we store the width and height set by the page developer into integer variables, since these are stored as Unit types in the Control properties, and converting these variables into integers every time we use them would be a hassle and would incur a performance hit as well because of the repeated castings. The Value property of the Unit type returns a double value; hence, we use the System.Convert class's shared ToInt32() method to convert the double into an integer type.

Revisiting the functional specifications of this control, we had mentioned that when the user clicks on the thumbnail image, a zoomed-in clip of the image, the same size as the thumbnail, is shown. Now, when the user clicks again to further zoom the image clip, we need a way to map the mouse coordinates of the clip shown to the actual size of the thumbnail. Since we are not sure at what location the image was clipped during the previous postback, we store the start coordinates of the previous clip rectangle in ViewState.

The prevX and prevY variables are restored with the starting X and Y coordinates of the previous clip rectangle respectively.

Now, we map the user's mouse click coordinates in the image clip to the respective coordinates in the new thumbnail. You'll notice that the prevX and prevY values have been added to the respective X and Y values (passed as arguments for the method) that contain the coordinates of the user's click. To get the Y coordinate of the click as per the new thumbnail size, we multiply the *height* of the new thumbnail and the Y coordinate of the user's click and then divide it by the *height* of the previously displayed thumbnail. We follow a similar formula to calculate the *X* coordinate as per the new thumbnail, only this time we use the *width*.

```
Dim imgControlWidth As Integer = _
        Convert.ToInt32(Me.Width.Value)
Dim imgControlHeight As Integer =  _
        Convert.ToInt32(Me.Height.Value)


'Retrieve the Previous Clip Rectangle start coordinates
Dim prevX As Integer = 0
Dim prevY As Integer = 0
If Not (ViewState("rectX") Is Nothing) And _
                Not (ViewState("rectY") Is Nothing) Then
        'Parse the values from ViewState
        prevX = Integer.Parse(ViewState("rectX").ToString())
        prevY = Integer.Parse(ViewState("rectY").ToString())
End If


'Get the clipping path
'Map the X & Y coordinates on the newly created thumbnail
'based  on the point where the user clicked
Dim y As Integer = CInt(thumbImage.Height * (coordY + prevY) /_
        Integer.Parse(ViewState("newHeight").ToString()))
Dim x As Integer = CInt(thumbImage.Width * (coordX + prevX) /_
        Integer.Parse(ViewState("newWidth").ToString()))
```

Once we get the exact X and Y coordinates as per the new thumbnail image, we need to find the start coordinates of the clip rectangle that will be used to display the zoomed image. Since the size to show the magnified image will always be smaller than the full thumbnail size, we need to clip an appropriate part from the thumbnail. This clipped image will be of the size of the ImageMagnify control's display area, and it should be centered on the point where the user clicked.

The following code listing calculates the start X and Y coordinates for the new clip rectangle based on the new thumbnail. The rectX and rectY variables will hold reference to the X and Y coordinates of the starting point of the clipping rectangle. Remember our goal is to calculate the appropriate start coordinates of the clipping rectangle so that the user-selected point is centered.

The complex looking If...Else blocks in the following code are the ones that allow us to calculate the exact starting point of the clipping rectangle. There are three possibilities for each coordinate, as follows:

- The user has clicked at the bottom or extreme right (or both) portion of the image. In that case, the clipping rectangle cannot center the click point and, hence, has to stick to the bottom or right (or both) edge of the image.

- The user has clicked at the top or extreme left (or both) portion of the image. In that case, the clipping rectangle cannot center the click point and, hence, has to stick to the top or left (or both) edge of the image.

- Lastly, the user has clicked anywhere other than the two previously described possibilities. In that case, we can easily center the clipping rectangle on the click point.

Once the coordinates of the clipping rectangle are found, they are saved to ViewState so that we can use them upon postback, to recalculate the exact coordinates of the user click.

```
Dim rectX As Integer = 0
Dim rectY As Integer = 0

'Temporary helper variables
Dim halfWidth As Integer = imgControlWidth / 2
Dim halfHeight As Integer = imgControlHeight / 2

'Calculate the Start point of the clipping rectangle
If (thumbImage.Width - x) < halfWidth Then
        rectX = x - (imgControlWidth - (thumbImage.Width - x))
Else
        If x < halfWidth Then
                rectX = 0
        Else
                rectX = x - halfWidth
        End If
End If

If (thumbImage.Height - y) < halfHeight Then
        rectY = y - (imgControlHeight - (thumbImage.Height - y))
```

```
    Else
            If y < halfHeight Then
                    rectY = 0
            Else
                    rectY = y - halfHeight
            End If
    End If


    'Save the Rectangle start coordinates
    ViewState("rectX") = rectX
    ViewState("rectY") = rectY
```

Having calculated the clipping rectangle's start coordinates, now we only need to create and save the clipping image using GDI+ libraries. First, we create a new `Rectangle` object (found in the `System.Drawing` namespace) and pass it the `rectX` and `rectY` values we just calculated, as well as the width and height of the clipping rectangle, which would actually be the width and height defined on the `ImageMagnifier` control. Since there is no direct method to clip a certain section off an existing image, we create a new image of the clip size and fill it with the clipped portion of the thumbnail.

A new blank `Bitmap` object is created with dimensions similar to the clipping rectangle, for the purposes described previously. The `Bitmap` object contains the data for the image as well as other image attributes. Next, we create a new `TextureBrush` object, passing the thumbnail image and the clipping rectangle as parameters. A TextureBrush is a GDI+ brush to paint using an image or clip of an image. Since we have provided the clipping rectangle, the brush will only paint the selected clip from the thumbnail image. The `FromImage()` shared method of the `Graphics` object is used to get a reference to the `Graphics` handle to the blank `Bitmap` image. The `Graphics` object is one of the most important objects in the GDI+ library, and it's used when we want to draw or paint. In our case, since we want to paint the clipped image, we call the `FillRectangle()` method and pass it the `clipBrush` variable so that it uses the `TextureBrush` to fill the new image; the next two parameters instruct the X and Y coordinates to start painting the new rectangle. Since we want to start from the top-left corner, we pass zeros for both; lastly, the width and height to paint are passed. Since the width and height are the same as the clipped image's width and height, we have essentially painted the clipped image onto our new `Bitmap` object. Once the painting is complete, we save the new `Bitmap` in the temporary directory using the JPEG encoder. The width and height values of the thumbnail are saved to `ViewSate` so that they can be used upon postback.

As mentioned earlier, `Graphics` objects are resource intensive and should be released manually. We call the `Dispose()` methods on all the GDI+ objects that consume resources. Finally, the `ImageUrl` property is set to point to the newly created file that contains the clipped image.

```vb
                    'Create a new Rectangle object
                    Dim clipRect As New Rectangle(rectX, rectY, _
                            imgControlWidth, imgControlHeight)
                    'Create a blank Bitmap of the size specified by the user
                    clipImage = New System.Drawing.Bitmap( _
                            imgControlWidth, imgControlHeight)
                    'Create a new TextureBrush and select the clip part from
                    'the thumbnail
                    clipBrush = New TextureBrush(thumbImage, clipRect)
                    'Create a Graphics object for the blank bitmap
                    imgGraphics = Graphics.FromImage(clipImage)
                    'Paint the selected clip on the Graphics of the
                    'blank bitmap
                    imgGraphics.FillRectangle(clipBrush, 0, 0, _
                            imgControlWidth, imgControlHeight)
                    'Save the bitmap at the specified temporary path
                    clipImage.Save(Me._thumbPath + Me._fileName, _
                            ImageFormat.Jpeg)
                    'Save the thumbnail images values
                    ViewState("newWidth") = thumbImage.Width
                    ViewState("newHeight") = thumbImage.Height

            Catch exc As Exception
                    'Rethrow the exception
                    Throw New Exception("An exception occurred while " + _
                            "creating the ImageMagnifer Control", exc)
            Finally
                    'Never forget to release the resources
                    clipBrush.Dispose()
                    imgGraphics.Dispose()
                    clipImage.Dispose()
                    orgImage.Dispose()
                    thumbImage.Dispose()
            End Try
            'Set the ImageUrl to the thumbnail image created
            Me.ImageUrl = Me.TempPath + "/" + Me._fileName
    End Sub
```

This completes the implementation of our ImageMagnifier control. Now let's see how to build and use this control on our Web applications.

Demonstration

Add the `ImageMagnify` control to the toolbox of your favorite IDE. Then drag the control to an ASP.NET page and view the generated HTML. It should look like the following:

```
<%@ Page Language="VB" %>
<%@ Register TagPrefix="cc" Namespace="Apress.Toolkit" Assembly="Apress.Toolkit" %>
<html>
        <body>
                <form runat="server" ID="Form1">
                        <h1>Image Magnifier Test Page</h1>
                        <h1>
                                <cc:ImageMagnifier id="ImageMagnifier1"
 runat="server" Height="252px" Width="240px"
TempPath="images" ImageUrl="photo.jpg"/>
                        </h1>
                </form>
        </body>
</html>
```

As you can see from the previous HTML, the `@Register` directive specifies the assembly name containing the control and its namespace. Now set the `ImageUrl` and `TempPath` properties to the URL of the image to display and the path to the temporary directory, respectively. Also, remember to set the `Height` and `Width` of the control so that it can display a thumbnail image of the original image. This can be easily accomplished using the Properties browser after having selected the control from within the Web form. Now you can try the ASP.NET page by browsing to the page. Remember that the directory specified in the temporary path should exist and the account under which ASP.NET is running should have *write* permissions to it.

Limitations

The `ImageMagnifier` server control doesn't allow users to zoom out. The only way to return to the original image is by using the Back button of the browser. To add support for this, the control could offer a small UI (showing zoom-in and zoom-out radio buttons) that the user could use to specify the type of zoom before clicking the desired portion of the image. When the page posts back, our code should check which radio button was selected and then perform the appropriate zoom-in or zoom-out operation.

Under some scenarios, giving ASP.NET proper permission to write files to a temporary folder—as required by our control—may be not possible due to actual security policies. In this case, we can move the image generation code contained in our control to an HTTP handler (an IHttpHandler-derived class) and modify it to just write the generated image to the response stream instead of writing it to a file. Then our control will use the src attribute of the img element to point to the new handler (using the query string to pass any additional parameters that the handler may need) instead of including a path to the temporary image file as it is doing now.

Extensions

You could extend the ImageMagnifier server control by adding a property that indicated the zoom factor. So you could create not only 2x zoomed images, but also 4x, 6x, 8x, etc. Already, we are using a private variable to store the zoom factor; all you need to do is expose this as a public property. Moreover, a DropDownList control could be added to the UI to allow for the zoom factor to be selected in a graphic way.

CHAPTER 9

■ ■ ■

Chart

The Chart base class allows developers to easily add histogram and pie charts to Web pages. The class analyzes data from a DataSet containing a Table filled with records through a SQL statement or a stored procedure. It then outputs the chart data as a GIF image allowing the chart to be included in any Web page. To do this, we'll need to use a slightly different technique from the server controls you'll find throughout most of this book; instead of creating a new control, we'll be using page inheritance to provide our core functionality.

Scenario

Analyzing data and then presenting it in a graphic way is often more useful than presenting a raw list of numbers and labels, because data trends are easier to spot and comparisons are easier to make. For example, we can identify the winner of an election result much more quickly by glancing at a histogram or pie chart than by reading the poll statistics from a table. Many companies invest a lot of time and money developing applications that provide user-friendly data analysis and presentation tools.

Technology

Using .NET to generate images isn't that hard, as we've seen in Chapter 8. However, when we want the generated image to depend on a lot of parameters, as our charts will, we're going to find it hard to pass all the relevant data from a server control to the image-generating page using the query string.

An alternative solution, which we're going to use here, is to use page inheritance. We will be creating a Page-derived class, named Chart, including the code to generate a chart on the fly based on user-specified values by setting properties on it. Note that the content served by our custom Chart page will not be HTML; it will be of image/gif type and will consist of a GIF image containing the on-the-fly generated chart.

The page developer then needs to create one page for each different chart he wants to offer. These pages should derive from our base Chart class (instead of deriving directly from System.Web.UI.Page) and their properties should be set accordingly (e.g., type of chart to generate, source data to be used, etc.).

After this, all that remains is to include the chart in any page we may want and for this we use an img element whose src attribute points to the page representing the chart.

Design

The output produced by the Chart class consists of a bitmap image that is divided into two parts: On the left, the chart itself (a pie or histogram) is rendered. The right-hand side of the image contains the legend for the chart, consisting of the title of the plot, labels for each slice or bar, and a "total" value corresponding to the number of items included in the analysis. The charts are color coded: in other words, each label is associated with a color, which is the color used to fill the bar or pie slice in the chart.

The Chart class contains fields that hold the following values:

- Type of chart (pie or histogram)

- Background color of chart

- Height of chart

- The title string

- Font size for labels and title

- The database connection string

- The dataset containing the values to analyze and chart

Each of these values can be set via Properties.

The Chart class also contains several methods. These can be divided into two types: drawing methods and data-loading methods.

We override the Render() method, which is called to render the image. This method, in turn, calls the DrawChart() method, which draws the chart. The DrawChart() method calls the DrawLegend() method, which renders the legend. These use Graphics methods, such as FillRectangle() and FillPie(), that make graphic operations really easy and straightforward.

The DrawChart() method uses the Bitmap.Save() method, which allows developers to save a bitmap image either to disk or to a stream. So, in theory, we could implement two possible approaches for our charting class.

- *Drawing the chart and saving it to disk*: For each user requiring a chart, a file with a unique name is created on the server and, later on, that file is referenced by the src attribute of an img element in any HTML page. After a timeout, or when the user session ends, the created image files should be removed from disk. This is the approach we took in Chapter 8 when creating the zoomed images.

- *Drawing the chart and saving it to the output stream of the ASP.NET page*: For each user that requires a chart, the ASP.NET output stream (accessed by the Response.OutputStream property of Page) is used to output the image.

As we have already demonstrated the first approach when we coded the Image Magnifier control, we are now going to follow the second approach for our Chart class.

The DrawChart() method also makes use of the return value of the CalculateTotal() method, which calculates the number of items included in the analysis. The CalculateTotal() method uses the DataColumn class to append a new column to the DataTable; this column will contain the "total" value.

There are two data loading methods; these can be called by pages inheriting from Chart, in order to pull data from a database and place it into a DataSet. One of them accepts a SQL statement as input and uses it to connect to a database and then fill a DataSet. The other also creates a DataSet, but accepts the name of a stored procedure to invoke as input, as well as an array containing the parameters that need to be passed to the stored procedure.

ADO.NET provides all the necessary classes to connect and query data from a database. More precisely, ADO.NET provides OLE DB classes to manage all databases that offer OLE DB providers (Oracle, Microsoft Access, and so on), SQL Server classes that implement direct database API calls, and ODBC classes, that support some ODBC drivers. Our Chart base class will make use of OLE DB classes to execute both stored procedures and SQL statements. The OLE DB data provider supports almost all popular databases. Naturally, when the target database is SQL Server, the performance will be lower than using the custom ADO.NET provider for SQL Server.

Implementation

We start by creating a class file in the IDE of your choice. This will be the file containing our Chart base class so we will name it Chart.

The Chart Class

The first thing we need to do is import all the necessary namespaces in order to use bitmap and database classes.

```
Imports System.Drawing
Imports System.Drawing.Imaging
Imports System.Data
Imports System.Data.OleDb
```

Now we can start to add some code to implement the ChartType property, which defines whether the chart to be created should be a pie chart or a histogram. Using an Enum, we can define some constants representing the chart type that the control will have to draw.

```
Namespace Apress.Toolkit

Public Class Chart
    Inherits System.Web.UI.Page

  Public Enum ChartTypeValue
    Pie
    Histogram
  End Enum

  Private _type As ChartTypeValue

  Public Property ChartType As ChartTypeValue
    Get
      Return _type
    End Get
    Set
      _type = Value
    End Set
  End Property
```

We also need to define some other properties. ConnectionString is used to both get and set the connection string to the database. Background gets and sets the background color used by the chart. Height and Width are used to control the dimensions of the bitmap, while the FontSize property controls the size of the text used in the chart legend. Finally, the DataSource property is used to get and set a DataSet.

```
  Private _connString As String
  Private _background As Color = Color.White
  Private _height As Integer
  Private _width As Integer
  Private _fontSize As Integer
  Private _title As String
  Private _ds As DataSet
```

```vb
    Public Property Height As Integer
      Get
        Return _height
      End Get
      Set
        _height = Value
      End Set
    End Property

    Public Property Width As Integer
      Get
        Return _width
      End Get
      Set
        _width = Value
      End Set
    End Property

    Public Property FontSize As Integer
      Get
        Return _fontSize
      End Get
      Set
        _fontSize = Value
      End Set

    Public Property Title As String
      Get
        Return _title
      End Get
      Set
        _title = Value
      End Set
    End Property

    End Property

    Public Property ConnectionString As String
      Get
        Return _connString
      End Get
      Set
        _connString = Value
```

```
    End Set
  End Property
  Public Property Background As Color
    Get
      Return _background
    End Get
    Set
      _background = Value
    End Set
  End Property

  Public Property DataSource() As DataSet
    Get
      Return _ds
    End Get
    Set(ByVal Value As DataSet)
      _ds = Value
    End Set
  End Property
```

Drawing the Chart

The main method at the core of our Chart class is DrawChart(). This method accepts three
parameters: a chart title, the index of the column containing the data to display, and the index
of the column containing labels for the chart. It uses these to actually create the bitmap with
the chart on it.

```
Private Sub DrawChart(ByRef ds As DataSet, ByVal title As String, _
                      ByVal iColumn As Integer, ByVal iLabel As Integer)
```

Inside the method, we first have to inform the ASP.NET page that the content will be
a GIF image, as follows:

```
Response.ContentType = "image/gif"
```

The code then creates a new bitmap image with the dimensions specified by the Width
and Height properties, as well as a new Graphics object that will enable us to manipulate
it. After that, it fills this new image with the background color.

```
'Create BMP canvas
Dim bmp As New Bitmap(Width, Height)
Dim objGraphic As Graphics = Graphics.FromImage(bmp)
objGraphic.FillRectangle(New SolidBrush(Background), 0, 0,_
                                            Width, Height)
```

Before we go on, we also want to check that there is some data for us to analyze. If there is, then we find out how many items are included in the analysis by adding together the contents of all of the columns in the DataTable. This is done by calling the CalculateTotal() method (which we will implement in a moment). This method adds another column to the DataTable containing the total value.

```
If Not _ds Is Nothing Then
  'Calculate the total
  CalculateTotal(1)
```

Next we create an array of random colors that will be used to fill either histogram bars or pie slices.

```
'Generate random colors
Dim I As Integer
Dim colors As New ArrayList()
Dim rnd As New Random()
For I = 0 To _ds.Tables(0).Rows.Count - 1
  colors.Add(New SolidBrush(Color.FromArgb(rnd.Next(255), _
                                           rnd.Next(255), _
                                           rnd.Next(255))))
Next
```

We will divide the bitmap image in half, one half containing the chart itself, the other the legend.

```
Dim iChartWidth As Integer = (Width / 2)
Dim iChartHeight As Integer = Height
```

We also find the number of columns contained in the Table.

```
Dim iTotalColumnPos As Integer = ds.Tables(0).Columns.Count - 1
```

The ChartType property value is used to decide whether to draw a pie chart or histogram.

```
Select Case ChartType
```

In the case of the pie chart, we start by finding out how much space we have to draw the pie in.

```
case ChartTypeValue.Pie

  'Check maximum pie width available
  Dim iPieWidth As Integer = iChartWidth
```

```
        If iChartWidth > iChartHeight Then
          iPieWidth = iChartHeight
        End If
```

Then a For...Next loop is used to read through the DataTable records, pulling out the data for each row, and calculating the size of the pie slice using this value. The FillPie() method provided by the Graphics class allows developers to draw and fill a slice of the pie with the specified color.

```
        'Draw pie
        Dim degree As Single
        Dim pieRect As New Rectangle(0, 0, (iPieWidth-10), _
                                           (iPieWidth-10))

        For I=0 To ds.Tables(0).Rows.Count - 1
          objGraphic.FillPie(colors(I),pieRect, _
              degree, ds.Tables(0).Rows(I)(iColumn) / _
              ds.Tables(0).Rows(I)(iTotalColumnPos) * 360)
          degree = degree + _
              ((ds.Tables(0).Rows(I)(iColumn) / _
              ds.Tables(0).Rows(I)(iTotalColumnPos)) * 360)
        Next
```

If a histogram chart has been selected, the Chart class calculates the coordinates (X,Y) of the top of each histogram bar, as well as its height and width. Finally, the FillRectangle() method of the Graphics class is used to draw the histogram. This method accepts a Brush object set with the fill color for the rectangle, and a Rect structure with the histogram bar dimensions.

```
        case ChartTypeValue.Histogram

          'Find number of columns in chart
          Dim noColumns As New Integer()
          noColumns = _ds.Tables(0).Rows.Count

          'Find max column height
          Dim maxHeight As Integer = 0
          For I = 0 To _ds.Tables(0).Rows.Count - 1
              If (_ds.Tables(0).Rows(I)(iColumn) > maxHeight) Then
                  maxHeight = _ds.Tables(0).Rows(I)(iColumn)
              End If
          Next
          Dim histogramRect As New Rectangle
          histogramRect.Width = CInt((iChartWidth / noColumns)) - 1
```

```
        For I = 0 To _ds.Tables(0).Rows.Count - 1
            Dim dbl As Double
            histogramRect.X = CInt(I *(iChartWidth /
_ds.Tables(0).Rows.Count))
            dbl = 1 - CInt(_ds.Tables(0).Rows(I)(iColumn)) / maxHeight
            histogramRect.Y = CInt(iChartHeight * dbl)
            dbl = CInt(_ds.Tables(0).Rows(I)(iColumn)) / maxHeight
            histogramRect.Height = CInt(iChartHeight * dbl)
            objGraphic.FillRectangle(CType(colors(I), Brush), histogramRect)
        Next
End Select
```

The code then draws the chart legend. We pass the DataSet, the Graphics object, the colors used in the chart, the title, and the index of the labels column to the DrawLegend() private method.

```
    DrawLegend(ds, objGraphic, colors, title, iLabel)
```

The Save() method provided by the Bitmap class is used to copy the stream containing the bitmap image to the ASP.NET page. Using the Page.Response.OutputStream as the destination stream, we can save the bitmap image directly onto the HTTP response without needing to save it onto the disk first.

```
    bmp.Save(Page.Response.OutputStream, ImageFormat.Gif)
    End If
```

Finally, we need to remove the bitmap object from memory so that we conserve server resources. Therefore we call the Dispose() method provided by both the Bitmap and Graphics objects.

```
    bmp.Dispose()
    objGraphic.Dispose()
  End Sub
```

Calculating the Total

The CalculateTotal() method is used to add a new column to the specified DataSet (specified as the first parameter passed to the method). This new column will contain the sum of all of the values contained in another column (specified as the second parameter passed to the method).

```
Private Sub CalculateTotal(ByRef ds As DataSet, _
                                    ByVal iColumn As Integer)
```

The Expression property provided by the DataColumn class allows developers to specify a SQL aggregate expression. The code uses this property to calculate the sum of the specified column.

```
'Add a column that will contain the total
Dim cTotal As New DataColumn("Total")
cTotal.Expression = "Sum("& _
                    ds.Tables(0).Columns(iColumn).ColumnName & ")"
cTotal.DataType = Type.GetType("System.Single")
ds.Tables(0).Columns.Add(cTotal)
End Sub
```

Drawing the Legends

The DrawLegend() method is called to draw the chart legend. The method accepts the following five parameters:

- a DataSet containing a DataTable filled with records

- a reference to the Graphics object that will be used to draw rectangles and labels

- an ArrayList object containing the colors used to paint the chart

- the title of the chart

- the index of the column containing the labels to display

Let's take a look at the code now, starting by the method signature.

```
Private Sub DrawLegend(ByRef ds As DataSet, ByRef objGraphics As _
                Graphics, ByRef colors As ArrayList, _
                ByVal title As String, _
                ByVal iColumn As Integer)
```

Two Font objects are declared, which will be used to write the labels and title.

```
Dim I As Integer
Dim f As New Font("Tahoma", FontSize)
Dim fTitle As New Font("Arial", FontSize, FontStyle.Bold)
```

A new rectangle, with a width half that of the bitmap image, is created to contain the legend. The DrawRectangle() and DrawString() methods are used to draw a frame around the legend and the title, respectively.

```
Dim solidBlack As New SolidBrush(Color.Black)
Dim iLegendWidth As Integer = (Width / 2)
Dim iLegendHeight As Integer = Height
Dim rect As New Rectangle()
rect.X = iLegendWidth
rect.Y = 0
rect.Height = iLegendWidth - 1
rect.Width = iLegendWidth - 1

objGraphics.DrawRectangle(new Pen(Color.Black, 1), rect)
objGraphics.DrawString(title, fTitle, solidBlack, _
                                        (iLegendWidth + 1), 0)
```

Next, we create a little colored square for each color used in the chart, and we write the label for each bar in the histogram or each slice in the pie chart. We use a For...Next loop to cycle through all of the bars or slices.

```
For I = 0 To ds.Tables(0).Rows.Count - 1
  rect.X = iLegendWidth + 5
  rect.Y = 30 + f.Height * I
  rect.Height = 10
  rect.Width = 10
  objGraphics.FillRectangle(colors(I), rect)

  objGraphics.DrawString(ds.Tables(0).Rows(I)(iColumn).ToString(), _
                                    f, solidBlack, iLegendWidth+20 , _
                                    30 + f.Height * I - 3)
Next
```

Finally, the control prints the total number of items used in the analysis at the bottom of the legend rectangle.

```
Dim iTotalColumnPos As Integer = ds.Tables(0).Columns.Count - 1
objGraphics.DrawString("Total: " & _
                ds.Tables(0).Rows(0)(iTotalColumnPos).ToString(), _
                f, solidBlack, iLegendWidth, _
                (iLegendWidth + 1) - f.Height - 5)

End Sub
```

Rendering the Chart

After having drawn the chart, all we have to do is render it. For that we need to hook into the rendering stage and override the Render() method. There we will be adding a call to the DrawChart() method, which is, in turn, the one in charge of outputting the chart image to ASP.NET's response stream.

```
Protected Overrides Sub Render(_
                    ByVal writer As System.Web.UI.HtmlTextWriter)
  DrawChart(Title, 1, 0)
End Sub
```

Demonstration

Having created the Chart class, we now need to create a page that derives from it so that we can see it in action.

Create a new Web form named TestChart.aspx, and edit its code-behind file to make sure the class inherits from our Chart class.

```
Public Class TestChart
    Inherits Apress.Toolkit.Chart
```

We can then use the Page_Load event handler to set properties and call the control's methods. First of all, we set the ConnectionString property to connect to the Northwind Microsoft SQL Server database.

```
Private Sub Page_Load(ByVal sender As System.Object, _
                                        ByVal e As System.EventArgs)
  ConnectionString = "Provider=SQLOLEDB.1;" & _
                    "Persist Security Info=False;User ID=sa;" & _
                    "Initial Catalog=Northwind;Data Source=."
```

The Northwind database contains the SalesByCategory stored procedure that queries for products belonging to a category and their related sales. This stored procedure accepts two parameters: the category name and the sale year. We can specify the parameters' names and values using OleDbParameter() constructors. In the following snippet of code, the @OrdYear parameter value is omitted because the stored procedure declares a default value (1998) for it:

```
'Load data source
Dim p1 As New OleDbParameter("@CategoryName", _
                                OleDbType.VarChar, 15)
```

```
Dim p2 As New OleDbParameter("@OrdYear", OleDbType.VarChar, 4)
p1.Value = "Beverages"
```

The LoadDataSourceBySP() method accepts an ArrayList object filled with stored procedure parameters. We can use the Add() method of the ArrayList class to prepare this array by adding the OleDbParameter objects to it.

```
Dim arParams As New ArrayList()
arParams.Add(p1)
arParams.Add(p2)
```

Then we set the Chart's DataSource property to the DataSet returned by a call to the LoadDataSourceBySP() method.

```
Me.DataSource = LoadDataSourceBySP("SalesByCategory", arParams)
```

Finally, the code sets the control's properties to draw a 550 × 320 pie chart with a white background, and a font size of 10. When the page reaches its rendering phase, the DrawChart() method draws the chart using these values.

```
Background = Color.White
ChartType = ChartTypeValue.Histogram
Title = "Sales By Category - Beverages"
Height = 400
Width = 650
FontSize = 10


  End Sub
End Class
```

There is one more thing you should do if you are using code behind. Edit the TestChart.aspx file, and modify its Page directive with the following:

```
<%@ Page Language="vb" AutoEventWireup="false" Codebehind="TestChart.aspx.vb"
Inherits="TestChart"%>
```

The Codebehind attribute has to point to the file containing the class derived by the Chart base class. The Inherits attribute has to contain the full type name of the child class specified in the code file.

If you now run TestChart.aspx, you should see the histogram chart in Figure 9-1 appear in a browser.

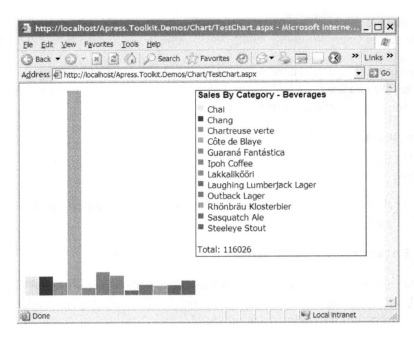

Figure 9-1. *Chart output using the* Histogram *type*

As you can see, the chart is normalized so that the tallest bar is the same height as the chart itself. Now try using the pie chart to display the data by modifying the following line of code in TestChart.aspx.vb:

```
...
Background = Color.White
ChartType = ChartType.Pie
Height = 320
...
```

This time you should see Figure 9-2 appear in a browser.

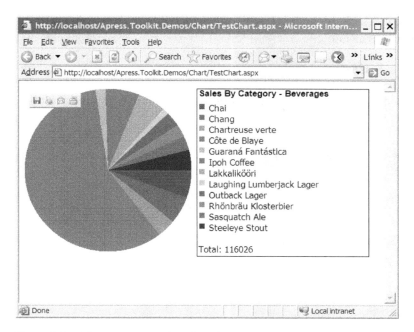

Figure 9-2. *Chart output using the* Pie *type*

Try changing the width and height of the chart. You'll see that the pie chart resizes itself according to the space available to it. Also, try increasing the size of the font. Eventually, some of the text will become too large to fit inside the legend, and this text will be cut off.

We can, of course, simply include the chart in any HTML page pointing the src attribute of an <img> tag to the chart page. For example, create the following HTML page named TestChart2.htm:

```
<!DOCTYPE HTML PUBLIC "-//W3C//DTD HTML 4.0 Transitional//EN">
<html>
  <head>
    <title>TestChart2</title>
  </head>
  <body MS_POSITIONING="GridLayout">
    <h1>Here's a dynamically generated chart:</h1>
    <img src="TestChart.aspx">
  </body>
</html>
```

As you can see, we can include the TestChart page (which inherits from our Chart base class) in a page using the line

```
<img src="TestChart.aspx">
```

When browsing TestChart2.htm, the chart will appear (see Figure 9-3) thanks to the use of the img element.

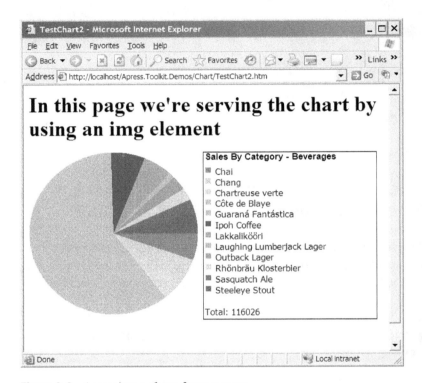

Figure 9-3. *Accessing a chart from a page*

Limitations

Our Chart base class has a few limitations.

- It only natively supports the OleDb-managed data provider.

- It doesn't currently take advantage of caching the chart image. Using the current design, it must access the database each time it wants to generate the same image.

- It is difficult to extend to include other types of charts without having to significantly modify Chart's source code. A more extensible approach would be to define an IChart interface that contains the declaration of the DrawChart() method. Then you could create classes such as HistogramChart, PieChart, and so on, each one providing its own implementation of the DrawChart() method. Then we don't need to modify Chart if we want to add functionality to create new types of charts: we simply create a new chart that implements the IChart interface.

- Finally, as we noted before, it is up to us to choose the correct font size so that all of the legend text fits nicely inside the legend without being cut off.

Extensions

The following are some ideas for extending our Chart class:

- Adding more properties to customize colors and fonts used to draw the chart and the legend. Perhaps you could modify the Chart class to automatically select the correct font size to use so that the legend text fits neatly inside the legend box, or to select colors from predesigned palettes, rather than at random.

- Adding support for more chart types (such as 3D charts). This would involve adding more enumeration values to the ChartType enum, and adding extra Case clauses to the Select statement in DrawChart() to draw these extra chart types (or better yet, follow the interface-based approach just described in the previous section).

- Adding properties to the Chart base class that get and set the database access parameters. Then classes that use the Chart class won't need to call its LoadDataSourceXXX() methods directly.

- Adding support for data sources different than a database could be a useful extension in case you need, for example, to bind to an array of values. For this you should follow the approach we used for implementing the DataSource property for the Bindable Bullet List control in Chapter 3.

CHAPTER 10

Image Map Generator

One very interesting feature of HTML is its support for client-side image maps. In this chapter, we'll develop an ASP.NET custom control that simplifies the process of creating such image maps.

We're all familiar with HTML hyperlinks, and how it's possible to replace the text of a hyperlink with an image, making the image act like a button. But HTML also supports the more complex scenario of making parts of an image respond to clicks, allowing us to specify "hot" regions on the image, and associate them with hyperlink references.

In this chapter we'll examine how the HTML map element works, and then create a control that will generate the required HTML while allowing us to define graphically the "hot" regions of our image, rather than having to use a process of trial and error, or laboriously work with a paint package and a calculator, to obtain correct coordinates.

Scenario

One very common need for Web sites is to display a mapped image. Clicking in different regions of an image takes the user to different areas of the site. A perfect example of this is a virtual tour of a university campus. You might want to provide an overhead photo of the campus and make each building in the image a hyperlink to its own specific Web page that would provide all the information about that building. Using standard HTML this task is not too difficult, but it can be time consuming to do by hand. A sample of such HTML is as follows:

```
<img src="myimage.jpg" usemap="#Map1">
<map id="Map1">
  <area shape="rect" coords="3,25,56,76" href="http://www.Apress.com">
</map>
```

Here an image tag has been defined to show myimage.jpg. In addition, we have indicated that the image is to use a map. The map allows you to define "hot" regions on the image with an associated URL that is navigated once clicked.

A region of this image has been defined that will navigate to the homepage of the Apress Web site when clicked; this region is defined by the coords attribute. The first two integers define the x and y position of the top-left corner of the rectangle. The last two define the x and y position of the bottom right-hand corner of the rectangle. In the shape property, we have specified the region to be a rectangle (we could have also specified an ellipse or a polygon). These other shapes expect different parameters for the coords.

While it does not seem overly difficult to set up an image tag with a map of coordinates, finding the coordinates for each region of the image that you want to make clickable can be a time-consuming process. What would be useful is to be able to simply outline the regions graphically on the image itself at design time in order to define the regions. The image map would be done in a fraction of the time, and you would be able to move on to more interesting aspects of Web site development. This is the scenario we are in, and in this chapter we will build a custom control including its own design-time support to easily handle definitions of image maps.

Technology

Our control will provide the ability to define areas of an image to be clickable. Therefore, we need to be able to define these areas at design time in a simple way.

> **Tip** It is required that you have an IDE with design-time support services compatible with Visual Studio .NET to fully experience the design-time support offered by this control.

The .NET Framework already comes with lots of classes that can be used by any control for enhancing the design-time experience. For example, for every property that provides an ellipsis button when you select it in the property browser, you get a graphic interface that lets you edit the property. This is called a *UI editor*. Examples of these editors are the color palettes for font colors, background colors, and so on. The URL editor is another editor that provides a file system browser to navigate to a file and get the URL to the file. All of these editors derive from the base class UITypeEditor, found in the System.Drawing.Design namespace. By inheriting from this class, we can provide a custom UI to edit any of our control properties. We will leverage this in order to provide a custom UI editor that will be used to define the "hot" regions on the image. The following UITypeEditor methods will be overridden in order to provide part of our custom editor functionality:

- GetEditStyle(): This method is called automatically by the IDE to determine what type of editor it should provide. Available options are the following members of the UITypeEditorEditStyle enumeration: Modal (a modal dialog), DropDown (a drop-down list for properties that expose an enumeration, for example), and the default, which is None.

- EditValue(): This is the method that is supposed to do the actual editing of the value. It will be called automatically by the IDE when the ellipsis button is clicked.

The ellipsis button will be drawn automatically by the IDE when a specific attribute is applied to the property telling it a custom editor is provided. This attribute is System.ComponentModel.EditorAttribute; it's very simple to use and you can find more information about it in the .NET Framework documentation.

At run time, our control will use the postback mechanism provided by ASP.NET to receive a notification when a region of the image is clicked. This can be achieved by making our control implement the IPostBackEventHandler interface. This interface contains only one method, RaisePostBackEvent, that will be called automatically by ASP.NET if the postback was initiated by our control. We will be discussing this method in more detail later during our control implementation.

Design

The most important feature of this control is the enhanced design-time support that it will offer to developers. As we have already noted, it will provide a user interface that will allow the developer to easily draw the areas of the image that will be clickable using the mouse. With the information we gather from the mouse, we will translate the selected areas of the image into the standard HTML <area> element. Of course, since our control is relying on coordinates within the image, it is also very important that it is rendered correctly, so let's examine how we can achieve that.

Our control class will derive from the System.Web.UI.Control base class, as it is going to render only very simple HTML without needing any of the fancy stuff offered by more powerful base classes like System.Web.UI.WebControls.WebControl.

We will expose a string property to provide our control with the location of our image file (a design-time absolute path) and a property to provide the URLs for the image used (any standard URL that maps to the file for the Web application). To make this latter property easier to work with, we will use the built-in Image URL editor.

We also need to expose another string property that will provide the coordinates of the selected regions. This string will be semicolon-delimited and contain comma-delimited lists of rectangle coordinates. The property will use a helper class to parse the different string portions representing the rectangle regions.

To obtain the mentioned rectangle regions, we will provide a graphic interface so the developer can define them on the image by simply using the mouse. For this, we will code a custom UI editor for the property.

Finally, we need to provide some mechanism for the developer to take the appropriate actions when a region is clicked on in the image. We will provide them with a `RegionClicked` event that they can subscribe to and will be raised every time an image region is clicked. As part of the information provided with this event, we will be sending a `RegionID` to let the page developer easily identify which, of all regions, was the one clicked by the user.

The design and technology have now been defined. Let's roll up our sleeves and get into the code.

Implementation

Let's start by creating a new class file named `ImageMap.vb`. Our main class will be named `ImageMap` and there will be other supporting classes defined in this file. The required namespaces are imported.

```
Imports System
Imports System.ComponentModel
Imports System.Web.UI
Imports System.Web.UI.HtmlControls
Imports System.Web.UI.Design
Imports System.Drawing.Design
Imports System.Drawing
Imports System.Windows.Forms.Design
Imports System.Windows.Forms
Imports System.Collections
Imports Microsoft.VisualBasic

Namespace Apress.Toolkit
```

We will also need to add additional references for the following three assemblies to our project: `System.Web.dll`, `System.Windows.Forms.dll` and `System.Design.dll`.

As we mentioned in our design, a supporting class is needed to provide custom event arguments. Let's add the code necessary for this class now.

```
Public Class ImageMapEventArgs
    Inherits EventArgs

    Private _RegionID As String
    Public ReadOnly Property RegionID() As String
        Get
```

```
            Return _RegionID
        End Get
    End Property

    Public Sub New(ByVal RegionID As String)
        MyBase.New()
        _RegionID = RegionID
    End Sub
End Class
```

This is a very simple class. We inherit from `EventArgs` as convention dictates, and we just add a single property named `RegionID` of type `String` that will contain the—guess what—ID of the clicked region.

The ImageMap Control

This is the class defining our control.

```
<ToolboxData("<{0}:ImageMap runat=server />"), _
    DefaultEvent("RegionClicked")> _
Public Class ImageMap
    Inherits Web.UI.Control
    Implements IPostBackEventHandler, INamingContainer

    Public Event RegionClicked(ByVal sender As Object, _
                               ByVal e As ImageMapEventArgs)

    Private _imagePath As String = ""
    Private _imgTag As New HtmlImage()
    Private _fullPathToImage As String = ""
    Private _imageMapProperties As New ImageMapProperties("")
```

Note how in this code we have marked the class with the `ToolboxData` attribute to inform the IDE that we want this control to show up in the toolbox.

We also defined a few private member variables. We have a string to hold the URL to the image for the HTML `<img>` tag. We define a reference to an `HtmlImage` tag that we will ultimately be rendering. We have another string property that will hold the fully qualified path and name of the image. The last member variable is of type `ImageMapProperties`, which carries information to and from our custom editor. We will define it in just a moment.

Next, we will expose the following properties. Add the following lines of code after the member declaration:

```
<Editor(GetType(ImageUrlEditor), GetType(UITypeEditor)), _
Description("Relative path to Image file.")> _
Public Property ImageSrc() As String
    Get
        Return _imagePath
    End Get

    Set(ByVal value As String)
        _imagePath = value
        ChildControlsCreated = False
    End Set
End Property
```

We have used the Editor attribute to specify that we want the IDE to use the
ImageUrlEditor to edit this property, thus providing the user with a nice editor that
allows for URL browsing instead of the default textbox.

```
<Editor(GetType(ImageMapEditor), GetType(UITypeEditor))> _
Public Property ImageMap() As String
    Get
        Return _imageMapProperties.ToString()
    End Get

    Set(ByVal value As String)
        _imageMapProperties = New ImageMapProperties(value)
        ChildControlsCreated = False
    End Set
End Property
```

The ImageMap property has an Editor attribute applied associating it with our
custom ImageMapEditor, which we have not built yet. This property uses the helper
class ImageMapProperties.ToString() method in order to return a human-readable form
for all required data for the image map (coordinates, regions, etc.).

```
<Description("Absolute path to image")> _
Public Property AbsoluteImagePath() As String
    Get
        Return _fullPathToImage
    End Get

    Set(ByVal Value As String)
        _fullPathToImage = Value
    End Set
End Property
```

This property, `AbsoluteImagePath`, is required so that the image map editor can load in the image from the local file system; it should point to a local copy of the same image we will be using on the Web site.

Creating the Child Controls

As we explained back in Chapter 1, there is only one place where the child controls of a composite control should be created and that is in the overridden `CreateChildControls` method.

```
Protected Overrides Sub CreateChildControls()
    Controls.Clear()
```

First, we clear the `Controls` collection that is provided by the base class to ensure that we don't just keep adding our controls over and over again; before starting to add our children, we want an empty control collection. The first child control we will create is an `HtmlImage` that will output an `<img>` tag.

```
_imgTag.ID = "Img"
_imgTag.Src = _imagePath
Dim id As String = Me.ClientID
_imgTag.Attributes.Add("usemap", "#" & id & "Map")
Controls.Add(_imgTag)
```

Next, we set up the `HTMLImage` object, `_imgTag`, to get its image from the private `_imagePath` field. Other attributes are then attached to it, including `usemap`, to point to the relevant `<map>` tag for this image. The second child control is `HtmlGenericControl` that will output the corresponding `<map>` tag.

```
Dim map As New HtmlControls.HtmlGenericControl("map")
map.Attributes.Add("name", id & "Map")
map.Attributes.Add("id", id & "Map")

Dim numRegions As Integer = _
        _imageMapProperties.RectCoords.Count
```

The previous code also defines a variable called `numRegions`, which retrieves the number of rectangles specified in the `_imageMapProperties.RectCoords` property.

```
If numRegions > 0 Then
    'we estimate the size of our string builder
    'to preserve resources for memory allocations
    Dim r As Rectangle
    Dim counter As Integer
```

```
          For counter = 0 To numRegions - 1
              Dim area As New HtmlGenericControl("area")
              area.Attributes.Add("shape", "rect")
              r = CType( _
                  _imageMapProperties.RectCoords(counter), _
                  Rectangle)
              Dim coordString As String = r.Left & "," & _
                                          r.Top & "," & _
                                          r.Right & "," & _
                                          r.Bottom
              area.Attributes.Add("coords", coordString)
              Dim jscriptString As String = "javascript:" & _
                      Page.GetPostBackEventReference(Me, _
                      (counter + 1).ToString())
              area.Attributes.Add("href", jscriptString)
              map.Controls.Add(area)
          Next
          Controls.Add(map)
      End If
  End Sub
```

Then we iterate through the `ImageMapProperties` object's `RectCoords` property (we will be implementing this class shortly). This property contains an `ArrayList` of `Rectangle` objects that define each region. We proceed to iterate through the `ArrayList` of rectangles to create one child of type `HtmlGenericControl` (this time representing an `<area>` tag) for each rectangle found, and add them as children of the previously created `HtmlGenericControl` representing the `<map>` tag.

Also, in the previous code, we defined the `href` attribute of the `<area>` tag to be a JavaScript function. This function causes a postback when the image is clicked. We get the body for the JavaScript function by calling `Page.GetPostBackEventReference()` with the parameters `Me` (which is the sender of the event), and an optional argument that in this case will be the ID of the region that was clicked (we will see how the regions are defined when we discuss how to create the custom property editor). The `href` property for the `<area>` element will look something like the following when rendered to a browser:

```
href="javascript:__doPostBack('ImageMap1','1')"
```

Raising Our Custom Event

We have to provide our implementation of the `IPostBackEventHandler.RaisePostBackEvent()` method, which ASP.NET will call in case our control initiated a postback. This will happen whenever the client-side JavaScript function we mentioned earlier is called, which will happen when an active region of the image is clicked. At that time, we want to raise our custom `RegionClicked` event.

```
Public Sub RaisePostBackEvent(ByVal eventArgument As String) _
    Implements IPostBackEventHandler.RaisePostBackEvent
    RaiseEvent RegionClicked(Me, _
                    New ImageMapEventArgs(eventArgument))
End Sub
```

Rectangles and Strings

Now it's time to introduce our helper `ImageMapProperties` class, which will be in charge of converting an `ArrayList` containing `Rectangle` instances to a string representation, and vice versa. Let's take a look at the code for this class, as follows:

```
Public Class ImageMapProperties
    Private _coords As ArrayList

    Public Sub New(ByVal designerString As String)
        Dim stringRepresentation As String
        If designerString Is Nothing Then
            stringRepresentation = ""
        Else
            stringRepresentation = designerString
        End If

        Dim vals() As String = stringRepresentation.Split(";"c)

        Dim rects As New ArrayList()
        Dim coords() As String
        Dim valsLength As Integer = vals.Length
        Dim r As Rectangle
        Dim counter As Integer
        If valsLength > 0 Then
            For counter = 0 To valsLength - 1
                coords = vals(counter).Split(","c)
                If coords.Length = 4 Then
                    r = New Rectangle(CInt(coords(0)), _
                CInt(coords(1)), CInt(coords(2)), CInt(coords(3)))
                    rects.Add(r)
                End If
```

```
            Next
        End If
        _coords = rects

    End Sub

    Public Sub New(ByVal rectCoordinates As ArrayList)
        _coords = rectCoordinates
    End Sub
    Public Overrides Function ToString() As String
        If _coords Is Nothing Then Return ""
        Dim rectCoordsCount As Integer = _coords.Count
        Dim counter As Integer
        Dim stringRep As New System.Text.StringBuilder()
        If rectCoordsCount > 0 Then
            For counter = 0 To rectCoordsCount - 1
                Dim r As Rectangle
                r = CType(_coords(counter), Rectangle)
                If counter > 0 Then stringRep.Append(";")
                stringRep.Append(r.X & ",")
                stringRep.Append(r.Y & ",")
                stringRep.Append(r.Width & "," & r.Height)
            Next
        End If
        Return stringRep.ToString()
    End Function
```

We're defining two constructors. One constructor accepts a string while the other accepts an ArrayList. The two constructors are required for the custom UI editor to work according to our design.

```
    Public Property RectCoords() As ArrayList
        Get
            Return _coords
        End Get

        Set(ByVal value As ArrayList)
            _coords = value
        End Set
    End Property

End Class
```

The property in the `ImageMap` class that holds the information about the regions and the full path to the image is a semicolon-delimited string. So, when we instantiate the class and the string is passed in, the object will know what it has to do because the constructor that accepts the string as a parameter will be executed. So, if the first constructor is called, then the code to translate the string into an `ArrayList` of rectangles is executed. When the other constructor is called, the `ArrayList` is stored. We can then obtain the string again by calling the `ToString()` method. This class is the glue between the custom UI property editor and the `ImageMap` class.

You may be wondering already why we haven't implemented this class as a `TypeConverter`-derived class, which is the .NET proper way of converting between different representations of a given type. We considered this but decided against it because of the added complexity involved by this approach that would go far beyond the scope of this book. If you're interested in learning more about type converters, please see the .NET Framework documentation.

Our Custom Type Editor

There is one more class that is required to complete the glue, and this is our custom UI editor class named `ImageMapEditor` that derives from the base class `UITypeEditor`. This class provides us with two methods that we need to override. Both were previously outlined in the "Technology" section of this chapter: the `GetEditStyle()` and `EditValue()` methods.

```
Public Class ImageMapEditor
    Inherits UITypeEditor

    Public Overloads Overrides Function GetEditStyle( _
            ByVal context As ITypeDescriptorContext) _
                                As UITypeEditorEditStyle
        Return UITypeEditorEditStyle.Modal
    End Function
```

The `GetEditStyle()` method tells the IDE what style of property editor we are providing. In our case, we will be using a modal dialog so we return `UITypeEditorEditStyle.Modal`.

```
    Public Overloads Overrides Function EditValue( _
            ByVal context As ITypeDescriptorContext, _
            ByVal provider As IServiceProvider, _
            ByVal value As Object) As Object
        Dim returnvalue As Object = value
        Dim srv As IWindowsFormsEditorService
```

```
        If Not provider Is Nothing Then
            srv = CType(provider.GetService( _
                    GetType(IWindowsFormsEditorService)), _
                    IWindowsFormsEditorService)
        End If

        If Not srv Is Nothing Then
            Dim ImageMapEd As New ImageMapEditorForm
            Dim stringRep As String = CType(value, String)
            Dim imgMapProps As New ImageMapProperties(stringRep)
            With ImageMapEd
                .ImagePath = CType(context.Instance, _
                        ImageMap).AbsoluteImagePath
                .Regions = CType(imgMapProps.RectCoords.Clone(), ArrayList)
                .StartPosition = FormStartPosition.CenterScreen
                If srv.ShowDialog(ImageMapEd) _
                        = DialogResult.OK Then
                    Dim newimgMapProps As _
                            New ImageMapProperties(.Regions)
                    Return newimgMapProps.ToString
                End If
            End With
            Return imgMapProps.ToString()
        End If
    End Function
```

The next method, shown previously, is the EditValue() method. This is called by the IDE when the ellipsis button is clicked. The work that is done in this method is as follows:

1. First, we instantiate our property editor form.

2. Then we pass in any values that are required by the form to initialize by setting properties that have been exposed on the form.

3. Then we show our form.

4. If the dialog result of our form is OK, then we get the properties that we had previously set because they most likely have changed.

5. Then we return our new property value.

The `ImageMap` property set accessor will automatically be called with the return value of this method. We can see our two constructors of the `ImageMapProperties` class at work here. The parameter that is received by the method is the value of the property when the ellipsis button is clicked. Since the form that we have created exposes two properties that are objects not fully compatible with the type of property we are editing, we use the constructor of the `ImageMapProperties` object that will accept those objects and translate them into the string value we need for our property. Once our `ImageMap` receives this string, it will create a new instance of the `ImageMapProperties` class so that it will have a reference to the `ArrayList` of rectangle objects to work with.

Coding the Editor Form

We are still missing the main piece of the puzzle. We need to implement the UI for our custom property editor. As we mentioned earlier, this will be a Windows Form, so add one to your project and set it up to look like Figure 10-1.

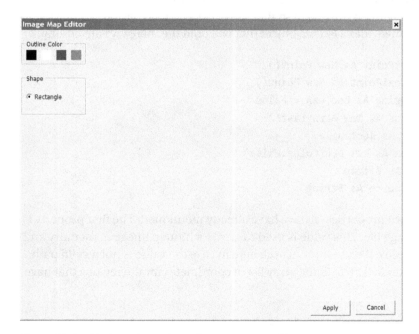

Figure 10-1. *Design-time view of our custom Editor*

The form (found in the `ImageMapEditorForm.vb` file) consists of four labels we're using as buttons (`lblBlack`, `lblWhite`, `lblBlue`, and `lblRed`) that have their background color set to different shades so that the outline of the rectangle can be changed to something perhaps more visible, such as a `PictureBox` or a `Button`, depending on the background color of the image. Lastly, though it is not visible here, you'll need to add a Context menu (make sure that the ContextMenu property of the PictureBox is set to your Context menu) with a single item, Delete, called DeleteMenu. This will be used to remove regions that have previously been defined. Let's take a look at the code for this form.

```
Imports System.Drawing
Imports System.Windows.Forms
Imports System.Collections
Imports System

Namespace Apress.Toolkit
    Public Class ImageMapEditorForm
        Inherits System.Windows.Forms.Form
```

First, some class-level variables are declared. These are some Point objects that we will use to keep a reference to where the mouse is on our image, an ArrayList called coords that will hold a rectangle object for each defined region, a Pen object that will be used to draw the rectangles on the image so that the developer has a visual cue of what regions have been defined, and a Bitmap object that will hold the image we are editing.

```
        Private startPoint As New Point()
        Private contextPoint As New Point()
        Private dragging As Boolean = False
        Private coords As New ArrayList()
        Private rect As Rectangle
        Private myPen As New Pen(Color.White)
        Private img As Bitmap
        Private imgSource As String
```

Then we expose two properties that we have already mentioned. The first property is the full path to the image file. This value is used to create a bitmap image in memory and assign it to the PictureBox. We use a Try...Catch here in case the value is not a valid path. The other property is Regions. This is the array list of coordinates for the regions that have been defined.

```
        Public Property ImagePath() As String
            Get
                Return imgSource
            End Get

            Set(ByVal value As String)
                Try
                    Dim bmp As New Bitmap(value)
                    img = bmp
```

```
                picture.Image = bmp
                picture.Invalidate()
                imgSource = value
            Catch ex As Exception
                MessageBox.Show(ex.Message & " " & value)
            End Try
        End Set
    End Property

    Public Property Regions() As ArrayList
        Get
            Return coords
        End Get

        Set(ByVal value As ArrayList)
            coords = value
        End Set
    End Property
```

Next, we implement the MouseMove event handler. In this method, we check if we are in a dragging operation. If we are, then we need to get the X and Y coordinates of the mouse. Then we build a rectangle object in case this is the last point that will be collected before the MouseUp event is fired. We also invalidate the PictureBox so that it is forced to repaint itself. This will give the effect of the mouse actually drawing the rectangle on the bitmap image.

```
    Private Sub Picture_MouseMove(ByVal sender As Object, _
                        ByVal e As MouseEventArgs) _
                        Handles picture.MouseMove
        If dragging Then
            Dim width As Integer = e.X - startPoint.X
            Dim height As Integer = e.Y - startPoint.Y
            rect = New Rectangle( _
                startPoint.X, startPoint.Y, width, height)
            picture.Invalidate()
        End If
    End Sub
```

In the MouseDown event handler, we check if it was the left mouse button that was clicked. If it was, we set our class-level boolean variable dragging to True. This way, we will know that the developer is beginning to define a region. We also instantiate the StartPoint to denote the X and Y coordinates of the mouse when the dragging began. If it was the right mouse button that was clicked, we just grab the current coordinates of the mouse for use by the ContextMenu's popup event handler.

```
Private Sub Picture_MouseDown(ByVal sender As Object, _
                              ByVal e As MouseEventArgs) _
                              Handles picture.MouseDown
    If e.Button = MouseButtons.Left Then
        dragging = True
        startPoint = New Point(e.X, e.Y)
    Else
        dragging = False
    End If

    If e.Button = MouseButtons.Right Then
        'get point of mouse for context menu
        contextPoint.X = e.X
        contextPoint.Y = e.Y
    End If
End Sub
```

The final mouse event we add is the MouseUp event handler. In this method, we check if it was the left mouse button that was released. If it was and we are in a dragging state, then we add the rectangle to the ArrayList. Then we invalidate the PictureBox so that it is, again, forced to repaint itself.

```
Private Sub Picture_MouseUp(ByVal sender As Object, _
                            ByVal e As MouseEventArgs) _
                            Handles picture.MouseUp
    If e.Button = MouseButtons.Left Then
        If dragging Then
            dragging = False
            coords.Add(rect)
            picture.Invalidate()
        End If
    End If
End Sub
```

Next, we look at the PictureBox Paint event. This method is invoked whenever the Invalidate() method on the PictureBox is called. In this event, we iterate through all the regions that have been defined so far and draw them on the bitmap image. Then, we check to see if we are in a dragging state. If we are, then we draw the rectangle that is currently being defined with a dotted-line border, and write the region ID next to the rectangle.

```
        Private Sub PictureBox1_Paint(ByVal sender As Object, ByVal e As_
                        System.Windows.Forms.PaintEventArgs) Handles
PictureBox1.Paint
            Dim r As Rectangle
            Dim counter As Integer
            Dim g As Graphics = e.Graphics
            For counter = 1 To Coords.Count
                p.DashStyle = Drawing.Drawing2D.DashStyle.Solid
                r = CType(Coords.Item(counter - 1), Rectangle)
                g.DrawRectangle(p, r)
                'draw a label on the rectangle
                g.DrawString(counter.ToString(), New Font("Arial", 12),
Brushes.Gray,_
                                        r.X, r.Y)
            Next
            If dragging Then
                p.DashStyle = Drawing.Drawing2D.DashStyle.Dash
                g.DrawRectangle(p, rect)
            End If
        End Sub
```

Then we define a handler for the click event of all the labels. By using the `Handles` keyword, we define one method to handle the click event for all the labels. This method will simply change the color of the pen that we are drawing the rectangles with.

```
        Private Sub ChangeColor_Click(ByVal sender As System.Object, ByVal e As_
            System.EventArgs) Handles Label1.Click, Label2.Click, Label3.Click,
Label4.Click
            p.Color = CType(sender, Label).BackColor
        End Sub
```

Here's the click event handler for the Delete menu option:

```
Private Sub DeleteRect_Click(ByVal sender As Object, ByVal e_
                        As System.EventArgs) Handles DeleteRect.Click
        Dim r As Rectangle
        Dim Counter As Integer
        For Counter = 0 To Coords.Count - 1
            r = CType(Coords.Item(Counter), Rectangle)
            If r.Contains(ContextPoint) Then
                Coords.Remove(r)
                PictureBox1.Invalidate()
                Exit For
```

```
            End If
        Next
    End Sub
```

Demonstration

Create a new Web form, drop a Label control, and edit it with the following code:

```
Public Class ImageMap
    Inherits System.Web.UI.Page
  Protected WithEvents ImageMap1 As Apress.Toolkit.ImageMap
  Protected WithEvents Label1 As System.Web.UI.WebControls.Label

'Web Form designer generated code omitted here

    Private Sub Page_Load(ByVal sender As System.Object, ByVal e_
                    As System.EventArgs) Handles MyBase.Load
        'Put user code to initialize the page here
    End Sub

    Private Sub ImageMap1_RegionClicked(ByVal sender As System.Object, ByVal e_
                    As ImageMapEventArgs) Handles
ImageMap1.RegionClicked
    Label1.Text = "You clicked region " & e.RegionID
    End Sub
End Class
```

Next, drag and drop an ImageMap control onto the designer. Click on the control, and then move to the Properties window. You need to set these properties for the ImageMap now. Make sure that you have an image file in your Web folder (we're using one of a cat, Cati-Kitty.jpg, for this example in Figure 10-2), and set the FullImagePath and ImgSrc properties to both point to C:\Inetpub\wwwroot\ApressToolkit\Cati-Kitty.jpg.

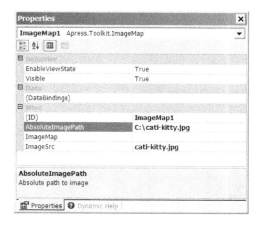

Figure 10-2. *Browsing the* ImageMap *properties*

Of course, in most cases, the path to the image will be a relative path or a root-relative path. This works well for the image source, but not for the FullImagePath: this must be a fully qualified path to an image file or it will not load in our editor. Once you have these two properties set, you'll see the image appear in the designer.

Now, we can select the ImageMap property by clicking on the ellipsis. This will pop up our custom designer, as shown in Figure 10-3.

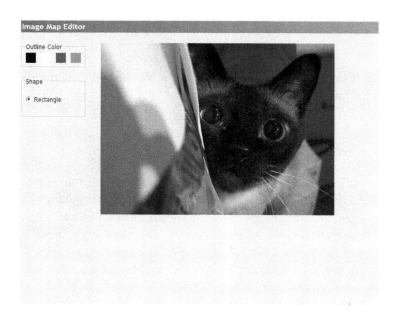

Figure 10-3. *The* ImageMapEditor *in action*

At this point, we can begin to define regions by dragging the mouse. Each region will be given a numeric ID in the order that they are defined. For this example (see Figure 10-4), we've selected each of Cati's eyes.

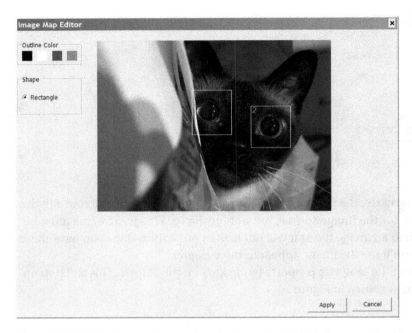

Figure 10-4. *Selecting regions using the* ImageMapEditor

Now simply click the Apply button and run the project. In the browser, you will notice the mouse cursor turn into the hand cursor over Cati's eyes.

Limitations

One limitation is the image size in the UI property editor, which must be the same size as the image that will be rendered to the browser. Otherwise, the coordinates for the regions will not be exact. Also, the properties in the Properties window must be set in a particular order. The full path to the image must be set before you can edit the ImageMap property.

Regions always post back to the server no matter if we need it or not. For example, if we would like a region to directly link to a specific URL, we still need to cause a postback to the server and then redirect from there to the target URL.

Finally, it's only possible to define rectangle regions, and not circle or polygon regions. In the previous example, it would have been nice to define a circle region for each of Cati's eyes instead of a rectangle region.

Extensions

As we just noted, our custom editor is a great candidate for extension. By using GDI+ classes, it would be possible to add support for other region types supported by the HTML specification. Moreover, the selection of regions itself could be improved by highlighting defined regions when the mouse passes over them, thus providing a nice visual cue of predefined regions.

In addition, allowing a region to link directly to a URL instead of always posting back to the server would be a good addition and one that doesn't require any real effort. You could easily add a new property, for example TargetUrl, that is specified alongside each region, and that—when provided—is used as the href attribute of the corresponding <area> tag. If the property is left blank, then we output the known _doPostBack function to cause a postback.

CHAPTER 11

■ ■ ■

Reviewing Controls

Most Web sites today give users the chance to voice their opinions regarding the content they offer. For example, an e-commerce Web site like Amazon.com will let you rate any book they sell on a scale of one to five stars, while a content-based Web site like MSDN lets you rate the published articles on a scale of one to nine points. Both of them will let users write a short text review and explain why they rated the item the way they did.

Having such review functionality for our own Web sites can be really useful for two main reasons: First, from the user's point of view, they can read the opinions of other users; this allows them to be better informed before they decide whether to purchase a product or subscribe to a service. Second, from the site owner's point of view, being able to read the comments and reviews that the customers have provided can be invaluable, as it allows them to quickly identify nonappealing offerings and act accordingly.

Scenario

A typical user interface for submitting a review has a textbox for the reviewer's name, a text area for the actual review, and a list of radio buttons to express a rating (for example, a selection consisting of "Superb," "Good," "Average," and "Poor"). We will build a user control named `ReviewerForm.ascx` to encapsulate the UI for getting this data.

Of course, we need a way to easily display all the data collected and store it in the database. For this we are coding two custom controls: `LastReview` and `Average`. `LastReview` will display the last review received for a given product plus a link that, when clicked, will show all of its available reviews. `Average` will simply display an image representing the current average rating of a given product.

Technology

Our controls will use a lot of ADO.NET classes to query a Microsoft SQL Server database. The ADO.NET library contains two useful namespaces that we will use: `System.Data` and `System.Data.SqlClient`.

The former contains the DataSet class definition that can represent a set of records returned by a SQL SELECT statement while being disconnected from the database. The latter contains a set of useful classes that perform all the classic ADO.NET operations and work against a Microsoft SQL Server database.

Design

We'll begin by looking at the database that will be used to store the reviews, then move on to explore every stored procedure used by the control to retrieve useful information, such as average rating and the last review written.

The sample database provided is currently a Microsoft SQL Server database. We chose to use Microsoft SQL Server because it is widely available even on desktop machines thanks to the MSDE engine. Take a look at the provided ReviewsDB database containing the Reviews table in Figure 11-1.

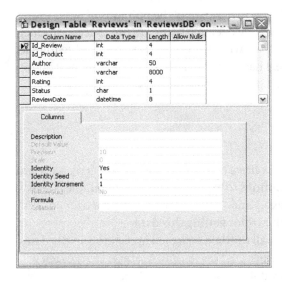

Figure 11-1. *Reviews table*

In Table 11-1, there is an explanation of each column.

Table 11-1. *Reviews Table Definition*

Column	Description
Id_Review	Primary key for the table. It is an autoincrement integer value.
Id_Product	Foreign key representing the product ID for which the review has been written.
Author	Name of the author submitting the review.
Review	The text for the review itself, allowing up to 8,000 characters.
Rating	Integer representing the rating given by the user.
Status	Indicates the current status of a review. It may be active status (zero), pending status (one), or rejected status (two).
ReviewDate	Represents the date and time the review was submitted.

Each time a new review is added to the database, its status value will be set to *pending*. This is done because we are assuming that an administrator, using a client application, will validate each review before letting it appear on the Web site (in order to make sure spam or obscene reviews aren't shown). If you don't want to implement this feature, you can simply change the last value of the INSERT statement from one to zero in the provided spInsertReview stored procedure.

Implementation

Our controls will use stored procedures either to retrieve data or to insert new reviews. We will need to implement four stored procedures: one to retrieve the average rating, one to get the last review, one to get all reviews, and one to insert a new review.

Let's start by writing the database code. Our first stored procedure, review_GetAverage, is used to obtain the average rating for a given product considering only already approved reviews.

```
CREATE PROCEDURE review_GetAverage
     @productid      int
AS
SELECT average = AVG(Rating)
          FROM Reviews WHERE Id_Product = @ProductId AND Status = 0
```

The next stored procedure, review_GetLastReview, uses the SQL TOP statement to retrieve just the first record of a selection ordered by review date in descending order.

```
CREATE PROCEDURE review_GetLastReview
     @productid      int
AS
SELECT TOP 1 author, review, rating, ReviewDate
          FROM Reviews
```

```
        WHERE ID_PRODUCT=@productid AND status=0
        ORDER BY ReviewDate DESC
```

The following is a simple stored procedure that can retrieve all the reviews for a specified product.

```
CREATE  PROCEDURE review_GetReviews
     @productid        int
AS
SELECT author, review, rating,ReviewDate
        FROM Reviews
        WHERE ID_PRODUCT=@productid AND status=0
```

Of course, we also need a way to actually add a review to the Reviews table and this is exactly what the review_InsertReview does: it accepts four parameters including a product ID, an author name, a review description, and a rating. Note that no status or review date is provided. In fact, the status is automatically set to *pending* while the review date is set to the value returned by the T-SQL getdate( ) function.

```
CREATE PROCEDURE review_InsertReview
        @productid       int,
        @author          varchar(50),
        @review          varchar(8000),
        @rating          int
AS

        INSERT INTO Reviews
                (ProductId, Author, Review, Rating, Status)
        VALUES
                (@productid, @author, @review, @rating, 1)
```

Now that we have our four stored procedures in place, we need to be able to execute them easily without any trouble. For this we will code a new class named exclusively for interacting with them, providing methods for inserting new reviews, retrieving a list of reviews for a given product, etc.

Let's name this new class ReviewerDB class. We begin by defining two properties needed to retrieve and set both the ConnectionString and the ProductID.

```
Public Class ReviewerDB
    Dim _connection As String

    Public Property ConnectionString() As String
        Get
            Return _connection
        End Get
```

```
        Set(ByVal Value As String)
            _connection = Value
        End Set
    End Property


    Dim _productid As Integer

    Public Property ProductID() As Integer
        Get
            Return _productid
        End Get

        Set(ByVal Value As Integer)
            _productid = Value
        End Set
    End Property
```

The code goes on to declare a method to insert a new review. It accepts three parameters: a string containing the author's name, a string containing the review description, and the rating value specified as an integer.

```
    Public Sub InsertReview(ByVal strName As String, _
                ByVal strReview As String, ByVal iRating As Integer)
```

We need to create an object from the `SqlCommand` class in order to execute the stored procedure.

```
Dim dbConn As New SqlConnection(ConnectionString)
Dim dbComm As New SqlCommand
```

Now we can prepare the code to execute the `review_InsertReview` stored procedure. We need to follow these steps:

1. Use the `SqlCommand` object to specify the connection to use and the stored procedure name, and to set the command type to `StoredProcedure`.

2. Use the `Parameters` collection provided by the `SqlCommand` class to specify each parameter in the stored procedure, following the exact order stated in the corresponding stored procedure.

3. Use the `Value` property of items from the `Parameters` collection to specify each parameter's value to store in the database.

Now let's see how all these look when translated into code.

```
dbComm.Connection = dbConn
dbComm.CommandText = "review_InsertReview"
dbComm.CommandType = CommandType.StoredProcedure

dbComm.Parameters.Add("@productid", SqlDbType.Int)
dbComm.Parameters.Add("@author", SqlDbType.VarChar, 50)
dbComm.Parameters.Add("@review", SqlDbType.VarChar, 8000)
dbComm.Parameters.Add("@rating", SqlDbType.Char, 1)

dbComm.Parameters(0).Value = ProductID
dbComm.Parameters(1).Value = strName
dbComm.Parameters(2).Value = strReview
dbComm.Parameters(3).Value = iRating
```

Finally, a Try...Finally block is used to ensure the connection always gets closed, whether or not any exceptions were raised during the record insertion.

```
Try
    dbConn.Open()
    dbComm.ExecuteNonQuery()
Finally
    If dbConn.State = ConnectionState.Open Then
        dbConn.Close()
    End If
End Try


End Sub
```

The rest of the class's code is similar to the previous one; each property calls a specific stored procedure to fill a DataSet with review records.

```
Public ReadOnly Property GetAllReviews() As DataSet
Get
    Dim dbConn As New SqlConnection(ConnectionString)
    Dim dbComm As New SqlCommand

    dbComm.Connection = dbConn
    dbComm.CommandText = "review_GetReviews"
    dbComm.CommandType = CommandType.StoredProcedure

    dbComm.Parameters.Add("@productid", SqlDbType.Int)
    dbComm.Parameters(0).Value = ProductID
```

```vbnet
        Dim da As New SqlDataAdapter(dbComm)
        Dim ds As New DataSet("REVIEWS")
        Try
            da.Fill(ds)
            Return ds
        Catch
            Return Nothing
        End Try

    End Get
End Property

        Public ReadOnly Property GetLastReview() As DataSet
    Get
        Dim dbConn As New SqlConnection(ConnectionString)
        Dim dbComm As New SqlCommand

        dbComm.Connection = dbConn
        dbComm.CommandText = "review_GetLastReview"
        dbComm.CommandType = CommandType.StoredProcedure

        dbComm.Parameters.Add("@productid", SqlDbType.Int)
        dbComm.Parameters(0).Value = ProductID

        Dim da As New SqlDataAdapter(dbComm)
        Dim ds As New DataSet("REVIEWS")

        Try
            da.Fill(ds)
            Return ds
        Catch
            Return Nothing
        End Try
    End Get
End Property
Public ReadOnly Property GetAverage() As Single
    Get
        Dim dbConn As New SqlConnection(ConnectionString)
        Dim dbCmd As New SqlCommand
        Dim dbReader As SqlDataReader
```

```
            dbCmd.Connection = dbConn
            dbCmd.CommandText = "review_GetAverage"
            dbCmd.CommandType = CommandType.StoredProcedure

            dbCmd.Parameters.Add("@productid", SqlDbType.Int)
            dbCmd.Parameters(0).Value = ProductID

            dbConn.Open()
            dbReader = dbCmd.ExecuteReader(CommandBehavior.CloseConnection)
            If (dbReader.HasRows) Then
                dbReader.Read()
                Dim avg As Object = dbReader.GetValue(0)
                If (TypeOf avg Is DBNull) Then
                    Return 0
                Else
                    Return (CType(dbReader.GetValue(0), Single))
                End If
            Else
                Return 0
            End If
        End Get
    End Property
End Class
```

The LastReview Control

This is the first custom control we will code to facilitate review functionality in your
ASP.NET application. This control will display a table with the last review written for
a specified product. In addition, it will implement a link to show all the reviews stored in
the database.

This control inherits from the WebControl base class and implements the
IPostBackEventHandler interface to support the raising of a custom event when the user
clicks on the link to show all reviews.

```
<ToolboxData("<{0}:LastReview runat=server></{0}:LastReview>")> _
Public Class LastReview
        Inherits System.Web.UI.WebControls.WebControl
        Implements IPostBackEventHandler
```

Other than two properties to retrieve and set the ProductID and ConnectionString,
this control provides a MaxChars property, which is useful to define how many characters
of the review description are allowed to be displayed.

```
Dim _maxchars As Integer

<Bindable(True), Category("Appearance"), DefaultValue("")> _
Property MaxChars() As Integer
    Get
        Return _maxchars
    End Get
    Set(ByVal Value As Integer)
        _maxchars = Value
    End Set
End Property
```

For the controls presented in this chapter, we have chosen to write their corresponding markup "by hand" using the HtmlTextWriter.Output method instead of other alternatives shown in previous chapters. The LastReview control implements two methods for taking care of its rendering: RenderLastReview and RenderAllReviews, both take an HtmlTextWriter parameter used to write the HTML.

The first render method, RenderLastReview, will render an HTML Table containing the information for the last review and a link to display all the reviews. The entire HTML to be rendered is contained in a string including placeholders that will be replaced later with the actual data for the review, such as the following:

```
Str = Str & "<FONT FACE='Verdana, Arial' SIZE='1'><B>Author:</B> [Author]<BR> _
<B>Review:</B> [Review] </FONT>"
```

In order to retrieve the information for last review, we can use the GetLastReview property of the ReviewerDB class. Before that, we have to indicate to this class the ConnectionString so it can establish a link to the database in the first place, and to the ProductID we're interested in getting reviews for.

```
Dim ds As DataSet
Dim dbutil As New ReviewerDB()
dbutil.ConnectionString = ConnectionString
dbutil.ProductID = ProductID
ds = dbutil.GetLastReview
```

When the retrieved DataSet is not Nothing, the code replaces the placeholders specified in the HTML string with values from the Reviews table. The MaxChars property is used to check whether the comment length is greater than the maximum value allowed. If it is too big, the string is cut and three dots are appended to the remainder, indicating the string has been truncated.

```
        If Not ds Is Nothing Then
                Dim row As DataRow
                Dim strReview As String
                For Each row In ds.Tables(0).Rows
                    'Replace placeholder with author
                   strHTML = strHTML.Replace("[Author]", row("author").ToString())

                    'Replace placeholder with review content
                    strReview = row("review").ToString()
                    If strReview.Length > MaxChars Then
                        strReview = strReview.Remove(MaxChars - 3,_
                                      strReview.Length - MaxChars) & "..."
                    End If
                    strHTML = strHTML.Replace("[Review]", strReview)
```

A Select Case block is used to analyze the rating value and to display the appropriate image (we are using stars, but you could use any image you want).

```
                    'Replace placeholder with image source and ALT
                    Select Case row("rating")
                        Case "1"
                            strHTML = strHTML.Replace("[ImageSrc]",_
                                                    "images/10star.gif")
                            strHTML = strHTML.Replace("[Vote]", "10 stars")
                        Case "2"
                            strHTML = strHTML.Replace("[ImageSrc]", _
                                                    "images/20star.gif")
                            strHTML = strHTML.Replace("[Vote]", "20 stars")
                        Case "3"
                            strHTML = strHTML.Replace("[ImageSrc]", _
                                                    "images/30star.gif")
                            strHTML = strHTML.Replace("[Vote]", "30 stars")
                        Case "4"
                            strHTML = strHTML.Replace("[ImageSrc]", _
                                                    "images/40star.gif")
                            strHTML = strHTML.Replace("[Vote]", "40 stars")
                        Case "5"
                            strHTML = strHTML.Replace("[ImageSrc]", _
                                                    "images/50star.gif")
                            strHTML = strHTML.Replace("[Vote]", "50 stars")
                    End Select
```

Finally, the GetPostBackEventReference() method is used to add a doPostBack() client function call, which is added to the onclick attribute of the anchor tag.

```
                'Replace placeholder with Link to show all reviews
                strHTML = strHTML.Replace("[Link]", _
                                    Page.GetPostBackEventReference(Me, _
                                    "GetAllReviews"))
        Next
        output.Write(strHTML)
```

When the DataSet object is equal to Nothing, meaning no data matching the given criteria was found, a simple message is displayed to indicate that no reviews for this product have been made.

```
        Else
            output.Write("No reviews for the specified product were found.")
        End If
    End Sub
```

The RaisePostBackEvent() method is necessary to get notified when the anchor's onclick event has been fired.

```
Sub RaisePostBackEvent(ByVal eventArgument As String)➥
Implements IPostBackEventHandler.RaisePostBackEvent
        If eventArgument = "GetAllReviews" Then
            _renderAllReviews = True
        End If
    End Sub
```

We inspect the value received in the eventArgument parameter to see which command our control should execute. We are only supporting one command named GetAllReviews, but you could easily add your own custom commands and process different actions for each one of them. After checking that we received the GetAllReviews command, we set an internal flag, _renderAllReviews, to True to signal that the user is requesting to see all the reviews and not just the last one.

But who will be paying attention to this flag? That's the job of the overridden Render method.

```
    Protected Overrides Sub Render(ByVal output As➥
System.Web.UI.HtmlTextWriter)
        If (_renderAllReviews) Then
            RenderAllReviews(output)
        Else
            RenderLastReview(output)
        End If
    End Sub
```

If the flag was set, then our control will render all reviews by calling the RenderAllReviews method or—in the case where the flag wasn't set—it will just call RenderLastReview to render the details about the last review.

As you may already have guessed, the RenderAllReviews method looks a lot like the RenderLastReview method we just saw, but with some minor differences. In this case, a TABLE tag is created for each review found (again, using placeholders that will be replaced later with real data taken from the database).

```
    If Not ds Is Nothing Then
        Dim row As DataRow
        strHTML = "<font face='arial'><h2>What people are saying
 about this product</h2><hr>"
        Dim strTABLE As String

        For Each row In ds.Tables(0).Rows
            strTABLE = strTABLE & "<table width='100%' border='0'
cellpadding='0'>
<tr><td width='60%'><b>[Author]</b> writes:<br>[Review]</td><td width='20%' align
='center'>[Date]</td><td width='20%' align='right'>Rating:<img src='[ImageSrc]'>
</td></tr>"
            strTABLE = strTABLE.Replace("[Author]", _
                                        row("author").ToString())
            strTABLE = strTABLE.Replace("[Review]", _
                                        row("review").ToString())
            strTABLE = strTABLE.Replace("[Date]", _
                            CType(row("ReviewDate"), Date).ToShortDateString())

            Select Case row("rating")
                Case "1"
                    strTABLE = strTABLE.Replace("[ImageSrc]", "images/10star.gif")
                Case "2"
                    strTABLE = strTABLE.Replace("[ImageSrc]", "images/20star.gif")
                Case "3"
                    strTABLE = strTABLE.Replace("[ImageSrc]", "images/30star.gif")
                Case "4"
                    strTABLE = strTABLE.Replace("[ImageSrc]", "images/40star.gif")
                Case "5"
                    strTABLE = strTABLE.Replace("[ImageSrc]", "images/50star.gif")
            End Select
            strTABLE = strTABLE & "</table><hr>"
        Next
        strHTML = strHTML & strTABLE & "</font>"
    End If
```

```
        output.Write(strHTML)
End Sub
```

The Average Control

Lots of Web sites use an image to indicate a product's average rating. This is a useful way for the user to get a quick and good idea about how well a given product is considered by the community. Our Average control will offer this functionality by displaying an HTML TABLE tag containing a bitmap image representing the average rating of a given product. The code needed is very similar to the code shown for the previous control, so we will not go into much detail this time.

The Render() method is used to display the table with the bitmap image. At the beginning of the code, a ReviewerDB object is used to call its GetAverage property to obtain the average rating for a specified product.

```
Protected Overrides Sub Render(ByVal output As System.Web.UI.HtmlTextWriter)
        Dim ds As DataSet
        Dim dbutil As New ReviewerDB
        dbutil.ConnectionString = ConnectionString
        dbutil.ProductID = ProductID
        Dim average As Single = dbutil.GetAverage
```

The retrieved number is casted to an integer and a Select Case block is used to replace the [ImageSrc] and [Vote] placeholders with the appropriate image.

```
        Select Case CInt(average * 4)
            Case 4
                strHTML = strHTML.Replace("[ImageSrc]", "images/10star.gif")
                strHTML = strHTML.Replace("[Vote]", "1 star")
            Case 5
                strHTML = strHTML.Replace("[ImageSrc]", "images/13star.gif")
                strHTML = strHTML.Replace("[Vote]", "1.25 stars")
            Case 6
                strHTML = strHTML.Replace("[ImageSrc]", "images/15star.gif")
                strHTML = strHTML.Replace("[Vote]", "1.5 stars")
            Case 7
                strHTML = strHTML.Replace("[ImageSrc]", "images/17star.gif")
                strHTML = strHTML.Replace("[Vote]", "1.75 stars")
            Case 8
                strHTML = strHTML.Replace("[ImageSrc]", "images/20star.gif")
                strHTML = strHTML.Replace("[Vote]", "2 stars")
```

```
            Case 9
                strHTML = strHTML.Replace("[ImageSrc]", "images/23star.gif")
                strHTML = strHTML.Replace("[Vote]", "2.25 stars")
            Case 10
                strHTML = strHTML.Replace("[ImageSrc]", "images/25star.gif")
                strHTML = strHTML.Replace("[Vote]", "2.5 stars")
            Case 11
                strHTML = strHTML.Replace("[ImageSrc]", "images/27star.gif")
                strHTML = strHTML.Replace("[Vote]", "2.75 stars")
            Case 12
                strHTML = strHTML.Replace("[ImageSrc]", "images/30star.gif")
                strHTML = strHTML.Replace("[Vote]", "3 stars")
            Case 13
                strHTML = strHTML.Replace("[ImageSrc]", "images/33star.gif")
                strHTML = strHTML.Replace("[Vote]", "3.25 stars")
            Case 14
                strHTML = strHTML.Replace("[ImageSrc]", "images/35star.gif")
                strHTML = strHTML.Replace("[Vote]", "3.5 stars")
            Case 15
                strHTML = strHTML.Replace("[ImageSrc]", "images/37star.gif")
                strHTML = strHTML.Replace("[Vote]", "3.75 stars")
            Case 16
                strHTML = strHTML.Replace("[ImageSrc]", "images/40star.gif")
                strHTML = strHTML.Replace("[Vote]", "4 stars")
            Case 17
                strHTML = strHTML.Replace("[ImageSrc]", "images/43star.gif")
                strHTML = strHTML.Replace("[Vote]", "4.25 stars")
            Case 18
                strHTML = strHTML.Replace("[ImageSrc]", "images/45star.gif")
                strHTML = strHTML.Replace("[Vote]", "4.5 stars")
            Case 19
                strHTML = strHTML.Replace("[ImageSrc]", "images/47star.gif")
                strHTML = strHTML.Replace("[Vote]", "4.75 stars")
            Case 20
                strHTML = strHTML.Replace("[ImageSrc]", "images/50star.gif")
                strHTML = strHTML.Replace("[Vote]", "5 stars")
        End Select

        output.Write(strHTML)
    Else
        output.Write("No average for the specified product.")
    End If
End Sub
```

The ReviewerForm User Control

The third control developed in this chapter, the ReviewerForm user control, is used to take the required information from the user wanting to fill in a review. It uses textboxes for the name and the review text, and a RadioButtonList to allow the user to specify their rating; in additon, two validation controls are added to check that all the required fields were filled in correctly.

Let's get into the code for this user control. When the user selects the Submit button, the Click event is raised and the ibSubmit_Click() event handler is called. We use this method to execute the review_InsertReview stored procedure that inserts a new review into the database.

```
Private Sub ibSubmit_Click(ByVal sender As System.Object, ByVal e As➡
System.Web.UI.ImageClickEventArgs) Handles ibSubmit.Click
```

First of all, we have to check that all the required fields have been correctly filled in. This is accomplished using the IsValid property provided by the Page class. This property will be set to True only if all validator controls also return True. A ReviewerDB object is then created and the InsertReview() method is called on it, with the user's input being passed in as its parameters.

```
    If Page.IsValid Then
        Dim dbcontrol As New ReviewerDB
        dbcontrol.ConnectionString = ConnectionString
        dbcontrol.ProductID = ProductID
        dbcontrol.InsertReview(txtName.Text, txtReview.Text, _
                               Integer.Parse(rblRating.SelectedItem.Value))
        _displayThankYouNote = True
    End If
End Sub
```

Note that we're setting an internal flag, _displayThankYouNote, to True after inserting the user's review into the database. We are doing this so when it comes to render time, the control can show a "Thank you" message instead of its regular UI with all the fields for taking user input.

Once again, we use the power of overriding the Render method for this.

```
Protected Overrides Sub Render(ByVal writer As System.Web.UI.HtmlTextWriter)
    If (_displayThankYouNote) Then
        RenderThankYouNote(writer)
    Else
        MyBase.Render(writer)
    End If
End Sub
```

If we find the flag has been set, then we call a helper render method (RenderThankYouNote) that just displays a nice message to the user; if the flag has not been set, meaning we need to render the UI for taking user input, then we just call the base implementation of Render, which will ultimately end up causing the rendering of all the children for our user control (its textboxes, radio button list, etc.).

Demonstration

Before we start demonstrating any of the controls developed in this chapter, we need to properly set up the ReviewsDB database.

Setting Up the ReviewsDB Database

Launch Microsoft SQL Server Enterprise Manager, select the Databases node of the target SQL Server within the tree view in the left pane, right-click over it, and select All Tasks ➤ Attach Database.... Enter the path to where you have extracted the ReviewsDB database file provided in the code download (see Figure 11-2).

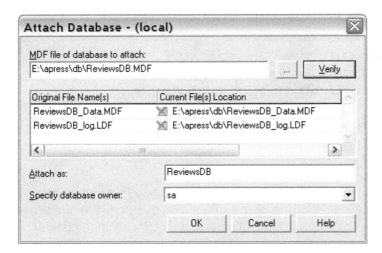

Figure 11-2. *Attach Database dialog box*

After accepting the previous dialog by clicking OK, a new ReviewsDB database will be attached to your SQL Server and you should see a message with the legend "Attaching database has completed successfully."

If you are running MSDE, or just happen to *not* have the Microsoft SQL Server Client Tools installed on your machine, you can still create the ReviewsDB database by using the osql.exe utility. Please read the instructions provided in the readme.txt file in the code download to learn how to do this. (You can find the code samples for this chapter in the Downloads section of the Apress Web site at http://www.apress.com.)

Testing Our Controls

Let's start with the LastReview control. Create a new blank Web form, drag a LastReview control from the toolbox, and set the following properties:

- ConnectionString to the Microsoft SQL Server database

- ProductID to 1

- MaxChars to 200

You should see the control transforming its output from "No reviews for the specified product were found" to a table containing the last review, as seen in Figure 11-3.

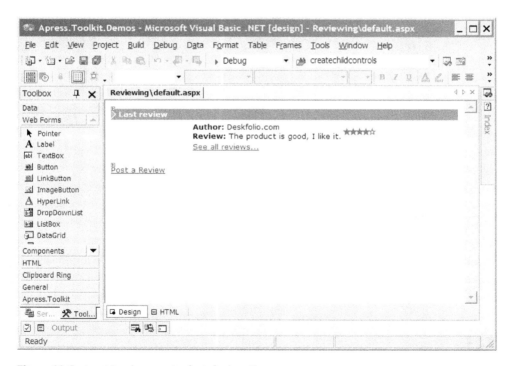

Figure 11-3. LastReview *control at design time*

Testing the Average control is almost identical to testing the LastReview control. Repeat the same steps we just described, this time dragging an Average control without setting the MaxChars property (as this control doesn't provide one).

Finally, let's see the ReviewerForm user control in action. Begin by creating a new blank Web form and drag the ReviewerForm.ascx over it. You won't be able to set the custom properties for this user control using the Property Inspector, as this is not supported by Visual Studio .NET, so you'll have to set the ConnectionString and ProductID properties either declaratively as attributes or from code in the Page_Load event handler. The results of browsing the review.aspx page containing the ReviewerForm.ascx user control are shown in Figure 11-4.

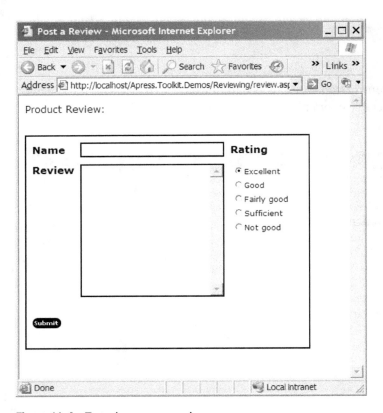

Figure 11-4. *Entering a new review*

Limitations

One of the major limitations of our design is that it does not take into account the possibility of badly behaved users who abuse the reviewing functionality by submitting multiple reviews on the same product, thus trying to cheat the results. As a measure against this, we could limit the review submissions to one review per IP address, but this may prevent valid users (those sharing the same proxy server for instance) from submitting their reviews. We could try using cookies as a way to detect when a user has already submitted a review for a given product, or we may want to limit reviewing to registered users. In the next chapter, we will take a detailed look at these options.

Extensions

As we have seen, when a user inserts a new review, its status is set to *pending*. We could code an admin page that would display a DataGrid showing all reviews with a pending status and a button to easily modify the page. A good start would be to add a parameter to the GetAllReviews stored procedure to specify the review status (currently, it is returning only approved reviews). Also, a trigger to the Reviews table could be added to send an e-mail to the administrator to inform her that a new review has been submitted and it's waiting for approval.

Another interesting extension would be to allow users to reply if a given review was helpful. This way you encourage serious reviewers to respond, while readers can trust the reviews done by those reviewers who have good reputations for making useful comments.

CHAPTER 12

■ ■ ■

Straw Poll

With the increasing interest in community sites of all kinds, an easy way to conduct polls is becoming an important feature of any such site. It helps you get to know your user base and to measure their views and opinions on different topics. In this chapter, you'll learn how to develop a set of controls that will make it easy to add this functionality to your Web applications.

Scenario

The purpose of a Straw Poll control is to display a multiple-choice question along with the relevant choices in a bulleted list. The user then selects one of the choices, usually anonymously. In addition, users can view the poll's current results. These results could be presented in many different ways, depending on the look and feel of the Web site.

One factor that needs to be taken into consideration to make the results as fair as possible is preventing users from casting multiple votes and thus rigging the results.

In this chapter, we'll build two custom controls—one to display the polls and another to display the poll results. This gives the developer who implements the control full freedom to customize the control as per the Web site needs.

Technology

We'll build the Straw Poll control as a composite custom control; we have already covered the requirements for such controls in Chapter 1. A working knowledge of XML and XML Schema will be helpful since the control uses an XML file as its data source (more on this in the next section). The control relies on the power of the DataSet object, which allows it to easily work with data from any source (in our case, an XML file). Even programmers who are not well versed in XML can utilize the DataSet object to easily access data. Another advantage derived from using the DataSet is that it can be cached very easily; this helps to increase overall performance.

Design

There are three main design decisions that need to be resolved before developing the Straw Poll control as they will affect its functional design: control separation, data source selection, and abuse prevention.

Control Separation

Straw Polls have two logical parts: the first part displays the poll question along with the relevant choices to allow the user to vote for an option, and the second part displays the results of the poll. We could package both these features into a single control, but easy customization is a key factor when developing controls. If you observe the usage of Straw Poll controls on existing Web sites, you'll find that most Web sites like to display the poll controls and their results separately. Taking a hint from the existing usage patterns, we are going to build two separate controls. Nevertheless, you can merge the two controls into a single one if you wish, and provide a way (an enumeration property for example) for the user to select which part or parts to display.

Data Source Selection

In Chapter 11, we made the choice to make the controls work against a database. In order to see a different approach, in this chapter we'll use a simple XML file instead. In this file, we are going to store the poll question and choice of answers plus the votes captured from users. Of course, if you wanted to, you could store any additional information, such as the IP address of the machine from where a vote has been submitted (in order to simplify this, our controls will expose an event that we can listen for).

Choosing an XML file as our data storage has some pros, such as being able to quickly and easily edit the file, for example, if you wanted to correct a typo in the poll question or change one of the available answers. On the cons side, the most obvious one is the problem arising from multiple instances of our controls trying to write to the same file at the same time. We will need to code with this in mind in order to avoid locking issues.

Abuse Prevention

Malicious users may try to rig the poll by casting multiple votes, so that their preferred choice wins. With the current Internet infrastructure, there is no way to totally prevent this sort of abuse if you are conducting anonymous polls. One technique is to record the IP address of the user casting the vote and to disallow any consecutive votes from the same address. This technique, although widely used, has two flaws. The first flaw concerns the privacy of the user; it might actually break privacy guidelines if you were to record the IP address, as your poll no longer remains anonymous. The second flaw is that many users share IP addresses with other users, maybe through a proxy server. This means that a legitimate user may be prohibited from voting if a proxy server is used; moreover, the same user could have a different IP address (and thus submit a new vote) every time he connects to his ISP.

Another technique is to restrict the user from voting more than once during a session. This technique prevents the basic abuse of poll results. The hack, in this case, consists of the user firing another browser instance, starting a new session, and voting again.

A different alternative is to store a cookie on the user's browser, so your control can track the user every time he returns to the voting page. However, some browsers do not support cookies, or some users explicitly turn them off—in these cases, we deny their vote. This should alienate only a very small user base and is the approach we are using for our control.

Implementation

As we just mentioned, the Straw Poll control will use an XML file as its backend data store. Therefore, we'll start by defining the XML Schema that the control will support, and then we'll follow with details on each one of the controls.

Poll Schema

Figure 12-1 is the diagrammatic representation of our schema file, as shown in VS .NET's editor.

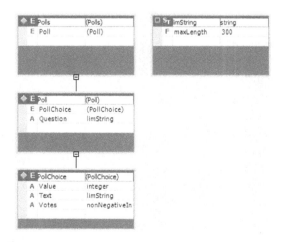

Figure 12-1. *Poll schema definition*

<Polls> is the root element. This element contains a single occurrence of the <Poll> element. We could have defined multiple occurrences here, but although it could be useful to use XSLT or some other code to merge numerous files together, it makes sense here

to keep each file small, so in the schema, the <Polls> element has exactly one <Poll> child. The <Poll> element holds all the crucial data for our control. It has an attribute called Question, which contains the poll question. Nested within the <Poll> element are the <PollChoice> elements that define the multiple-choice options for the poll. These elements have three attributes: Value, Text, and Votes. The Value attribute holds the value of the poll item, the Text attribute holds the actual text shown to the user, and the Votes attribute contains the number of votes for the particular PollChoice.

Inside the <Poll> element, a uniqueness constraint is defined. This specifies that the Value attributes of the <PollChoice> elements must be unique inside each Poll element. We have defined a new simple type called limString. This is used to limit the length of the string that can be used to phrase the question or poll choice to 300 characters.

```xml
<?xml version="1.0" ?>
<xs:schema id="Polls" targetNamespace="http://Apress.com/XmlPoll.xsd"
         xmlns:mstns="http://Apress.com/XmlPoll.xsd"
         xmlns="http://Apress.com/XmlPoll.xsd"
         xmlns:xs="http://www.w3.org/2001/XMLSchema"
         elementFormDefault="qualified">
  <xs:element name="Polls" >
    <xs:complexType>
      <xs:sequence>
        <xs:element name="Poll">
          <xs:complexType>
            <xs:sequence>
              <xs:element name="PollChoice"
                        minOccurs="1"
                        maxOccurs="unbounded">
                <xs:complexType>
                  <xs:attribute name="Value"
                              type="xs:integer" />
                  <xs:attribute name="Text"
                              type="xs:limString" />
                  <xs:attribute name="Votes"
                              type="xs:nonNegativeInteger" />
                </xs:complexType>
              </xs:element>
            </xs:sequence>
            <xs:attribute name="Question"
                        type="xs:limString" />
          </xs:complexType>
          <xs:unique name="uniqueValues">
            <xs:selector xpath="." />
            <xs:field xpath="PollChoice/@Value" />
```

```
        </xs:unique>
      </xs:element>
    </xs:sequence>
  </xs:complexType>
</xs:element>
<xs:simpleType name="limString">
  <xs:restriction base="xs:string">
    <xs:maxLength value="300" />
  </xs:restriction>
</xs:simpleType>
</xs:schema>
```

The following listing shows a sample XML file that conforms to the above XML Schema, and so is usable by the Straw Poll controls. This particular file is called PollDetails.xml. For each poll question used in your Web site, you will have a new XML file.

```
<?xml version="1.0" ?>
<Polls xmlns="http://Apress.com/PollDetails.xsd">
  <Poll Question="Which is your favorite .NET language?">
    <PollChoice Value="1" Text="C#" Votes="0" />
    <PollChoice Value="2" Text="VB.NET" Votes="0" />
    <PollChoice Value="3" Text="Managed C++" Votes="0" />
    <PollChoice Value="4" Text="JScript.NET" Votes="0" />
    <PollChoice Value="5" Text="J#.NET" Votes="0" />
    <PollChoice Value="6" Text="Other" Votes="0" />
  </Poll>
</Polls>
```

XmlPoll and XmlPollResult Controls

The two UI controls will have some similar functionality and so we create an abstract (MustInherit) class for them to derive from. We'll also declare an EventArgs object and delegate objects to deal with an event that is fired when a vote is cast.

Our first control will be a composite custom control named XmlPoll. Its job will be to load the user-specified XML file and build the relevant UI to display the poll question along with its multiple choices. In addition, this control will be responsible for saving the user's vote back to the XML file. It will also fire an event that may allow you to capture additional user information should you wish to.

In addition, we'll code another control, XmlPollResult, for dealing with the display of poll results in a graphic way.

Arguments of Our Custom Event

As previously mentioned, the XmlPoll control raises an event when a vote is cast. To be of any use for the code listening to that event, it should include information about the poll choice's value and text. Hence, we create a custom VoteEventArgs class, derived from System.EventArgs. As shown here, the VoteEventArgs class constructor takes two parameters: the text of the selected poll choice and its value, to initialize its private fields. It also exposes both of these values as properties.

The following is the VoteEventArgs class:

```
Imports System
Imports System.Web.UI
Imports System.Data
Imports System.IO
Imports System.Web.UI.WebControls
Imports System.Web.Caching
Imports System.Web

Namespace Apress.Toolkit
  Public Class VoteEventArgs
    Inherits System.EventArgs

    Private _voteValue As String
    Public Property VoteValue As String
      Get
        Return Me._voteValue
      End Get

      Set(ByVal value As String)
        Me._voteValue = Value
      End Set
    End Property

    Private _voteText As string
    Property VoteText As String
      Get
        Return Me._voteText
      End Get

      Set(ByVal value As String)
        Me._voteText = Value
      End Set
    End Property
```

```
   Sub New(ByVal voteText As String, ByVal voteValue As String)
     Me._voteValue = voteValue
     Me._voteText = voteText
   End Sub
End Class
```

The PollBase Base Class

As mentioned already, we'll define an abstract base class where our two controls will inherit from in order to gain some common functionality used by both of them. We'll name this class PollBase and make it inherit from Control. Contained within this class is a protected DataSet and some Style variables; these will enable the developer to easily modify the look and feel of the control. At the beginning of the code is a private property that will be used by the LoadXml() method later, in partnership with the Context.Cache object, to ensure the file system is not read from too often.

```
Public MustInherit Class PollBase
   Inherits Control

   Protected xmlSet As DataSet

   Private ReadOnly Property cacheString As String
     Get
       Return Me.UniqueID & "xmlSet"
     End Get
   End Property

   Private _questionStyle As Style = New Style()
   Private _tableStyle As TableStyle = New TableStyle()
   Private _headerItemStyle As TableItemStyle = New TableItemStyle()
   Private _bodyItemStyle As TableItemStyle = New TableItemStyle()
   Private _footerItemStyle As TableItemStyle = New TableItemStyle()
```

Now we create public properties to access these private fields, as follows:

```
Public Property QuestionStyle As Style
   Get
     Return Me._questionStyle
   End Get

   Set(ByVal value As Style)
     Me._questionStyle = value
```

```vbnet
      End Set
   End Property

   Public Property TableStyle As WebControls.TableStyle
      Get
         Return Me._tableStyle
      End Get

      Set(ByVal Value As WebControls.TableStyle)
         Me._tableStyle = value
      End Set
   End Property

   Public Property XmlFile As String
      Get
         If ViewState("xmlFile") Is Nothing Then
            Return String.Empty
         Else
            Return CType(ViewState("xmlFile"), String)
         End If
      End Get

      Set(ByVal value As String)
         ViewState("xmlFile") = value
      End Set
   End Property
```

The last property shown here, XmlFile, is one of the core properties required by our control. The XmlFile property holds the full path of the XML file, for example: C:\Inetpub\ wwwroot\ApressToolkit\PollDetails.xml. This file is used to populate the control. The rest of the properties just access the various private Styles variables defined previously, and so they are not all displayed in the previous listing.

Loading the Data

The LoadXml() method deals with the problem mentioned earlier: when multiple instances of the control access the XML file, there can be file-locking problems. To tackle this, the XML file is opened using a System.IO.FileStream object. The overload of the FileStream object's constructor, which takes a FileShare enumeration as a parameter, is used. Setting the FileShare enumeration to ReadWrite ensures there will be no file locking.

In addition, the SyncLock keyword is used to ensure that, at a given time, only one thread can execute the code inside the block. The code within the SyncLock block is executed only once, no matter how many different threads are calling this method. We use the string object returned from the XmlFile property for the exclusive lock.

```
SyncLock Me.XmlFile
```

Since it is not likely that every user visiting the site is going to cast a vote, the poll data remains moderately static. This fact is used to our advantage by caching the DataSet filled with data from our XML file to increase the performance of the control. ASP.NET's built-in caching features are quite extensive; we are using one of them that allows us to invalidate a cache based upon changes made to a dependent file. In our case, we would like the cache to be invalidated when the underlying XML file is updated; this can be done very easily using the CacheDependency class from the System.Web.Caching namespace. The following line of code adds a cache dependency on the XML file:

```
Dim cacheDepend As CacheDependency = New CacheDependency(Me.XmlFile)
```

The full listing of the LoadXml() method is shown next. This same method is used by our controls to read in the poll data.

```
Protected Sub LoadXml()
  If Context.Cache(Me.cacheString) Is Nothing Then
    If File.Exists(Me.XmlFile) Then
      Dim readStream As FileStream
      Try
        readStream = New FileStream(Me.XmlFile, FileMode.Open, _
            FileAccess.Read, FileShare.ReadWrite)
        Me.xmlSet = New DataSet()
        SyncLock Me.XmlFile
          Me.xmlSet.ReadXml(readStream)
        End SyncLock
        Dim cacheDepend As CacheDependency = _
            New CacheDependency(Me.XmlFile)
        Context.Cache.Insert(Me.cacheString, Me.xmlSet, _
                          cacheDepend)
      Finally
        readStream.Close()
      End Try
    Else
      Throw New ArgumentException("The XML data source file " _
          & "does not exist!")
    End If
```

```
        Else
            Me.xmlSet = CType(Context.Cache(cacheString), DataSet)
        End If
    End Sub
  End Class
End Namespace
```

The XmlPoll Control

Now we can start building the controls. The following is the code for the XmlPoll control:

```
Imports System
Imports System.Web.UI
Imports System.Data
Imports System.IO
Imports System.Web.UI.WebControls
Imports System.Web.Caching
Imports System.Web

Namespace Apress.Toolkit
  Public Class XmlPoll
    Inherits PollBase
    Implements INamingContainer
    Public Event VoteCast As VoteCastEventHandler
    Private optList As RadioButtonList
    Private _optionStyle As Style = New Style
    Private _buttonStyle As Style = New Style
    Private _renderView As RenderView = RenderView.Poll
```

The XmlPoll class implements the INamingContainer marker interface and derives from PollBase. We are also defining a new event, VoteCast, which—as we said before—is raised once a valid vote is cast. Two further properties need to be added to this control, and they are shown here:

```
    Public Property OptionStyle As Style
      Get
        Return _optionStyle
      End Get

      Set(value As Style)
        _optionStyle = value
      End Set
    End Property
```

```
    Property ButtonStyle As Style
      Get
        Return _buttonStyle
      End Get
Set(value As Style)
        _buttonStyle = value
      End Set
    End Property
```

These properties are straightforward and require no explanation.

Creating the XmlPoll's Child Controls

We are overriding the CreateChildControls() method in order to create the bulk of our control's UI. Depending on the current value of the _renderView private field, our control will create different child hierarchies. The first two cases are the simpler ones, and for both of them our control will create only one child, a Label control, used to output a message.

```
If (_renderView = RenderView.DuplicateVote) Then
   Dim lbl As Label = New Label
   lbl.Text = "You've already voted in this poll."
   Controls.Add(lbl)
   Return
ElseIf (_renderView = RenderView.ThankYouNote) Then
   Dim lbl As Label = New Label
   lbl.Text = "Thank you for voting!"
   Controls.Add(lbl)
   Return
End If
```

The real work happens when the _renderView field is set to RenderView.Poll. First, the LoadXml() method, inherited from the PollBase class, is called to load the data from the XML file.

```
    MyBase.LoadXml()

    Dim table As New Table()
    table.ApplyStyle(Me.TableStyle)
```

Once the data is loaded, a Table object is created and added to the Controls collection of the current control. We also apply the TableStyle to the Table using the ApplyStyle() method, which is inherited from the WebControl class. Hence, the consumer has full access to modify the style of the table generated by our XmlPoll control by merely changing the value of the TableStyle property.

```
Dim headerRow As TableRow = New TableRow()

Dim questionLabel As Label = New Label
questionLabel.ApplyStyle(QuestionStyle)
questionLabel.Text = Me.xmlSet.Tables("Poll").Rows(0)("Question").ToString()

Dim headerCell As TableCell = New TableCell
headerCell.Controls.Add(questionLabel)
headerRow.Cells.Add(headerCell)
headerRow.ApplyStyle(HeaderItemStyle)

table.Rows.Add(headerRow)
```

In this code, a new TableRow and Label are created. The Text property of the Label is set to the question of the poll retrieved from the DataSet. This occurs by retrieving the collection of tables using the Tables property, then retrieving the Poll table by name under the default property. Then we retrieve the specific row by accessing the RowCollection using the Rows property and using the default property to retrieve the first one. Finally, using the default property, we find the cell under the column named Question. Then the Label is added to a TableCell, which is inserted into a TableRow, which, ultimately, gets added to a Table.

```
Dim bodyRow As TableRow = New TableRow()

optList = New RadioButtonList()
With optList
  .ApplyStyle(OptionStyle)
  .DataSource = Me.xmlSet.Tables("PollChoice")
  .DataTextField = "Text"
  .DataValueField = "Value"
  .DataBind()
  .SelectedIndex = 0
End With

Dim bodyCell As TableCell = New TableCell()
bodyCell.Controls.Add(optList)

bodyRow.Cells.Add(bodyCell)
bodyRow.ApplyStyle(BodyItemStyle)
table.Rows.Add(bodyRow)
```

A new TableRow is used to hold the RadioButtonList control. The RadioButtonList control is populated from the DataSet and is databound to the Text and Value columns of the PollChoices table. Finally, the RadioButtonList is added to a TableCell, which is then added to the TableRow, which is inserted into the Table. Notice here as well that we are setting the Style for the TableRow and the RadioButtonList.

```
    Dim pollButton As Button = New Button()
    pollButton.ApplyStyle(ButtonStyle)
    pollButton.Text = "Vote!"

    AddHandler pollButton.Click, AddressOf Me.PollButton_Click

    Dim footerRow As TableRow = New TableRow()
    Dim footerCell As TableCell = New TableCell()

    footerCell.Controls.Add(pollButton)
    footerRow.Cells.Add(footerCell)
    footerRow.ApplyStyle(FooterItemStyle)
    table.Rows.Add(footerRow)

    MyBase.Controls.Add(table)
End Sub
```

In the final block of the CreateChildControls() method, one more TableRow is added and this time it is populated with a Button control. The event handler for the Click event of the button is defined and the button is added to the table.

Processing the Vote Submission

Now you can see the event handler for the pollButton.Click event.

```
Private Sub PollButton_Click(ByVal sender As Object, ByVal e As _
                             EventArgs)
  If Context.Request.Browser.Cookies Then
    Dim cookieKey As String = Me.UniqueID
    Dim cookieValue As Integer = _
      Me.xmlSet.Tables("Poll").Rows(0)("Question").GetHashCode()
```

The PollButton_Click() method is called when the user submits a vote. This method first checks if the user's browser supports cookies. If so, two important variables are created: cookieKey, which is based on the UniqueID property of the poll control to ensure that the cookie key remains unique across a Web application. The poll question is also retrieved from the DataSet, its hash is calculated from the string value, and this is stored in the cookieValue variable. The GetHashCode() method of the string class returns the hash of the string it references as an integer, which is calculated to be unique across all string instances you might create.

```
            Dim pollCookie As HttpCookie = _
                    Context.Request.Cookies.Item("pollCookie")
            If pollCookie Is Nothing Then
                AddVote(cookieKey, CStr(cookieValue))
            Else
                If Not pollCookie.Values(cookieKey) = CStr(cookieValue) Then
                    AddVote(cookieKey, CStr(cookieValue))
                Else
                    SetRenderView(RenderView.DuplicateVote)
                End If
            End If
        End If
    End Sub
```

First, a check is made to see if a cookie by the name of "pollCookie" exists. If not, then the user is voting for the first time, so a call to the AddVote method is made. The cookieKey and string representation of cookieValue are passed to this method.

If the cookie exists, we also compare the hash code stored in the cookie with the current hash code. If they don't match, the question must have changed and so the user is allowed to vote by calling the AddVote() method. Instead, if we detect a cookie containing a key that matches the current poll, then we prohibit the user from voting again and show a proper message by calling the SetRenderView method with RenderView.DuplicateVote as its parameter.

Let's see what AddVote looks like.

```
    Private Sub AddVote(ByVal cookieKey As String, ByVal cookieValue As String)
        SaveXml(cookieKey, CStr(cookieValue))
        WriteCookie(cookieKey, CStr(cookieValue))
        SetRenderView(RenderView.ThankYouNote)
        Me.OnVoteCast(New VoteEventArgs(Me.optList.SelectedItem.Text, _
        Me.optList.SelectedItem.Value))
    End Sub
```

First, it calls SaveXml to add the new vote to the data file. Then it calls WriteCookie, which will take care of writing the new key/value to a cookie to identify that the user has already voted for this particular pool. Finally, the proper view is set and the VoteCast event is fired.

Adding a New Vote

Now let's look at each one of the tasks performed by AddVote, starting with the SaveXml() method, which is used to save the user's vote to the XML file.

```
Private Sub SaveXml(ByVal cookieKey As String, _
                    ByVal cookieValue As String)
   Dim selRow As DataRow() = _
      Me.xmlSet.Tables("PollChoice").Select("Value = " & _
      Me.optList.SelectedItem.Value)
```

It first extracts the DataRow object from the DataTable using the DataTable.Select() method. Since the values from each poll item will be unique, it is safe to assume that only a single DataRow is returned from the Select() method as long as the XML file is valid. Let's continue with the code that updates the DataSet, as follows:

```
Dim votes As Integer = CType(selRow(0)("Votes"), Integer)
selRow(0)("Votes") = votes + 1

Me.xmlSet.AcceptChanges()

Dim writeStream As FileStream
Try
    writeStream = New FileStream(Me.XmlFile, FileMode.Truncate, _
            FileAccess.Write, FileShare.ReadWrite)
    SyncLock Me.XmlFile
        Me.xmlSet.WriteXml(writeStream)
    End SyncLock
Finally
    If Not writeStream Is Nothing Then
        writeStream.Close()
    End If
End Try
End Sub
```

Here, we retrieve the Votes column from the DataRow, increment its value, and set it back to the DataRow. The AcceptChanges() method is called on the DataSet to make the change permanent. Finally, the DataSet is written to the XML file using a FileStream object, in a similar way that is used for the LoadXml() method. You can see the SyncLock come into use here. This control can never read and write concurrently. If the LoadXml() method wants to read the file, it has to wait until this SaveXml() method has finished writing and releases the exclusive lock on the object, and vice versa.

After updating the XML file, we need to update the cookie sent to the client to indicate participation in a particular pool.

```
    Private Sub WriteCookie(ByVal cookieKey As String, _
ByVal cookieValue As String)
        Dim pollCookie As HttpCookie = Context.Request.Cookies("pollCookie")
```

```
        If (pollCookie Is Nothing) Then
            pollCookie = New HttpCookie("pollCookie")
        End If
        pollCookie.Values.Add(cookieKey, cookieValue)
        pollCookie.Expires = DateTime.MaxValue
        Context.Response.Cookies.Add(pollCookie)
    End Sub
```

First, we try to get an existing pollCookie to update and if none is found, we just create a new one. Its expiration is set to the maximum DateTime value so it does not expire. The cookieKey and cookieValue variables are added to the cookie and the cookie is added to the response that will be sent to the browser.

The next step is to set the proper render view using the simple SetRenderView method.

```
    Private Sub SetRenderView(ByVal renderView As RenderView)
        _renderView = renderView
        ChildControlsCreated = False
    End Sub
```

As a last step, all that remains is to cause the firing of the VoteCast event, for which a call to OnVoteCast is made.

```
    Me.OnVoteCast(New VoteEventArgs(Me.optList.SelectedItem.Text, _
    Me.optList.SelectedItem.Value))
```

The Text and Value of the user-selected poll choice are passed as parameters to the VoteEventArgs class.

The OnVoteCast method raises the VoteCast event, passing along the appropriate parameters.

```
    Protected Overridable Sub OnVoteCast(ByVal voteDetails As _
                                         VoteEventArgs)
        RaiseEvent VoteCast(Me, voteDetails)
    End Sub
  End Class
End Namespace
```

This method completes the implementation of the XmlPoll control.

Displaying Poll Results

As we have already mentioned, we are also coding an XmlPollResult control whose purpose will be to show a poll's result graphically. The design and implementation of this control is very similar to the earlier control, except that instead of displaying the RadioButtonList, it displays the results of the poll. There are a few different ways you can display the results to the user. These can range from showing the number of votes using plain text to using images (a pie chart, for instance). In this implementation, a 1×1 pixel GIF image (mostly single color) is used and the image stretches depending on the number of votes. This gives an effect of columns that change their size to match the number of votes. Also, the user of this control could choose a color for the image that matches the overall Web site design.

We'll code this control as a composite custom control; let's see the code for it now.

```
Imports System
Imports System.Web.UI
Imports System.Data
Imports System.IO
Imports System.Web.UI.WebControls
Imports System.Web.Caching

Namespace Apress.Toolkit
  Public Class XmlPollResult
    Inherits XmlPollBase
    Implements INamingContainer
```

Most of the properties and fields needed by this control are already derived from XmlPollBase, but we need to define a new one, ImageSrc, to hold the image used for the bar.

```
    Public Property ImageSrc() As String
      Get
        Dim o As Object = ViewState("imageSrc")
        If Not (o Is Nothing) Then
            Return CType(o, String)
        Else
            Return String.Empty
        End If
      End Get

      Set(ByVal value As String)
        ViewState("imageSrc") = value
      End Set
    End Property
```

As with the `XmlPoll` control, we'll be overriding `CreateChildControls()` in order to create the control's UI. We're also calling the inherited `LoadXml()` method in the overridden `CreateChildControls`, like we did with `XmlPoll`.

```
Protected Overrides Sub CreateChildControls()
    Controls.Clear()
    MyBase.LoadXml()

    Dim table As table = New table()
    table.ApplyStyle(TableStyle)

    Dim questionLabel As Label = New Label()
    questionLabel.ApplyStyle(QuestionStyle)
    questionLabel.Text = Me.xmlSet.Tables("Poll").Rows(0)("Question")

    Dim headerCell As TableCell = New TableCell()
    headerCell.Controls.Add(questionLabel)
    Dim noOfRows As Integer = _
                Me.xmlSet.Tables("PollChoice").Rows.Count
    headerCell.ColumnSpan = 3

Dim headerRow As TableRow = New TableRow()
    headerRow.Cells.Add(headerCell)
    headerRow.ApplyStyle(HeaderItemStyle)
    table.Rows.Add(headerRow)
```

Note that the first lines of this method are identical to the ones of `XmlPoll`'s `CreateChildControls()` method. The one difference is that the `ColumnSpan` property for the cell containing the question is equal to the number of columns in the table. This means it will straddle the entire graph.

```
Dim TotalVotes As Integer = 0
Dim pos As Integer
Dim dr As DataRow

For Each dr In Me.xmlSet.Tables("PollChoice").Rows
    TotalVotes += CType(dr("Votes"), Integer)
Next
```

Here, we iterate through each row in the data table and add the number of votes to a running total.

```
For Each dr In Me.xmlSet.Tables("PollChoice").Rows
    Dim pollRow As TableRow = New TableRow
```

```
Dim nameCell As TableCell = New TableCell
nameCell.Width = Unit.Percentage(50)
nameCell.Controls.Add(New LiteralControl(dr("Text").ToString()))

Dim imgCell As TableCell = New TableCell
imgCell.Width = Unit.Percentage(35)
```

The previous For Each loop creates a new row in each step, adds a new cell to contain the text of the poll question, and defines a new cell that will be used to contain the line. The code then dynamically resizes the Width property of the image specified to stretch the provided image according to the percentage of votes.

```
Dim voteCount As Integer
voteCount = CType(dr("Votes"), Integer)
Dim img As Image = New Image
img.ImageUrl = Me.ImageSrc
'Calculate the % for width
img.Width = Unit.Percentage((CDbl(voteCount) / _
        CDbl(TotalVotes)) * 100)
img.Height = Unit.Parse("15")
imgCell.Controls.Add(img)
```

The rest of the code flows in a similar fashion and should be simple to follow without requiring any additional explanation.

```
'Add the % and number of votes
Dim valueCell As TableCell = New TableCell
valueCell.Width = Unit.Percentage(15)
valueCell.Controls.Add(New LiteralControl( _
        img.Width.Value.ToString("0.00") & _
" (" & voteCount.ToString() & ")"))
        pollRow.Cells.Add(nameCell)
        pollRow.Cells.Add(imgCell)
        pollRow.Cells.Add(valueCell)
```

At the end of the method, the last rows are added to the table and the table is added as the child controls of the control.

```
        pollRow.ApplyStyle(BodyItemStyle)
        table.Rows.Add(pollRow)
    Next
    'Add footer
    Dim footerRow As TableRow = New TableRow
```

```
        Dim footerCell As TableCell = New TableCell
        footerCell.ColumnSpan = 3 ' Changed
        footerCell.Controls.Add(New LiteralControl("Total Votes: " & TotalVotes))

        footerRow.Cells.Add(footerCell)
        footerRow.ApplyStyle(FooterItemStyle)
        table.Rows.Add(footerRow)

        Me.Controls.Add(table)
    End Sub
End Class
```

This completes the implementation details of our controls.

Demonstration

Let's start by testing our XmlPoll control first; create a Poll.aspx page and add the following:

```
<%@ Page Language="VB" %>
<%@ Register TagPrefix="Apress" Namespace="Apress.Toolkit"➡
 Assembly="Apress.Toolkit" %>
<script runat="server">
  Private Sub Page_Load(ByVal sender As System.Object, _
                        ByVal e As System.EventArgs) Handles MyBase.Load
    StrawPoll.XmlFile = Server.MapPath("PollDetails.xml")
    StrawPoll.TableStyle.BorderColor = System.Drawing.Color.Red
    StrawPoll.TableStyle.BorderWidth = New Unit(2)
    StrawPoll.QuestionStyle.ForeColor = System.Drawing.Color.Gray
  End Sub
</script>
<html>
<head>
</head>
<body>
  <form runat="server">
    <Apress:XmlPoll id="StrawPoll" runat="server"></Apress:XmlPoll>
    <br><br>
    <asp:HyperLink id="HyperLink1" runat="server"
          NavigateUrl="PollResult.aspx">Result</asp:HyperLink>
  </form>
</body>
</html>
```

After browsing the page, you should get the following screen (see Figure 12-2) and be able to submit your vote.

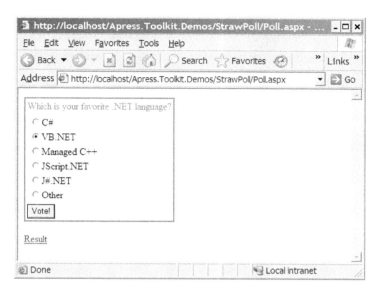

Figure 12-2. *Submitting a vote*

Now let's display the poll results with our XmlPollResults control. Create a new page named PollResult.aspx with the following code:

```
<%@ Page Language="VB" %>
<%@ Register TagPrefix="Apress" Namespace="Apress.Toolkit"➥
 Assembly="Apress.Toolkit" %>
<script runat="server">
  Private Sub Page_Load(ByVal sender As System.Object, _
                        ByVal e As System.EventArgs) Handles MyBase.Load
    StrawPollResult.XmlFile = Server.MapPath("PollDetails.xml")
    StrawPollResult.TableStyle.BorderColor = System.Drawing.Color.Red
    StrawPollResult.TableStyle.BorderWidth = New Unit(2)
    StrawPollResult.ImageSrc = Server.MapPath("bar.gif")
  End Sub
</script>
<html>
<head>
</head>
<body>
  <form runat="server">
```

```
    <Apress:XmlPollResult id="StrawPollResult" runat="server">
    </Apress:XmlPollResult>
  </form>
</body>
</html>
```

After browsing to the newly created page, you should get a screen showing the poll results, as shown in Figure 12-3.

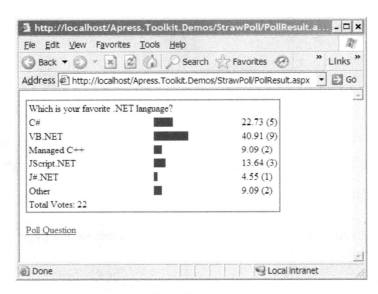

Figure 12-3. *Displaying the poll results*

Limitations

The main limitation for the current controls is related to the approach they take for storing data. They use an XML file for storing the answers to the questions and the number of votes cast and no other data source. Of course, this might not be a serious drawback, but some application implementations might require you to use a relational database. However, you could expose an XmlDataSet property where the user directly supplies a DataSet to the control, which could be fetched from any other data source, like SQL Server. Of course, you'll have to make a few changes in the SaveXml() method of the PollBase control to stop saving to the XML file. You could then handle the VoteCast event and update your data source with the user vote.

Extensions

As mentioned in the "Limitations" section, you can extend the controls by exposing the various databinding properties and methods to allow the user to bind the control to any sort of data source. You can also make the Straw Poll control expose events, where you can embed custom code to process the user's selection. In fact, you can use the Straw Poll control even in some forms when you want to redirect users to pages depending upon the selection made by the user.

One possible extension would be to hook this up to a Web service. This would enable multiple Straw Polls on many different sites to operate concurrently. It would require an update to the LoadXml() and SaveXml() methods to access the Web service methods in this case.

CHAPTER 13

RSS Reader

If you've ever created a portal Web site, you know how difficult it can be to integrate frequently changing content from multiple sources. In the past, Web developers have resorted to various tricks and workarounds to accomplish this goal, most of which require a considerable amount of custom code (mainly scrapping code) and are liable to break when the source Web site is modified in any way. The introduction of .NET and Web services improved the situation, but only partly. The problem is that even though Web services provide a consistent, cross-platform model for exchanging information, there is still no guarantee that different Web services will expose functionality in a similar way. This means that you may need to master dozens of similar, yet different, class models before you can aggregate third-party content.

The only way to solve this sort of problem is to adhere to a common format for exposing content. One of the most promising players is RSS, an XML markup designed for content syndication. RSS provides a consistent model for aggregating links in an XML document (for example, newspapers articles). This allows portal sites to integrate up-to-the-minute information from hundreds of different sites. For a basic overview of RSS formats and a FAQ document, you can refer to the material provided by Dave Winer at `http://backend.userland.com/stories/rss`.

This chapter shows a component that lets you leverage the RSS format with ASP.NET, and link to content feeds from any RSS source on the Internet. Best of all, you'll have complete control over the display formatting and use of this information.

Scenario

RSS was first developed by Netscape in 1999 for its My Netscape portal, to allow the site to quickly and generically combine a broad range of content. The idea was that users could choose their favorite sites and, provided they exposed RSS feeds, read the content from a single centralized location. Although RSS can theoretically be used to expose and describe any Web content, it's most commonly used for news syndication. The power of the format comes from the large base of existing RSS users. With RSS, you can find category-specific news from high-tech publishers like ZDNet, Wired, and Slashdot, traditional news sources like CNN, the BBC, and the *New York Times*, international media like *Le Parisien* and the *Arab News*, and specialized channels like *Scientific American, Linux French*, and even *The Matrix Online*!

A number of promising uses of the RSS format quickly come to mind, as follows:

- *You can create a news-browsing engine that allows the user to search through an enormous catalog of material, viewing articles from multiple sources*: We'll demonstrate this at the end of this chapter.

- *You could integrate a specific RSS feed into a part of your site*: For example, a Web site for developers might want to devote a small portion of real estate to the Visual Studio Magazine feed. You could even allow the user to choose a favorite RSS feed.

- *You can create a specialized news-searching program that checks the descriptions of articles in multiple feeds for important words, and displays the results*: For example, you could have it check for programming articles about ASP.NET.

- *You could retrieve RSS feed information and use it with any other .NET control*: For example, you might randomly select an article for a headline of the day, or incorporate a series of feed links into a scrolling news ticker.

All these scenarios can be implemented quite easily with the RSS Reader component developed in this chapter.

Technology

The RSS Reader builds upon the RSS format. The component will be developed to work with the first widely accepted version of the RSS Specification, v0.91. There are also other versions of RSS: 0.90, 0.92, 0.94, and 2.0. The basic RSS format defines a single `<channel>` element, which provides a linked image, title, description, and site URL. This information describes the RSS feed. In the `<channel>` element are multiple `<item>` elements, each of which identifies a single resource and provides a title, link, and description.

Tip RSS is not an acronym, although it has been called Rich Site Summary, RDF Site Summary, and Really Simple Syndication at different times. For information about the RSS format, refer to `http://backend.userland.com/rss091`.

The content provider updates its RSS file regularly. In fact, for many providers, the RSS file isn't actually a file at all—instead, it's generated dynamically (much like an .aspx page) by reading current information from a database. The RSS file has a simple goal: to describe one or more resources on the provider's Web site. The actual resource isn't contained in the RSS file. Instead, it can be found by following the embedded link.

For example, here's a shortened excerpt of what an RSS file looks like. It's been reduced to a single item, which corresponds to a news story.

```
<rss version="0.91">
  <channel>
    <title>Foo News Site</title>
    <link>http://www.FooNewsSite.com/</link>
    <description>This is the Foo News Site, always providing the most updated Foo
news to you.</description>
    <pubDate>Sun, 17 October 2004 04:10 PST</pubDate>

    <item>
    <title>A Foo News Title</title>
    <link>http://www. FooNewsSite.com/news/foo1.htm</link>
    <description>This is the description for the First Foo News.
By Catalina Angelinetti.</description>
    </item>

    <!-- Other items omitted. -->

  </channel>
</rss>
```

The goal of the RSS Reader component is simple. It needs to understand the RSS format in order to parse it and translate it into a more useful form. In this case, that more useful form will be a custom collection object that can easily be manipulated and bound to a control for display.

Of course, though it's useful to be able to read an RSS document, it still requires the end user (or the programmer) to know where to find useful RSS feeds. Several organizations have leaped to fill this gap, although there is no consistent standard. For example, Syndic8 provides an XML-RPC service that allows you to retrieve lists of feeds based on specific criteria (see http://www.syndic8.com/services.php). On the other hand, NewsIsFree (http://www.newsisfree.com) provides a list of popular feeds in an XML document, using a nonstandardized RSS-like format. Being able to access these feed lists is extremely useful, because it allows you to build an all-purpose news browser.

Design

The RSS Reader is implemented as a component, not a control, which gives the developer the complete control they need to use the information in any way. For example, the information can be displayed directly on screen in a formatted list, or used to power another component like a news ticker. Best of all, the RSS Reader can be used in any type of application, from an ASP.NET Web page to a simple Console command-line utility.

The RSS Reader implementation is divided into two parts. The core part is a set of custom data objects that model the different kinds of information found in an RSS document. These objects have three goals, as follows:

- *Make it easy to manipulate RSS content by offering strongly typed classes*: For example, thanks to IntelliSense, it's much easier to find a property like `RssItem.Title` than to try to find the corresponding element in an `XmlDocument` object.

- *Allow easy databinding by exposing key RSS data as properties*: The different RSS collection objects inherit from `CollectionBase`, meaning you can easily bind them to any Web or Windows control that supports databinding, including the ASP.NET `DataList` and `DataGrid` controls.

- *Hide the lower-level details of the actual format from the developer using our component*: Ideally, the RSS objects should be able to hold RSS information, regardless of the RSS Specification version used.

The RSS data objects include an `RssItem` (representing an individual link in a channel), `RssItemCollection` (a strongly typed collection of links), `RssChannel` (a document with a collection of links and additional information about their source), and `RssImage` (an image attached to a channel). You can find their source code in the file named `RssDataObjects.vb`. (You can find the code samples for this chapter in the Downloads section of the Apress Web site at `http://www.apress.com`.)

The second part of the RSS Reader component is the reader that will take a URL, parse an XML document, and return the appropriate RSS object. This class is named `RssReader`, and it derives from the base `Component` class in the `System.ComponentModel` namespace. This class is found in the file named `RssReader.vb`.

In addition, we will include classes that can model an RSS feed list and read it from a URL. These classes are considered tentative, because there is still not much agreement on how the underlying format should look. However, they are ready to use with current RSS feed documents. This set of classes includes the `RssFeedItem` and `RssFeedItemCollection` data objects, and the `RssFeedListReader` reader. They are all coded in the file named `RssFeedListUtility.vb`.

.NET provides several classes that can read XML documents, including XmlTextReader and XmlDocument. Both of these support retrieving a document directly from a URL. The RSS Reader uses the XmlDocument class, which makes it easier to extract specific node trees by name. Rather than use these classes, you could implement the RSS Reader component using the .NET Framework's support for XML serialization. However, this approach is not ideal in this situation. The key problem is that different versions of the RSS Specification use different element names for functionally equivalent pieces of information, including the link (which is included as a <link>, <enclosure>, or <guid> element depending on the version of the RSS Specification). By implementing a separate RssReader class, you gain the ability to handle these discrepancies using conditional code, and return a common set of standardized objects. Also, having the extra layer of indirection provided by the FeedReader class allows other features to be transparently implemented if needed, like validation or custom type conversion. Otherwise, these wouldn't be as easy to implement as with the higher-level serialization framework.

Implementation

The first part of the RSS Reader is the RssChannel class, which models the entire RSS document. It retains information like a title, site link, description, and an image, which is encapsulated in a separate RssImage object. The RssChannel also provides a collection of RssItem instances.

What follows is the code for the RssChannel. You'll notice that the property implementation code has been omitted for brevity. About every private member has a corresponding public property exposing it.

```
Public Class RssChannel

    Private _DocumentVersion As String
    Private _Title As String
    Private _Link As String
    Private _Description As String

    Private _Image As New RssImage()
    Private _Items As New RssItemCollection()

    '(Property procedures omitted.)

End Class
```

The RssImage class is similarly straightforward, as follows:

```
Public Class RssImage

    Private _PictureUrl As String
    Private _Title As String
    Private _Link As String

    '(Property procedures omitted.)

End Class
```

Each RssItem represents an individual resource in the RSS channel (typically a news article), like so:

```
Public Class RssItem

    Private _Title As String
    Private _Link As String
    Private _Description As String

    '(Property procedures omitted.)

End Class
```

Multiple RssItem objects could be grouped into an ArrayList or similar collection, but we use a strongly typed custom collection instead called RssItemCollection. This ensures that the wrong objects can't be added to the collection. The RssItemCollection inherits from CollectionBase, which gives it access to a protected List member (the collection of items). The Add() and Remove() methods access this List to change the contents of the collection.

```
Public Class RssItemCollection
    Inherits System.Collections.CollectionBase

    Public Sub Add(ByVal item As RssItem)
        List.Add(item)
    End Sub

    Public Sub Remove(ByVal index As Integer)
        If index > Count - 1 Or index < 0 Then
            Throw New ArgumentException( _
                "No item at the specified index.")
```

```
        Else
            List.RemoveAt(index)
        End If
    End Sub


    Default Public Property Item(ByVal index As Integer) As RssItem
        Get
            Return CType(List.Item(index), RssItem)
        End Get
        Set(ByVal Value As RssItem)
            list.Item(index) = Value
        End Set
    End Property
End Class
```

The next step is to define the RssReader class that can process an RSS document and generate the corresponding data objects. The RssReader class contains a single method, GetChannel(), which accepts a URL to an RSS feed. First, the document is loaded into an XmlDocument object. Then, the GetElementsByTagName() method is used to extract specific nodes. If the file is known to have only one instance of a given node (as with the <channel> element), then the first result is selected.

```
Imports System.Xml


Public Class RssReader


    Public Function GetChannel(ByVal channelUrl As String) _
        As RssChannel


        'Load the XML document from the specified URL.
        Dim Document As New XmlDocument()
        Dim Node As XmlNode, Nodes As XmlNodeList
        Document.Load(channelUrl)


        'Create and configure the Channel.
        Dim Channel As New RssChannel()


        'Point to <rss> element to get the version.
        Node = Document.GetElementsByTagName("rss")(0)
        Channel.DocumentVersion = Node.Attributes("version").Value
        'Point to <channel> element.
        Node = Document.GetElementsByTagName("channel")(0)
        Channel.Title = Node.Item("title").InnerText
```

```
            Channel.Link = Node.Item("link").InnerText
            Channel.Description = Node.Item("description").InnerText

            'Set the image.
            Node = Document.GetElementsByTagName("image")(0)
            If Not (Node Is Nothing) Then
                Channel.Image.Title = Node.Item("title").InnerText
                Channel.Image.PictureUrl = Node.Item("url").InnerText
                Channel.Image.Link = Node.Item("link").InnerText
            End If

            'Get all <item> nodes.
            Nodes = Document.GetElementsByTagName("item")
            For Each Node In Nodes
                Dim Item As New RssItem()
                Item.Title = Node.Item("title").InnerText
                Item.Link = Node.Item("link").InnerText
                If Not (Node.Item("description") Is Nothing) Then
                    Item.Description = Node.Item("description").InnerText
                End If
                Channel.Items.Add(Item)
            Next

        Return Channel
    End Function
End Class
```

The following is the basic outline of the expected RSS document structure:

```
<rss version="">
  <channel>
    <title />
    <link />
    <description />

    <image>
      <title />
      <url />
      <link />
    </image>

    <item>
      <title />
```

```
      <link />
      <description />
   </item>

   <!-- Other items omitted. -->

  </channel>
</rss>
```

The `<item>` element can be repeated any number of times.

Finally, the classes used for reading RSS feed lists use a similar approach. The feed list is made up of individual channel descriptions, which are similar to the `<channel>` element in the RSS file, but have less information (for example, no image). In the RSS Reader component, the `RssFeedItem` class represents the following:

```
Public Class RssFeedItem

    Private _Title As String
    Private _Link As String
    Private _Description As String

    '(Property procedures omitted.)

End Class
```

Tip The `RssFeedItem` class resembles the `RssItem` class. However, they have no relation, and so we won't use inheritance or any other type of object relationship. An `RssFeedItem` instance represents a link to an RSS document. An `RssItem` instance represents a link to another resource in an RSS document, typically a Web page.

There is also a dedicated `RssFeedItemCollection` class, which is shown here:

```
Public Class RssFeedItemCollection
    Inherits System.Collections.CollectionBase

    Public Sub Add(ByVal item As RssFeedItem)
        List.Add(item)
    End Sub
```

```
Public Sub Remove(ByVal index As Integer)
    If index > Count - 1 Or index < 0 Then
        Throw New ArgumentException( _
            "No item at the specified index.")
    Else
        List.RemoveAt(index)
    End If
End Sub

Default Public Property Item(ByVal index As Integer) _
  As RssFeedItem
    Get
        Return CType(List.Item(index), RssFeedItem)
    End Get
    Set(ByVal Value As RssFeedItem)
        list.Item(index) = Value

    End Set
End Property
```

End Class

Finally, an RssFeedListReader class exposes a GetFeedList() method that returns an RssFeedItemCollection for a specified URL.

```
Public Class RssFeedListReader
    Inherits System.ComponentModel.Component

    Public Function GetFeedList(ByVal feedUri As String) As
RssFeedItemCollection
        'Load the XML document from the specified URL.
        Dim Document As New XmlDocument
        Dim Node As XmlNode, Nodes As XmlNodeList
        Document.Load(feedUri)

        'Create and configure the feed list.
        Dim Feeds As New RssFeedItemCollection

        'Get all 'channel' nodes.
        Nodes = Document.GetElementsByTagName("channel")
        Dim x As Integer
        For Each Node In Nodes
```

```
            Dim Feed As New RssFeedItem
            Feed.Title = Node.Item("title").InnerText
            Feed.Link = Node.Item("link").InnerText
            Feed.Description = Node.Item("description").InnerText
            Feeds.Add(Feed)
        Next
        Return Feeds
    End Function

End Class
```

Demonstration

Now that the RSS Reader component is complete, it's time to see it in action. To demonstrate how easy it is to use to the RSS Reader, let's try a page that presents a list of feeds. This list will be rendered using a bound DataList displaying the feed title and description, plus a button to link to each feed.

Browse to the NewsBrowser.aspx file to see how the DataList is setup.

```
<asp:DataList id="listFeeds" runat="server" BorderColor="#CC9966" BorderStyle="None"
BackColor="White" CellPadding="6" GridLines="Both" BorderWidth="1px" Font-
Names="Verdana" Font-Size="X-Small" Width="460px">
    <ItemStyle ForeColor="#330099" BackColor="White"></ItemStyle>
    <ItemTemplate>
        <asp:Button CommandName="<%# CType(Container.DataItem, RssFeedItem).Link%>"
        Text="Select" runat="server" ID="Button1"/>
        <b><%# CType(Container.DataItem, RssFeedItem).Title %><br></b>
<font size="1"><%# CType(Container.DataItem, RssFeedItem).Description %></font>
        <br>
    </ItemTemplate>
</asp:DataList>
```

Note how, after properly casting the RssFeedItem instance, we're accessing its Link, Title, and Description properties to output their values as part of the ItemTemplate.

The code-behind file has the code to handle the source for the feed list and to bind it to a DataList; it also causes a redirect to the ViewFeed.aspx page to show the posts for a given feed when a button is clicked.

```
Private Sub Page_Load(ByVal sender As System.Object, ByVal e As System.EventArgs) _
                                                        Handles MyBase.Load

        If Not Me.IsPostBack Then
```

```
        Dim FeedReader As New RssFeedListReader()
        Dim Feeds As RssFeedItemCollection
        Feeds = FeedReader.GetFeedList("http://weblogs.asp.net/MainFeed.aspx")
        listFeeds.DataSource = Feeds
        listFeeds.DataBind()
    End If
End Sub

Private Sub listFeeds_ItemCommand(ByVal source As Object, ByVal e As _
                    DataListCommandEventArgs) Handles listFeeds.ItemCommand
    Response.Redirect("ViewFeed.aspx?url=" & Server.UrlEncode(e.CommandName))
End Sub
```

The output of this simple test is shown in Figure 13-1. No special formatting has been applied.

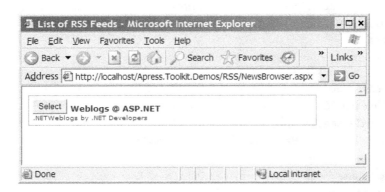

Figure 13-1. *Browsing for RSS feeds*

Once you click the Select button, a redirect to ViewFeed.aspx will happen and you should get a detailed view of each one of the contained items in the feed, as shown in Figure 13-2.

As you can see from the preceding image we're using a DataList again, this time to present each feed item.

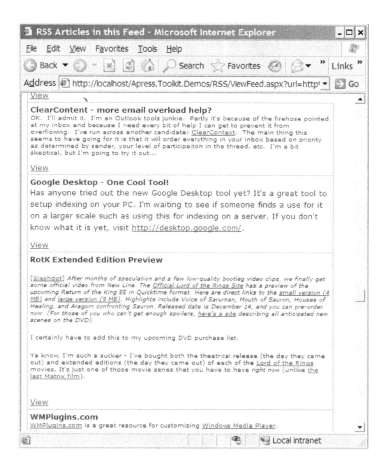

Figure 13-2. *Viewing an RSS feed*

```
<asp:datalist id="DataList1" runat="server" Font-Size="X-Small" Font-Names="Verdana"
BorderWidth="1px" GridLines="Both" CellPadding="4" BackColor="White"
BorderStyle="None" BorderColor="#CC9966"
Width="500px" Height="269px">
    <ItemStyle ForeColor="#330099" BackColor="White"></ItemStyle>
    <ItemTemplate>
        <b><%# CType(Container.DataItem, RssItem).Title %></b><br><font size="1">
        <%# CType(Container.DataItem, RssItem).Description %></font><br>
<a href="<%# CType(Container.DataItem, RssItem).Link %>">View</a><br>
    </ItemTemplate>
</asp:datalist>
```

And the code found in the code-behind file (ViewFeed.aspx.vb) takes care of binding the feed items to the DataList instance.

```
Private Sub Page_Load(ByVal sender As System.Object, ByVal e As System.EventArgs) _
                                                        Handles MyBase.Load
    If Not Me.IsPostBack Then
        Try
            Dim Rss As New RssReader
            Dim Channel As RssChannel
            Channel = Rss.GetChannel(Request.QueryString("url"))

            DataList1.DataSource = Channel.Items
            DataList1.DataBind()
        Catch Err As Exception
            lblError.Text = "Invalid feed format.<br><br>"
            lblError.Text &= Err.Message
        End Try
    End If
End Sub
```

Limitations

Currently, the RSS Reader component works well as a simple, flexible way to incorporate information from RSS feeds into your application. However, it lacks a few niceties, such as the following:

- *It doesn't provide any way to validate RSS documents, and if an error occurs while reading one, it doesn't provide specific error information that could be used to track the source of the incompatibility*: The System.Xml namespace includes some basic validation features that you could build on.

- *It's wasn't designed to support RSS versions higher than 0.91, the first widely accepted version of the RSS format*: It will also work with most other versions, but it could include more support. For example, there are still several optional RSS elements that are sometimes used, but aren't supported by the RssReader component.

- *The RSS component is designed only for reading RSS documents*: There is no support for authoring your own RSS documents, although this could be added.

Extensions

There are numerous directions you can take to extend the RSS Reader. You might want to develop a custom ASP.NET or Windows control that works with the RSS Reader component to display information in a customizable way. This would probably be implemented in a separate assembly, allowing the RSS Reader component to remain independent and free of any links to the Windows Forms or ASP.NET development platforms. Also, you might want to add increased support for other versions of the RSS standard and optional elements.

Support for newer versions of the RSS Specification, like v2.0, would be a great extension as more and more content providers are already switching to it.

One of the most interesting advances would be to improve the RSS Reader to allow RSS authoring. This would be a fairly straightforward task—you would simply implement an RssWriter class with a WriteDocument() method. The programmer would construct an RssChannel object, and convert it to an XML file with the WriteDocument() method. This method could save it directly to disk or, more usefully, return a stream or an XmlDocument instance that you could manipulate at will.

CHAPTER 14

■ ■ ■

Search Engine

Most large Web sites provide some sort of search capability. Often, this search feature is tailored to a specific type of content, like a repository of white papers or news articles, but it can also be used to search all the ordinary Web pages hosted on a site. There are dozens of ways to implement such a search technology, from custom server-side products like Microsoft Index Server (included in server versions of Windows), to handcrafted application-specific solutions. This chapter presents a solution between these two extremes, with a custom indexing component that can support multiple formats.

No matter what searching approach you take, you have to make compromises. Some of the questions you face include the following:

- *How much content do you index?* A full-text search may be more accurate, but it will be more time-consuming, and require more server resources for storage. It also might crowd out relevant keywords by the sheer number of indexed words.

- *How do you tailor the search to your type of content?* Often, information will be stored in a proprietary format like an XML document with a defined schema. If your indexing tool can understand this format, it can index the most relevant information. However, this requires the indexing code to be limited to a specific type of document, or be prohibitively complex.

- *How do you store the index information?* Index information, especially if large, is normally best stored in a relational database. But for small solutions, such as the one we'll present here, you might find that other options, such as a file-based index, work just as well.

- *How do you parse the search query?* Once you've created the index, you need a system for executing search queries. If your information is stored in a database, you may want to use SQL commands. Otherwise, it's up to you to handle the whole process, eliminate unimportant words, identify required and optional words, and rank the results.

In addition, you have to decide how often you'll generate the index, and how you'll generate it. This could be accomplished by using a dedicated long-running component, triggering a rebuild by invoking a Web service method, or by using some other mechanism. It is technically possible to index pages just before a search is conducted to ensure up-to-the-minute information, but this approach exerts such a performance burden on a Web server that it's almost never used.

This chapter will present a library of ASP.NET components that allow you to add simple search capabilities to your Web pages using HTML <meta> tags to seed the index. There will be two halves to the implementation, as follows:

- An *indexer*, which examines URLs and creates a list of keywords. Special care is taken to make the solution as generic and extensible as possible, so you can tailor it for specific types of documents. The only assumption the indexing component makes is that the document will be downloaded over HTTP. It can easily be a Web page, XML document, or even a proprietary binary file. The index, once created, is serializable, and could easily be stored in a file on disk, or as binary or XML data in an external database.

- A *searcher*, which performs searches against the indexed information, and retrieves a list of ranked results. It supports the following features:

  - Ranking of results based on proportion of matched terms. For example, if three out of five terms are matched in a search, the rank percentage will be 60%.

  - Support for phrases. Depending on the mode, terms can be grouped together in phrases using quotation marks. These terms will be evaluated as an atomic unit in the search, without losing the embedded space character.

  - Support for a basic *match-any* search mode, along with a more restrictive *match-all* mode.

  - Support for advanced queries where specific terms are designated as required, optional, or excluded.

  - Automatic stripping out of identified special characters and noise words from a phrase (like "a" and "and").

  - Canonicalization of terms into a standard format.

Of course, language parsing is a complex and subtle issue. There are numerous possible extensions to query syntax that the search component *doesn't* support. We'll look at these limitations at the end of this chapter, and consider some ways you can address them.

Scenario

It's not hard to realize uses for a search component. It can be used to index the pages on a single Web site, or specific related resources on a variety of sites. You might choose to index every `.html`, `.aspx`, and `.asp` page on your site, or you might restrict it to a set with specific resources.

The value of such a search engine depends on how easily it can be incorporated into existing solutions, and the quality of the generated results. The search component in this chapter relies on a relatively small set of page-specific keywords, rather than indexing all the words in a document. This means that it works best in scenarios where the number of indexed pages is large; otherwise, there is a strong possibility that many queries will be executed without returning any results. This is less of a risk when using a search technology that indexes entire pages, because there will be a much larger number of indexed keywords.

There is both a short and a long path to incorporating the functionality from the search component into your own Web sites. The short path involves adding `<meta>` tags to all your existing HTML pages. The search component can then work with these pages, because the indexer (which actually creates the indexes) would recognize `<meta>` tag information. The longer path involves creating a specialized indexer that will work with the search component to generate keywords for proprietary types of content (like a product record in a company-specific XML format). In theory, there is no limit to the type of content the indexer can process, although you won't be able to work with complex third-party formats (like a Microsoft Word document), unless you know exactly how they are structured.

Typically, the search component will be used in conjunction with the search indexer to provide access to pages on a single Web site. The search hits are returned using `SearchHit` and `SearchHitCollection` objects that support databinding. Thus, you can quickly take the retrieved matches, and bind them to a control like the `DataGrid` or `DataList` to create a basic search page.

A search component like this needs to walk a fine line between simplicity and customizability. Commonly used search options, like phrase matching, are implemented using public properties. By modifying these properties, the consuming application can change the behavior of the search. However, lower-lever features, like the steps performed by the parsing engine, cannot be customized as easily, and may require a component rewrite.

Technology

There are two main aspects to this control, indexing and query parsing, so we'll look at each part individually.

Indexing

The large search engines of the Internet, like Yahoo!, AltaVista, Excite, and Google, each use a variety of techniques for indexing pages. Some search engines make use of the <meta> tags that are located in the head of a Web page to derive information about a page's content. AltaVista, for example, indexes this information. More complex modern search systems don't trust a page to tell the truth in its <meta> headers, and rely on other factors to rate a site's usefulness for a particular search. However, for our basic indexing purposes, <meta> tags will do fine.

The <meta> tags used for content description only require a couple of lines of HTML code, and are easy to add to any existing Web page. These <meta> tags also have a well-known, identifiable format. For example, the following are the <meta> tags describing the MSDN site:

```
<META NAME="Description" CONTENT="MSDN Home"/>
<META NAME="Keywords" CONTENT="MSDN, microsoft, developer, network, developer
resources, microsoft developer resources"/>
```

<meta> tags are found in the <head> section of an HTML document, and are never displayed in the browser. Their ease of use, and the fact that they are used by a majority of Web sites, makes them a good choice for index information in the search component.

In addition to <meta> tags, the component relies on .NET platform technologies, such as the WebRequest and WebResponse classes (for downloading information), regular expressions (for locating <meta> tags in a Web page), and serialization (for storing index information). This means the search component will not be tightly coupled to a specific data store (like SQL Server). It's entirely up to you how you want to store the index data. Because the index is serializable, you can use a file (as our examples will), or store it directly in a database field.

Query Parsing

Search engines often include fairly advanced parsing logic to analyze queries. Unfortunately, there is no tool in the .NET Framework that can automate this kind of processing. You'll need to code this logic manually. The search component used in this chapter does save some steps by using the built-in enumerating capabilities of the String object and the specialized StringCollection, which provides a Contains() method that allows you to quickly search the collection for the occurrence of a specific string.

The search component breaks its work into four discrete tasks, which are executed by separate procedures. The steps are as follows:

1. Begin by stripping out special characters that should be ignored. This task is performed first, because the query is still contained in a single string.

2. Next, break down the query into word elements. Depending on the type of search mode, this may return a collection of optional, required, and excluded words.

3. Normalize the query words. Because the search component uses text matching, you must agree on a standard form for all words. This includes stripping off extra spaces, converting the string to lowercase, and removing any unimportant noise words. At the same time, you could use smart synonym substitution to get preferred terms, or strip off word suffixes to normalize verb forms such as "programming" to the root "program."

4. Perform the search with the query terms. Each page will be ranked according to how many terms it matches.

Design

As mentioned earlier, the search component is divided into two parts, a search indexer (described in this chapter) and a search parser. This separation provides flexibility in how the index will be created and stored, without affecting how the index information will be parsed in a search. This division also makes it impractical to carry out a real-time search, because the index generation takes time. Instead, as with most search systems, searches must be performed using a preexisting index that has been stored in a file or database. This limitation is acceptable, because a real-time search would be typically quite slow, and would waste valuable server processing time, especially for a high-traffic Web site.

The rest of the design follows these guidelines:

- *The indexing process is customizable*: That means you can plug in your own indexers that examine certain types of documents and specify the proper keywords. Or, you can use the default, which works with <meta> tag keywords.

- *The index objects are serializable*: That means you can store index information easily, using a local file, a field in a database, or some other type of data source. In this chapter, we'll simply store the index information in a flat file on the Web server.

- *An indexer can be invoked through a variety of helper methods*: That means you have the flexibility to index an individual page, a list of pages, or an entire group of pages in a specific directory.

The search component is optimized for simplicity. This means that the query processing steps identified previously are performed in separate passes. This can add to the amount of time needed to process a query, but it ensures that the code is much easier to alter, enhance, and troubleshoot. Where possible, some tasks are collapsed into a single pass. For example, noise words are identified at the same time that words are converted to a common representation, because this is all part of the query normalization.

The search component exposes some details publicly, making it possible to specify the following information:

- The collection of indexed pages to use

- Restrictive (match all) or permissive (match any) search mode

- Phrase matching

- Characters that will be ignored

- Characters that will be converted to spaces

- Noise words that will be removed

- Whether to treat single-character words as noise words

In order to determine the appropriate defaults for the search component, you must consider the type of indexing. By default, the index is generated using <meta> tags, which include only a small set of words. For this reason, it makes sense to default the query component to *match any*; otherwise, more detailed queries will probably find no results, because the number of indexed keywords is fairly small. We can increase the value of searches of this sort by scoring pages more highly if they match more keywords in the search.

Implementation

We'll start with the indexer project.

Indexer

Figure 14-1 gives a bird's eye view of all the classes in the indexing part of our component. The classes shaded in gray represent data objects that store index information, while the other classes work together to implement the indexing functionality. Both the SearchIndexer and the IndexFileUtility class derive from System.ComponentModel.Component.

All of these classes are grouped into the Apress.Toolkit.SearchEngine namespace. So, our first task is to create a class library to hold all these types.

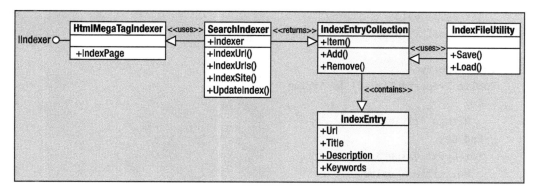

Figure 14-1. Indexing classes

The first step is to define the custom classes used to store index information. In this case, two custom classes are required: IndexEntry (which stores index information for a single page), and a corresponding IndexEntryCollection (a strongly typed collection that stores IndexEntry instances).

The IndexEntry object stores four pieces of information: the URL of the page, the title of the page, a description for the page, and a list of comma-separated keywords. These are implemented using properties (rather than public member variables), which ensures that the class can be used with databinding, and follows good design practices. Finally, the <Serializable> attribute is added to the class to ensure that the framework can serialize the data. Let's see just a fragment of this class, as its implementation is pretty trivial.

```
Imports System

Namespace Apress.Toolkit.SearchEngine

  <Serializable()> _
  Public Class IndexEntry
    Private _url As String
    Private _title As String
    Private _description As String
    Private _keywords As String

    Public Property Url() As String
      Get
        Return Me._url
      End Get
```

```
      Set(ByVal value As String)
        Me._url = value
      End Set
    End Property
    Public Property Title() As String
      Get
        Return _title
      End Get
      Set(ByVal value As String)
        Me._title = value
      End Set
    End Property
```

The IndexEntryCollection also includes the <Serializable> attribute, ensuring that you will be able to serialize a group of indexed pages. As with any collection, you can also add and remove specific members, as well as iterate through the entire contents. The easiest way to create a custom collection is simply to derive from the CollectionBase class in the System.Collections namespace, and implement strongly typed methods as shown in the following code:

```
Imports System

Namespace Apress.Toolkit.SearchEngine
  <Serializable()> _
  Public Class IndexEntryCollection
    Inherits System.Collections.CollectionBase

    Public Sub Add(ByVal item As IndexEntry)
      List.Add(item)
    End Sub

    Public Sub Remove(ByVal index As Integer)
      If index > Count - 1 Or index < 0 Then
        Throw New ArgumentException( _
            "No item at the specified index.")
      Else
        List.RemoveAt(index)
      End If
    End Sub
```

```
   Default Public Property Item(ByVal index As Integer) As IndexEntry
      Get
         Return DirectCast(List.Item(index), IndexEntry)
      End Get
      Set(ByVal value As IndexEntry)
         List.Item(index) = value
      End Set
   End Property
   End Class
End Namespace
```

The next component is the indexer that examines the page and creates the corresponding `IndexEntry` object. As discussed earlier, there are a number of ways that a list of keywords can be derived from a document. A truly flexible search engine would be able to support several different indexing approaches, and be able to use different indexers with different types of content. However, you must be able to describe the resource using the properties in the `IndexEntry` class.

To facilitate this design, we'll create an interface that defines an indexer class. In order to function as an `IIndexer`, a class must provide a method that reads a stream of information and returns the `IndexEntry` object with the keyword information.

```
Imports System.IO

Namespace Apress.Toolkit.SearchEngine

   Public Interface IIndexer
      Function IndexPage(ByVal pageContent As Stream, _
                         ByVal url As String) As IndexEntry
   End Interface
End Namespace
```

You can now create `IIndexer` classes to index any document you desire. For our example, we'll simply build an `IIndexer` that works with `<meta>` tags. This indexer needs to read a stream, and find the `<meta>` tag elements shown earlier to determine the description and keywords. In addition, it will retrieve the title, if defined.

There are a number of ways to extract this information from a supplied stream. One approach would be to read the stream character-by-character, searching for the start of the tag. Another approach would be to retrieve the entire document as a string variable, and search the string with a regular expression, which allows for much more straightforward coding. The drawback is that the memory usage will be increased, especially if the page is large. However, the indexing process only deals with one page at a time, and will not be executing in parallel in service of multiple Web requests, so this is the approach used in the `HtmlMetaTagIndexer` in this example.

The following code is the declaration of the `HtmlMetatagIndexer`:

```
Imports System.IO
Imports System.Text.RegularExpressions

Namespace Apress.Toolkit.SearchEngine

    Public Class HtmlMetaTagIndexer
        Implements IIndexer
```

The next step is to craft the regular expression that will be used to find the `<meta>` tag keywords. It might occur to you to use the following simple expression:

```
<meta name="keywords" content=".*"
```

This regular expression matches any string that starts with `<meta name="keywords" content=` followed by a variable-length string of characters, and then a closing quotation mark. The sequence `.*` means "any number of non-newline characters" (technically, the period represents "any non-newline character," and the asterisk means "any number of the preceding character"). However, this expression is extremely inefficient, because it performs its matching by counting backward from the end of the document. It also can't cope with multiple whitespace characters between tag attributes.

A better approach is to divide the regular expression into two strings, which can be added to the `HtmlMetaTagIndexer` as private constants. The first string matches the initial portion of the tag with the name attribute.

```
    Private Const NameRegexPattern As String = _
        "<meta\s+name\s*=\s*(""|')"
```

The second string matches the content attribute, and retrieves the required information into a group named `<match>`.

```
    Private Const ContentRegexPattern As String = _
        "\1\s+content\s*=\s*(""|')\s*(?<match>.*?)\s*\2\s*/?>"
```

Finally, a third pattern is required to create the regular expression that will match the `<title>` element.

```
Private Shared TitlePattern As String = _
    "<title>(?<match>.*?)</title>"
```

You can now add the regular expression objects that use these patterns as private shared members, as follows:

```
Private Shared MetaKeywords As New Regex(NameRegexPattern _
    & "keywords" & ContentRegexPattern, _
    RegexOptions.IgnoreCase Or RegexOptions.Singleline)

Private Shared MetaDescription As New Regex(NameRegexPattern _
    & "description" & ContentRegexPattern, _
    RegexOptions.IgnoreCase Or RegexOptions.Singleline)

Private Shared TitleRegex As New Regex(TitlePattern, _
    RegexOptions.IgnoreCase Or RegexOptions.Singleline)
```

The IndexPage function will use these objects to retrieve information to configure a new IndexEntry object. First, it retrieves the HTML from the page as a string.

```
Public Function IndexPage(ByVal pageContent As Stream, ByVal url As String) As _
IndexEntry Implements IIndexer.IndexPage

        Dim Reader As New StreamReader(pageContent)
        Dim Html As String = Reader.ReadToEnd()
        Reader.Close()
```

Next, it retrieves the keywords for the page. Note that if no keywords can be located, a null reference is returned instead, indicating that the page cannot be cataloged.

```
    Dim KeywordMatch As Match = MetaKeywords.Match(Html)
    Dim Keywords As String
    If KeywordMatch.Success Then
      Keywords = KeywordMatch.Groups("match").Value
    End If

    If Keywords = String.Empty Then
      'This page should not be indexed.
      Return Nothing
    End If
```

Now, the code uses the same approach to retrieve the description, as seen here:

```
    Dim DescriptionMatch As Match = MetaDescription.Match(Html)
    Dim Description As String
    If DescriptionMatch.Success Then
      Description = DescriptionMatch.Groups("match").Value
    End If
```

Finally, it retrieves the title and returns a new `IndexEntry` object that encapsulates all the page information.

```
Dim TitleMatch As Match = TitleRegex.Match(Html)
Dim Title As String
If TitleMatch.Success Then
  Title = TitleMatch.Groups("match").Value
End If

Dim Entry As IndexEntry = New IndexEntry(url)
Entry.Title = Title
Entry.Description = Description
Entry.Keywords = Keywords
Return Entry
    End Function
  End Class
End Namespace
```

At this point, the search indexer functionality is all in place. However, it's also helpful to create a utility class that will start the indexing process at the client's request. This class should accept a user-supplied `IIndexer`, and use it to catalog a single URL, or a group of URLs by repeatedly calling the `IIndexer.IndexPage()` method.

It includes a public `IndexUrl()` method that calls a private `IndexPage()` method with the supplied URL. (The reason for this division will become clear in the next example. It allows you to create a variety of indexing methods without repeating the same code.)

```
Imports System
Imports System.Net
Imports System.IO

Namespace Apress.Toolkit.SearchEngine

  Public Class SearchIndexer
    Inherits System.ComponentModel.Component

    Private _indexer As IIndexer

    Public ReadOnly Property Indexer() As IIndexer
      Get
        Return _indexer
      End Get
    End Property
```

```vb
Public Sub New()
  Me.New(New HtmlMetaTagIndexer())
End Sub

Public Sub New(ByVal indexer As IIndexer)
  If indexer Is Nothing Then
    Throw New ArgumentNullException("indexer", _
        "Must pass in an IIndexer object.")
  Else
    Me._indexer = indexer
  End If
End Sub

Public Function IndexUrl(ByVal url As String) As IndexEntry
  Return IndexPage(url)
End Function

Private Function IndexPage(ByVal url As String) _
                        As IndexEntry

  If url Is Nothing Then
    Throw New ArgumentNullException("url", _
      "Url can't be null")
  ElseIf url = String.Empty Then
    Throw New ArgumentException("url", _
      "Url can't be an empty string")
  End If

  Dim Request As HttpWebRequest = WebRequest.Create(url)
  Dim Response As WebResponse = Request.GetResponse()
  Return _indexer.IndexPage(Response.GetResponseStream(), url)
End Function
```

When indexing pages, the SearchIndexer uses the IIndexer specified by the Indexer property, which can be passed in through a constructor argument at run time.

NOTE The SearchIndexer utility class does not handle the exceptions that will be thrown for invalid URLs or network troubles. These errors will be propagated directly to the client, which has the ability to correct them accordingly. If you wanted to, you could catch exceptions and rethrow them with additional information.

This is the basic form of the SearchIndexer, but it can be easily improved by adding new indexing methods. For example, consider the following method, which allows you to create an index for an entire collection of pages by submitting an array of URL strings:

```
Public Function IndexUrls(ByVal urls() As String) _
               As IndexEntryCollection

    Dim Index As New IndexEntryCollection()
    Dim Url As String
    For Each Url In urls
      Dim Page As IndexEntry = IndexPage(Url)
      If Not (Page Is Nothing) Then Index.Add(Page)
    Next
    Return Index
End Function
```

Or consider the IndexSite() method, which provides an easy way to automate index creation for a single virtual directory. You supply the base URL and the physical directory, and the method automatically indexes all .aspx, .asp, .htm, and .html files it finds. Note that each page is still opened over HTTP using the URL (rather than directly from the hard drive). Although this is slower, it ensures that the URL is correct and the page is accessible.

```
Public Function IndexSite(ByVal baseUrl As String, _
    ByVal physicalPath As String) As IndexEntryCollection
    If Not baseUrl.EndsWith("/") Then baseUrl &= "/"
    Dim Index As New IndexEntryCollection()
    Dim SiteDirectory As New DirectoryInfo(physicalPath)
    Dim File As FileInfo
    For Each File In SiteDirectory.GetFiles()
      If File.Extension.ToLower = ".aspx" Or _
        File.Extension.ToLower = ".asp" Or _
        File.Extension.ToLower = ".htm" Or _
        File.Extension.ToLower = ".html" Then

        Dim Page As IndexEntry
        Page = IndexPage(baseUrl & File.Name)

        If Not (Page Is Nothing) Then
          Index.Add(Page)
        End If
      End If
    Next
    Return Index
End Function
```

Another useful variant is the UpdateIndex() method, which looks at a current index and recreates it. This is a helpful method when serializing the index—it allows you to build an updated copy of an existing index by using an old, serialized copy, rather than by remembering and resubmitting all the links.

```
Public Function UpdateIndex(ByVal currentIndex _
            As IndexEntryCollection) As IndexEntryCollection

    Dim NewIndex As New IndexEntryCollection()
    Dim Page As IndexEntry
    For Each Page In currentIndex
      Dim NewPage As IndexEntry = IndexPage(Page.Url)
      If Not (NewPage Is Nothing) Then NewIndex.Add(NewPage)
    Next
    Return NewIndex
  End Function
 End Class
End Namespace
```

So far we've dealt with index creation. Using SearchIndexer and HtmlMetaTagIndexer, you can easily index one or multiple Web pages. But what about saving the index information for later use? Because the IndexEntry and IndexEntryCollection classes are serializable, they can easily be converted to a stream of bytes and stored in a file or in a database record.

Generally, developers will use this ability to save the index according to their needs. However, to complete this demonstration, you can create a simple utility class with Save() and Load() methods that allow index information to be stored in a file and retrieved later. These methods use the BinaryFormatter in order to serialize the data. For more flexibility, you can write your own serialization code, as you would with any other serializable type.

The complete code for the IndexFileUtility is shown here:

```
Imports System.IO
Imports System.Runtime.Serialization.Formatters.Binary

Namespace Apress.Toolkit.SearchEngine

  Public Class IndexFileUtility
    Inherits System.ComponentModel.Component

    Public Sub Save(ByVal index As IndexEntryCollection, _
      ByVal filePath As String, ByVal overwrite As Boolean)

      Dim Mode As FileMode
      If overwrite Then
```

```
      Mode = FileMode.Create
    Else
      Mode = FileMode.CreateNew
    End If
    Dim fs As New FileStream(filePath, Mode)
    Dim bf As New BinaryFormatter()

    bf.Serialize(fs, index)
    fs.Close()
  End Sub

  Public Function Load(ByVal filePath As String) _
    As IndexEntryCollection

    Dim fs As New FileStream(filePath, FileMode.Open)
    Dim bf As New BinaryFormatter()

    Dim Index As IndexEntryCollection
    Index = CType(bf.Deserialize(fs), IndexEntryCollection)
    fs.Close()
    Return Index

  End Function

  End Class
End Namespace
```

That completes the indexing components. We'll see how to generate an index with them in the "Demonstration" section, a little later on.

Searcher

Searcher is a smaller class library than Indexer. The first step is to define the custom classes used to store search results. In this case, two custom classes are required: SearchHit (which represents a single page match) and a corresponding SearchHitCollection (a strongly typed collection that stores SearchHit instances).

The SearchHit object stores all the same information presented in the IndexEntry object introduced in the previous section, along with two additional properties: a Rank that counts the number of matched words, and a Percent that gauges the relative success of the search. Because the SearchHit class is so similar to IndexEntry, we can use inheritance to extend IndexEntry. In addition, a constructor is added that allows a SearchHit instance to be created using an IndexEntry. This allows the search component to quickly generate a SearchHit whenever a page is matched, simply by specifying the ranking information.

```
Imports System

Namespace Apress.Toolkit.SearchEngine

  <Serializable()> _
  Public Class SearchHit
    Inherits IndexEntry

    Private _rank As Integer
    Private _percent As Decimal

    Public ReadOnly Property Rank() As Integer
      Get
        Return _rank
      End Get
    End Property
    Public ReadOnly Property Percent()
      Get
        Return _percent
      End Get
    End Property

    Public Sub New(ByVal page As IndexEntry, _
      ByVal rank As Integer, ByVal percent As Decimal)
      MyBase.New(page.Url)
      _rank = rank
      _percent = percent
      Me.Description = page.Description
      Me.Keywords = page.Keywords
      Me.Title = page.Title
    End Sub

  End Class

End Namespace
```

The code for the SearchHitCollection class is about the same as the one for the IndexEntryCollection class we just saw in the previous section, so we are avoiding listing it here.

The next step is to define two enumerations that will be used by the search component. These include the SearchType enumeration, which has three values as follows:

- MatchAll: The query consists of separate required words.

- MatchAny: The query consists of separate words, and at least one word must match.

- MatchAdvanced: The query is treated as MatchAny, but it may contain the keyword "and" to indicate linked terms, and it may contain "not" to indicate excluded words.

and the PhraseMatch enumeration, which also has three values:

- SinglePhrase: The query contains a single contiguous phrase. Thus, MatchAll and MatchAny will work equivalently.

- None: The query contains separate unrelated words.

- InlineQuotes: The same as None, but quotation marks (") may be used to delimit contiguous phrases.

The two definitions are as follows:

```
Public Enum SearchType
   MatchAll
   MatchAny
   MatchAdvanced
End Enum

Public Enum PhraseMatch
   SinglePhrase
   None
   InlineQuotes
End Enum
End Namespace
```

The SearchParser performs the actual parsing, searching, and ranking. The following is the opening of the declarations for this class:

```
Imports System.Collections.Specialized

Namespace Apress.Toolkit.SearchEngine

   Public Class SearchParser
      Inherits System.ComponentModel.Component
```

Now, we need to declare a series of properties that will allow the user of the class to access its members. First, we let them choose what kind of search to perform through these two properties.

```
Private _searchType As SearchType = SearchType.MatchAny

Public Property SearchType() As SearchType
  Get
    Return _searchType
  End Get
  Set(ByVal Value As SearchType)
    _searchType = Value
  End Set
End Property

Private _phraseMatch As PhraseMatch = PhraseMatch.InlineQuotes

Public Property PhraseMatch() As PhraseMatch
  Get
    Return _phraseMatch
  End Get
  Set(ByVal Value As PhraseMatch)
    _phraseMatch = Value
  End Set
End Property
```

Next, we provide access to three collections of strings, representing the set of words the parser will ignore in queries, the set of characters it removes from queries altogether, and the set of characters it treats as word breaks.

- NoiseWords: will be removed entirely from the query (unless they are part of a phrase)

- StripChars: will be removed from any word (even if they are part of a phrase)

- SpaceChars: will be converted to spaces (even if they are part of a phrase)

What follows is the code to implement the properties to access the previously mentioned collections:

```
Private _noiseWords As New StringCollection()
Public ReadOnly Property NoiseWords() As StringCollection
    Get
        Return _noiseWords
    End Get
End Property


Private _stripChars As New StringCollection()
Public ReadOnly Property StripChars() As StringCollection
    Get
        Return _stripChars
    End Get
End Property


Private _spaceChars As New StringCollection()
Public ReadOnly Property SpaceChars() As StringCollection
    Get
        Return _spaceChars
    End Get
End Property
```

We also allow the client to specify whether all single-character words should be auto-matically discarded.

```
Private _treatSingleCharAsNoise As Boolean = True

Public Property TreatSingleCharAsNoise() As Boolean
  Get
    Return _treatSingleCharAsNoise
  End Get
  Set(ByVal Value As Boolean)
    _treatSingleCharAsNoise = Value
  End Set
End Property
```

Finally, we provide access to the collection of index entries that the parser will use.

```
Private _index As IndexEntryCollection

Public Property Index() As IndexEntryCollection
  Get
    Return _index
  End Get
```

```
   Set(ByVal Value As IndexEntryCollection)
     _index = Value
   End Set
End Property
```

Here is the constructor, which initializes the collections of strings we just met:

```
Public Sub New()

   Dim Noise() As String = _
     {"the", "a", "an", "or", "and", "to", "of"}
   Dim Strip() As String = _
     {"?", "@", "$", "%", "^", "&", "*", "(", ")"}
   Dim Space() As String = {",", ";", ":", "/", "\"}

   'We copy the arrays into string collections.
   'This simplifies the code, because you can check for a
   'character using the Contains() method, instead of iterating
   'through the array manually.
   Me.NoiseWords.AddRange(Noise)
   Me.StripChars.AddRange(Strip)
   Me.SpaceChars.AddRange(Space)
End Sub
```

Now, we come to the key entry point into the parser. The Search() method remains fairly simple because it uses several private procedures to perform each stage of the query processing.

```
Public Function Search(ByVal query As String) _
  As SearchHitCollection
```

We'll follow the parsing process as it goes through the steps we enumerated earlier.

1. Strip out special characters.

```
query = FilterCharacters(query)
```

2. Break down the query into words. This procedure updates the RequiredWords, OptionalWords, and ExcludedWords string arrays based on the query and the SearchType. Note that excluded words are only supported for SearchType.MatchAdvanced queries.

```
Dim RequiredWords, ExcludedWords, OptionalWords _
  As StringCollection
ParseQuery(query, RequiredWords, ExcludedWords, OptionalWords)
```

3. Convert all words to a standard form, and remove noise words.

```
CanonicalizeWords(RequiredWords)
CanonicalizeWords(OptionalWords)
CanonicalizeWords(ExcludedWords)
```

4. Now perform the search. This ranks each page that is a match.

```
Dim Matches As SearchHitCollection
Matches = MatchTerms(RequiredWords, ExcludedWords, OptionalWords)

Return Matches

End Function
```

The first step uses the FilterCharacters() function to remove unwanted characters (those defined in the StripChars collection). Note that this technique removes the characters wherever they appear, even if they are embedded inside another word or phrase. The procedure works by iterating through the query string, copying the information into a new string if it meets the restriction criteria. In the same pass, space-equivalent characters (those identified in the SpaceChars collection) are replaced with real spaces, and spaces throughout the string are collapsed. This ensures that there is exactly one space between each query term.

```
Private Function FilterCharacters(ByVal query As String) As String

Dim StrippedQuery, LastChar As String
Dim i As Integer

For i = 0 To query.Length - 1

  If Me.StripChars.Contains(query.Chars(i)) Then
    'Do nothing (strip out special characters).

  ElseIf (Me.PhraseMatch <> PhraseMatch.InlineQuotes _
        And query.Chars(i) = """") Then
    'Do nothing (strip out quotations if they aren't used.)

  Else
    'Continue with further processing.

    If Me.SpaceChars.Contains(query.Chars(i)) Then
      'Convert space characters to spaces. This takes
      'effect even inside phrases in InlineQuotes mode.
```

```
        If LastChar <> " " Then
          StrippedQuery &= " "
          LastChar = " "
        End If

    Else
      If LastChar = " " And query.Chars(i) = " " Then
        'Duplicate spaces are ignored (collapsed).
      Else
        'The character was not a filter or space
        'character. Copy the character as is.
        StrippedQuery &= query.Chars(i)
        LastChar = query.Chars(i)
      End If
    End If
  End If

Next

Return StrippedQuery

End Function
```

The second step is to take the adjusted query string and separate out the required words, optional words, and excluded words into separate collections. This step is somewhat complicated by the fact that the processing needs to follow different rules depending on the search mode.

- In SinglePhrase mode, all words are collapsed into a single term for the RequiredWords collection.

- In MatchAll mode, all words are added to the RequiredWords collection.

- In MatchAny mode, all words are added to the OptionalWords collection.

- In MatchAdvanced mode, the ParseQuery() procedure looks for AND and NOT keywords. If AND precedes a word, it becomes a required term. If NOT precedes a word, it becomes an excluded term. Otherwise, all words are added to the OptionalWords collection.

To actually split the query into an array of words, you could use the Split() method of the String class. Unfortunately, this approach is not useful if you are using inline phrases (in which case you need to allow spaces in identified phrases) or if you are using an advanced search, which can use the "not" and "and" operators, which should not be treated as search words. For these reasons, we implement a character-by-character parser instead.

```
Private Sub ParseQuery(ByVal query As String, _
    ByRef requiredWords As StringCollection, _
    ByRef excludedWords As StringCollection, _
    ByRef optionalWords As StringCollection)

    'Parse query for required, optional, and excluded words.
    requiredWords = New StringCollection()
    optionalWords = New StringCollection()
    excludedWords = New StringCollection()

    'First, handle the special case (single phrase mode).
    If Me.PhraseMatch = PhraseMatch.SinglePhrase Then
      requiredWords.Add(query)
      Return
    End If

    'In all other search modes, the query must be examined more
    'closely.
    Dim InQuotedPhrase, Required, Excluded As Boolean
    Dim CurrentWord As String

    Dim i As Integer
    For i = 0 To query.Length - 1

      'Special handling at end of string.
      If (query.Chars(i) = " " And Not InQuotedPhrase) _
        Or (i = query.Length - 1) Then

        'Make sure we catch the last character.
        If i = query.Length - 1 And query.Chars(i) <> " " _
          And query.Chars(i) <> """" _
          Then CurrentWord &= query.Chars(i)

        'Check for special words in advanced mode.
        If Me.SearchType = SearchType.MatchAdvanced And _
          Not InQuotedPhrase And CurrentWord.ToLower = "and" Then

          'The next word is required.
          Required = True
```

```vb
    ElseIf Me.SearchType = SearchType.MatchAdvanced And _
      Not InQuotedPhrase And CurrentWord.ToLower = "not" Then

      'The next word is excluded.
      Excluded = True

    Else
      'The word is complete.
      'Add it to the appropriate collection.
      Select Case Me.SearchType

        Case SearchType.MatchAny
          optionalWords.Add(CurrentWord)

        Case SearchType.MatchAll
          requiredWords.Add(CurrentWord)

        Case SearchType.MatchAdvanced
          If Required Then
            requiredWords.Add(CurrentWord)
          ElseIf Excluded Then
            excludedWords.Add(CurrentWord)
          Else
            optionalWords.Add(CurrentWord)
          End If

          Required = False
          Excluded = False

      End Select
    End If

    InQuotedPhrase = False
    CurrentWord = ""

  ElseIf query.Chars(i) = """" And _
    Me.PhraseMatch = PhraseMatch.InlineQuotes Then
    'A quote phrase has started or ended.
    'If started, do not complete the word until another
    'quote is found.
    InQuotedPhrase = Not InQuotedPhrase
```

```
      Else
         'This is an ordinary character.
         'Add it to the current word.
         CurrentWord &= query.Chars(i)

      End If
   Next


End Sub
```

To save a pass through the string, you could combine this code with that in the FilterCharacters() procedure. However, the code would be less flexible and more complicated.

The third step is to convert all words into an agreed upon format. In this case, the words are trimmed of all preceding and trailing spaces (which could thwart keyword comparisons), and converted to lowercase. In addition, you could use this step to substitute words using the preferred synonym. For example, this common search technique might replace VS.NET and Visual Studio.NET with a common, agreed upon variant: Visual Studio .NET. This way, a search for either term would find the full set of results. However, in order to implement these rules, you would need to read information from some sort of large synonym database. Keyword canonicalization only works if you apply it to both query terms *and* indexed page keywords.

```
Private Sub CanonicalizeWords(ByVal words As StringCollection)

   Dim WordsToDelete As New StringCollection()

   Dim i As Integer
   For i = 0 To words.Count - 1
      If Me.NoiseWords.Contains(words(i)) Then
         WordsToDelete.Add(words(i))
      ElseIf Me.TreatSingleCharAsNoise And words(i).Length = 1 Then
         WordsToDelete.Add(words(i))
      Else
         words(i) = words(i).Trim().ToLower()
      End If
   Next

   Dim Word As String
   For Each Word In WordsToDelete
      words.Remove(Word)
   Next

End Sub
```

Note that this code does not enumerate through the StringCollection using For Each syntax. That's because this form of enumeration is read-only. Also, words that will be removed are flagged in a separate collection and deleted in a separate step to avoid index renumbering glitches.

Finally, in the fourth step, the MatchTerms() function compares the query term collections against the indexed page keywords. This method is exposed as a public method so it can be consumed directly. For example, see AltaVista's advanced search page (http://www.altavista.com/sites/search/webadv), which uses separate textboxes for required words, excluded words, and so on. In this case, the class-level properties related to parsing a query won't be used, because the query is already reduced.

```
Public Function MatchTerms(ByVal RequiredWords As StringCollection, _
    ByVal ExcludedWords As StringCollection, _
    ByVal OptionalWords As StringCollection) As SearchHitCollection

  Dim Hits As New SearchHitCollection()

  Dim Page As IndexEntry
  For Each Page In Index
    Dim Keywords As New StringCollection()
    Keywords.AddRange(GetKeywordsForPage(Page))

    'Optionally, this step could be performed when indexing.
    'However, performing it later ensures the latest
    'canonicalization settings always take effect.
    CanonicalizeWords(Keywords)

    Dim Rank, TotalWords As Integer
    TotalWords = RequiredWords.Count + OptionalWords.Count

    Rank = RankPage(RequiredWords, ExcludedWords, _
                    OptionalWords, Keywords)

    If Rank > 0 Then
      Hits.Add( _
        New SearchHit(Page, Rank, Rank / TotalWords * 100))
    End If
  Next

  Return Hits

End Function
```

The GetKeywordsForPage() function breaks up the long keyword string.

```
Private Function GetKeywordsForPage(ByVal page As IndexEntry) _
    As String()
  Return page.Keywords.Split(",")
End Function
```

Finally, the RankPage() function compares a single page to the query criteria. It ensures that no excluded words are present, and that all required words are found. In addition, the Rank is incremented by 1 for every word that matches. The final percentage is calculated by comparing the rank against the total number of supplied words (in other words, the possible number of matches the query could have).

```
Private Function RankPage( _
      ByVal requiredWords As StringCollection, _
      ByVal excludedWords As StringCollection, _
      ByVal optionalWords As StringCollection, _
      ByVal keywords As StringCollection) As Integer

  Dim Rank As Integer

  'Check for excluded words.
  'If any are found, the rank is automatically 0.
  Dim Word As String
  For Each Word In excludedWords
    If keywords.Contains(Word) Then
      Return 0
    End If
  Next

  'Check for required words.
  'If any are not found, the rank is automatically 0.
  For Each Word In requiredWords
    If keywords.Contains(Word) Then
      Rank += 1
    Else
      Return 0
    End If
  Next

  'Check for optional words.
  For Each Word In optionalWords
    If keywords.Contains(Word) Then
```

```
        Rank += 1
      End If
    Next

    Return Rank

    End Function

  End Class
End Namespace
```

Note that queries that have no matching terms will also receive a Rank of 0, and any page that has a Rank of 0 will not get added to the SearchHitCollection.

Demonstration

We're going to build a simple Web application with two Web pages: index.aspx will allow us to run the indexer and generate a serialized index file for a selection of Web sites; search.aspx will allow us to use the searcher components to run queries against the index.

The Index Page

Set the page's layout to FlowLayout, and we can start adding components to the page.

1. Add a command button to the page. Set its Text property to Create Index, and its ID to cmdCreate.

2. Add a second button beside it. Set its Text property to Load Index, and its ID to cmdLoad.

3. On the next line, add a new DataList control to display the retrieved results, and set its ID to ListIndex.

4. Click on the SearchIndexer item, and drag it onto the design surface. Rename SearchIndexer1 to Indexer.

5. Click on the IndexFileUtility item, and drag it onto the design surface. Rename IndexFileUtility1 to Util.

6. Next, add two buttons, one named cmdReload and one named cmdRefresh.

Our DataList needs a template for each item. Add the following import directive to the top of the page in HTML view:

```
<%@ Import Namespace="Apress.Toolkit.SearchEngine" %>
```

Then change the body of the DataList element to read as follows:

```
<asp:DataList id="ListIndex" runat="server">
  <ItemTemplate>
    <b>
      <%# CType(Container.DataItem, IndexEntry).Title %>
    </b>
    <br>
    <font size="1"><b>Description: </b>
      <%# CType(Container.DataItem, IndexEntry).Description %>
      <br>
      <b>Keywords: </b>
      <%# CType(Container.DataItem, IndexEntry).Keywords %>
      <br>
      <b>URL: </b>
      <u><%# CType(Container.DataItem, IndexEntry).Url %></u>
    </font>
    <br>
  </ItemTemplate>
</asp:DataList>
```

This specifies how each item we bind to the DataList will be displayed. Notice that in order to create a databinding expression that uses a property of IndexEntry, you must cast the DataItem object to IndexEntry.

```
<%# CType(Container.DataItem, IndexEntry).Title %>
```

Finally, you need to add the code for the Web page. Switch to the code-behind file, and import the search engine namespace.

```
Imports Apress.Toolkit.SearchEngine
```

Here's the code that creates the index when the first button is clicked and saves it to a file:

```
Private Sub cmdCreate_Click(ByVal sender As System.Object, _
    ByVal e As System.EventArgs) Handles cmdCreate.Click
  Dim Urls(6) As String
  Urls(0) = "http://www.apress.com"
  Urls(1) = "http://msdn.microsoft.com"
  Urls(2) = "http://www.ebay.com"
  Urls(3) = "http://www.w3.org"
  Urls(4) = "http://www.pcmag.com"
  Urls(5) = "http://www.amazon.com"

  Dim Index As IndexEntryCollection = Indexer.IndexUrls(Urls)
  ListIndex.DataSource = Index
  ListIndex.DataBind()

  Util.Save(Index, Request.PhysicalApplicationPath & _
      "index.bin", True)
End Sub
```

and here's the code for the second button, which simply loads in a previously saved index and displays it:

```
Private Sub cmdLoad_Click(ByVal sender As System.Object, _
  ByVal e As System.EventArgs) Handles cmdLoad.Click
  Dim Index As IndexEntryCollection
  Index = Util.Load(Request.PhysicalApplicationPath & "index.bin")
  ListIndex.DataSource = Index
  ListIndex.DataBind()
End Sub
```

Figure 14-2 shows the page in action.

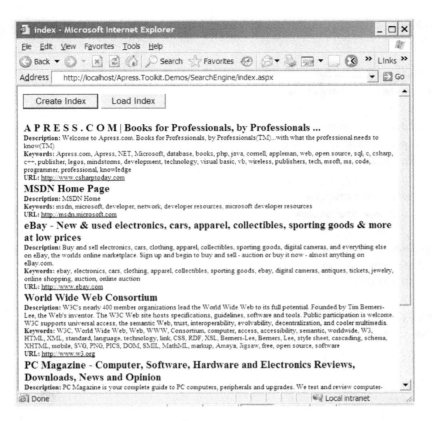

Figure 14-2. Managing the index

The Search Page

Testing the search component is easy—it simply requires a basic page that allows you to submit a query string and to optionally specify SearchParser properties. When the Search button is clicked, an index file is loaded (the same file that was created by index.aspx), and the search is performed.

Again, set search.aspx to FlowLayout mode, and we'll drag some components onto the page.

1. Drag a textbox onto the page. Set its ID to txtQuery.

2. Now add two list boxes, each with its Rows property set to 1, to the right of the textbox. Name the first lstPhraseMatch and the second lstSearchType.

3. Next, add a button, with the label Search, and the ID cmdSearch.

4. Then, on the next line, add a DataList and set its ID to ListMatches.

5. Now, add another `IndexFileUtility` and set its name to `Util`.

6. Finally, add a `SearchParser` and name it `Searcher`.

Again, we need to add a template to the `DataList` control, and we also need to add elements to our list box controls. In HTML mode, add the import directive and change the other elements as follows:

```
<%@ Import Namespace="Apress.Toolkit.SearchEngine" %>
<%@ Page Language="vb" AutoEventWireup="false" Codebehind="search.aspx.vb"
Inherits="SearchEngine.search"%>
<!DOCTYPE HTML PUBLIC "-//W3C//DTD HTML 4.0 Transitional//EN">
<HTML>
  <HEAD>
    <title>index</title>
  </HEAD>
  <body>
    <form id="Form1" method="post" runat="server">
      <P>
        <asp:TextBox id="txtQuery" runat="server"></asp:TextBox>
        <asp:ListBox id="lstSearchType" runat="server" Rows="1">
          <asp:ListItem Value="MatchAll">Match All</asp:ListItem>
          <asp:ListItem Value="MatchAny"
              Selected="True">Match Any</asp:ListItem>
          <asp:ListItem
              Value="MatchAdvanced">Advanced Search</asp:ListItem>
        </asp:ListBox>
        <asp:ListBox id="lstPhraseMatch" runat="server" Rows="1">
          <asp:ListItem
              Value="SinglePhrase">Match whole phrase</asp:ListItem>
          <asp:ListItem Value="None"
              Selected="True">Match individual words</asp:ListItem>
          <asp:ListItem
            Value="InlineQuotes">Match quoted phrases</asp:ListItem>
        </asp:ListBox>
        <asp:Button id="cmdSearch"
                runat="server" Text="Search"></asp:Button></P>
      <P>
        <asp:DataList id="ListMatches" runat="server">
          <ItemTemplate>
            <b>
              <%# CType(Container.DataItem, SearchHit).Title %>
```

```
          <br>
        </b><font size="1"><b>Description: </b>
          <%# CType(Container.DataItem, SearchHit).Description %>
          <br>
          <b>Keywords: </b>
          <%# CType(Container.DataItem, SearchHit).Keywords %>
          <br>
          <b>URL: </b><u>
            <%# CType(Container.DataItem, SearchHit).Url %>
          </u>
          <br>
          <b>Percent Match: </b>
          <%# CType(Container.DataItem, SearchHit).Percent %>
          %   <b>Rank: </b>
          <%# CType(Container.DataItem, SearchHit).Rank %>
        </font>
        <br>
      </ItemTemplate>
    </asp:DataList></P>
  </form>
 </body>
</HTML>
```

Now we can add the searching logic to our code-behind file. We need to import
Apress.Toolkit.SearchEngine at the top of the file, but all the logic goes in the Click
event handler for the cmdSearch button.

```
Private Sub cmdSearch_Click(ByVal sender As System.Object, _
    ByVal e As System.EventArgs) Handles cmdSearch.Click
  Dim index As IndexEntryCollection
  index = Util.Load(Request.PhysicalApplicationPath & "index.bin")

  Searcher.PhraseMatch = lstPhraseMatch.SelectedIndex
  Searcher.SearchType = lstSearchType.SelectedIndex

  Searcher.Index = index

  Dim Matches As SearchHitCollection = Searcher.Search(txtQuery.Text)

  ListMatches.DataSource = Matches
  ListMatches.DataBind()

End Sub
```

Figure 14-3 shows the search page in action.

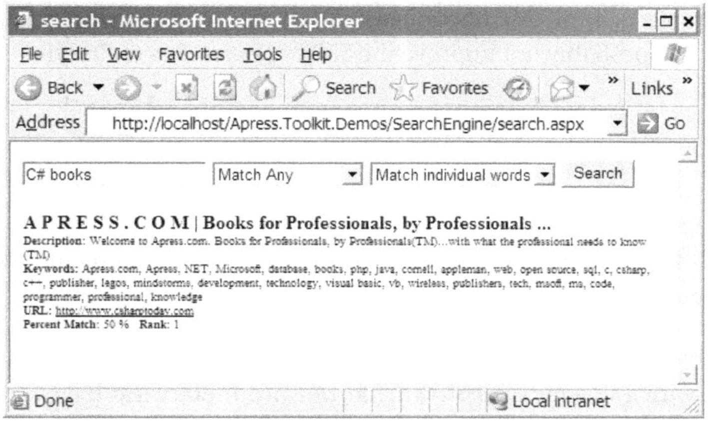

Figure 14-3. The Search page

Limitations

As with any search indexing technology, the search component makes some difficult compromises. These are mitigated by the expandable design that allows you to extend the indexing system. However, there are still a few possible drawbacks.

One problem is that the search component lacks a generic way to store index information. It's possible to store it in a file, but this raises possible concurrency problems if not handled carefully. You could develop a database-specific extension, but this requires more work.

Another limitation is the index size. Before you can search an index with this component, it must be loaded into memory. This limits the practical size of the index, which is one of the main reasons that the indexer uses keywords instead of a full-text search. To store and search an extremely large amount of data would require a relational database product like SQL Server. Quite simply, there is no practical way to implement an in-memory component that uses a full-text search without encountering memory issues and user concurrency problems.

The query parser has its own problems. String handling in the .NET Framework is not exceedingly fast. However, in several cases, our code uses a simplified, factored design rather than a more performance-optimized design. This means that sometimes multiple passes are made through a query. This could be improved, although it typically isn't a significant factor unless parsing extremely large indexes.

The separate design also enforces some limitations on the ways that queries can be analyzed. For example, the query engine supports the syntax X AND Y OR Z but it does not support (X AND Y) OR (A AND B). That's because it only allows for one collection of required, excluded, and optional words. To allow for more complex queries, you would have to abandon the three-collection approach used in the search component. Instead, you would analyze the query, canonicalize terms, and store the result in some sort of expression form (perhaps even a custom XML document). This is much more complex, and in the case of metatags, will probably not improve the ability of searches to find the desired resources.

Extensions

There are a number of possible improvements and extensions that you could implement with the indexer. These include the following:

- *Creating other implementations of* IIndexer *to index other types of documents*: You might use this to deal with a specific type of XML file, or a proprietary text file.

- *Creating other* IIndexer *implementations to optimize the indexing process*: For example, you could create an indexer that uses a different algorithm to find <meta> tags in a Web page. You might be able to develop a higher-performance indexer that only reads the stream one character at a time and closes the stream as soon as it locates the information it needs.

- *Adding some kind of* DataSet *interface that would make it easier to serialize index information to a database*: This would also have a benefit with searches, which could use the SQL query language and full-text search commands including LIKE.

- *Extending the* IndexEntry *object to store additional information*: Possibilities include size, the first 100 characters, time last updated, and so on.

- *Adding new features to allow the* SearchIndex *class to work like a spider, automatically following links that are on the same domain and adding the information to the index*: This would require a significant amount of code, because URLs can be found in several different elements (for example, in the <a> anchor element or the onClick attribute). Further complicating the issue are relative URLs, which can include sequences like ..\ or \\ that must be interpreted according to the current page's URL.

- *Extending the advanced query syntax to add new operators*: Currently, punctuation marks, such as the period (.), colon (:), semicolon (;), and comma (,), are treated as word breaks and are ignored during a search.

- *Adding smart synonym substitution*: This is particularly useful for terms like VB.NET and VB .NET, which are frequently confused. However, you would have to populate the synonym database by hand.

- *Attempting to find phrases that include spaces, even if quotes are not used*: This is particularly useful for identifying terms like VB .NET, which would otherwise be separated into two words unless quotation marks are used.

- *Adding the ability to sort a* `SearchHitCollection`: This would be one of the easiest enhancements to add, and it would allow you to order search results by rank or percentage.

Index

www.ingramcontent.com/pod-product-compliance
Lightning Source LLC
Chambersburg PA
CBHW062057050326

40690CB00016B/3121

* 9 7 8 1 5 9 0 5 9 4 4 6 9 *